Tourism and Resilience

TOURISM ESSENTIALS

Series Editors: Chris Cooper, *Oxford Brookes University, UK*, C. Michael Hall, *University of Canterbury, New Zealand* and Dallen J. Timothy, *Arizona State University, USA*

Tourism Essentials is a dynamic new book series of short accessible volumes focusing on a specific area of tourism studies. It aims to present cutting-edge research on significant and emerging topics in tourism, providing a concise overview of the field as well as examining the key issues and future research possibilities. This series aims to create a new generation of tourism authors by encouraging young researchers as well as more established academics. The books will provide insight into the latest perspectives in tourism studies and will be an essential resource for postgraduate students and researchers.

Full details of all the books in this series and of all our other publications can be found on http://www.channelviewpublications.com, or by writing to Channel View Publications, St Nicholas House, 31–34 High Street, Bristol BS1 2AW, UK.

TOURISM ESSENTIALS: 5

Tourism and Resilience

Individual, Organisational and Destination Perspectives

C. Michael Hall, Girish Prayag and Alberto Amore

CHANNEL VIEW PUBLICATIONS
Bristol • Blue Ridge Summit

DOI 10.21832/HALL6300

Library of Congress Cataloging in Publication Data
Names: Hall, Colin Michael, 1961- author. | Prayag, Girish, author. | Amore, Alberto, author.
Title: Tourism and Resilience: Individual, Organisational and Destination Perspectives/C. Michael Hall, Girish Prayag and Alberto Amore.
Description: Bristol, UK; Blue Ridge Summit, PA, USA: Channel View Publications, [2018] | Series: Tourism Essentials: 5 | Includes bibliographical references and index.
Identifiers: LCCN 2017029166| ISBN 9781845416300 (hbk : alk. paper) | ISBN 9781845416294 (pbk : alk. paper) | ISBN 9781845416317 (pdf) | ISBN 9781845416324 (epub) | ISBN 9781845416331 (kindle)
Subjects: LCSH: Tourism—Management. | Tourism—Planning. | Sustainable tourism. | Organizational resilience.
Classification: LCC G155.A1 H3474 2018 | DDC 910.68/4—dc23 LC record available at https://lccn.loc.gov/2017029166

British Library Cataloguing in Publication Data
A catalogue entry for this book is available from the British Library.

ISBN-13: 978-1-84541-630-0 (hbk)
ISBN-13: 978-1-84541-629-4 (pbk)

Channel View Publications
UK: St Nicholas House, 31–34 High Street, Bristol BS1 2AW, UK.
USA: NBN, Blue Ridge Summit, PA, USA.

Website: www.channelviewpublications.com
Twitter: Channel_View
Facebook: https://www.facebook.com/channelviewpublications
Blog: www.channelviewpublications.wordpress.com

Copyright © 2018 C. Michael Hall, Girish Prayag and Alberto Amore.

All rights reserved. No part of this work may be reproduced in any form or by any means without permission in writing from the publisher.

The policy of Multilingual Matters/Channel View Publications is to use papers that are natural, renewable and recyclable products, made from wood grown in sustainable forests. In the manufacturing process of our books, and to further support our policy, preference is given to printers that have FSC and PEFC Chain of Custody certification. The FSC and/or PEFC logos will appear on those books where full certification has been granted to the printer concerned.

Typeset by Nova Techset Private Limited, Bengaluru and Chennai, India.

Contents

	List of Figures and Tables	vii
	List of Boxed Cases and Insights	xi
	Acknowledgements	xiii
	List of Acronyms	xv
1	Disturbance and Change in the Tourism System	1
	Introduction: From Stability to Change	1
	All Change?	2
	Systems Thinking and the Tourism System	19
	Chapter Summary and Outline of the Book	28
2	Resilience: Responding to Change	32
	Introduction: Responding to Change	32
	Resilience	33
	Resilience and Tourism	53
	Chapter Summary	58
3	Individual Resilience	61
	Introduction	61
	Definitions and Conceptualisations of Individual Resilience	62
	Trait or Psychological and Process Resilience	66
	Individual Resilience during Disasters: The 3Cs	68
	The Interface between Individual and Employee Resilience	69
	Tourism, Individual Resilience and Employee Resilience	73
	Conclusion	76
4	Organisational Resilience in Tourism	79
	Definitions and Conceptualisations of Organisational Resilience	81
	Organisational Resilience: The 'View' Inside the Organisation	84
	Critical Infrastructures for Developing Organisational Resilience	87

	Organisational Resilience: A Step Back to Ecological and Socio-ecological Systems	95
	Conclusion	101
5	Destination Resilience	104
	Introduction	104
	Conceptualising Destination Resilience	104
	Ecological Dimensions of Destination Resilience	107
	Summary and Conclusions	131
6	Conclusion: Is Resilience a Resilient Concept?	136
	Introduction	136
	Resilience as a Boundary Object and Bridging Concept	137
	Resilience and Tourism Systems	146
	Resilience: Sustainability 2.0?	149
	Resilience and System Thinking	151
	A Community-based Approach to Tourism Resilience?	154
	All Change? Or No Change?	155
	References	159
	Index	185

List of Figures and Tables

Figures

Figure 1.1	Spatial scales of change	18
Figure 1.2	Elements of a geographical tourism system	20
Figure 2.1	Metaphors of adaptive cycles	48
Figure 2.2	The influence of temporal and spatial resolution on assessing tourism-related phenomenon	50
Figure 2.3	Panarchy: Linked adaptive scales	51
Figure 2.4	Panarchy: Tourism and climate change	52
Figure 2.5	Linked adaptive scales in the tourism system	58
Figure 3.1	Diagrammatic representation of four waves of research on positive adaption in the context of adversity	65
Figure 4.1	Components of organisational resilience	88
Figure 4.2	Equilibrium model of single island biota	99
Figure 4.3	Island biogeographical perspectives on economic endemism, immigration, emigration and extinction	100
Figure 5.1	Representation of a complex tourism system	105
Figure 5.2	Elements in destination resilience	133
Figure 6.1	Progressing resilience in tourism	141
Figure 6.2	Awareness and knowledge of sources of change: Conceptual schema	142

Figure 6.3a Assessing resilience factors: Exposure and vulnerability   143

Figure 6.3b Assessing resilience factors: Hazard and risk change warning system and its relationship to tourism   143

Figure 6.3c Assessing resilience factors: Organisational structures and relationships   144

Figure 6.3d Assessing resilience factors: People   144

Figure 6.3e Assessing resilience factors: Mitigation and adaptation strategies   145

Figure 6.3f Assessing resilience factors: Communications and media   145

Figure 6.3g Assessing resilience factors: Recovery   146

Figure 6.4 Urban hotel design panarchy   156

Tables

Table 1.1 Resource use intensities in global tourism   5

Table 1.2 Important tourism regions facing biodiversity loss, water security threats   12

Table 1.3 The economic and human impact of disasters 2005–2014   14

Table 1.4 Global human impact by disaster types 2005–2014 (annual average)   15

Table 1.5 Top 10 countries most affected by disasters 2005–2014   16

Table 1.6 Properties of complex systems   24

Table 1.7 Basic stability concepts in socio-ecological systems   27

Table 1.8 Types of change in the tourism environment   29

Table 2.1 Use of 'resilience' in journal article titles, abstracts or keywords (as of August 2016)   34

Table 2.2 Modifications in the understandings of resilience at different levels of integration   40

Table 2.3 Different foci of engineering versus ecological resilience   42

Table 2.4 Stages of the adaptive cycle   47

Table 2.5 Use of 'resilience' and 'tourism' in journal article titles, abstracts or keywords (as of August 2016)	54
Table 2.6a Resilience and tourism in journal article titles, abstracts and keywords by key themes and foci as of August 2016	56
Table 2.6b Resilience and tourism in journal article titles, abstracts and keywords by key themes and foci as of August 2016	57
Table 3.1 Four waves of research on positive adaptation in the context of adversity	64
Table 3.2 Fundamental questions related to individual and employee resilience	77
Table 4.1 Fundamental questions related to organisation resilience	102
Table 5.1 Tourism in the resilience plans of the Rockefeller Foundation's 100 Resilient Cities	119
Table 5.2 Fundamental questions related to destination resilience	133
Table 6.1 Comparisons between resilience and sustainability	150
Table 6.2 Approaches to resilience and change	153

List of Boxed Cases and Insights

Box 1.1 The Great Barrier Reef Climate Change Action Plan 2007–2011 and beyond — 7

Box 1.2 Dealing with weather and climate stressors in southern Florida — 18

Box 1.3 Feedback mechanisms in the High Arctic — 22

Box 2.1 Disturbance ecology — 38

Box 2.2 Social resilience and socio-ecological resilience — 43

Box 3.1 The Antigua Boat Sheds & Café — 72

Box 3.2 The resilient tourist? — 75

Box 4.1 Improving tourism enterprises' responsiveness to extreme natural events — 80

Box 4.2 Public agency survival — 85

Box 4.3 Business resilience following the 2004 southeast Asia tsunami: Evidence from reef enterprises in Phuket (Thailand) — 91

Box 4.4 Winnie Bagoes: Gourmet pizza the Kiwi way! — 94

Box 4.5 Can post-disturbance business survival be explained ecologically? — 98

Box 5.1 Atlantic City — 109

Box 5.2 Assessing the socio-ecological vulnerability of destinations: Evidence from Khao Lak, Patong and Phi Phi Don (Thailand) — 111

Box 5.3 Long-term planning for tourism growth and destination resilience: Recommendations from the OECD — 113

Box 5.4 Building destination resilience in southeast Asia: The R3ADY Asia Pacific Programme — 114

Box 5.5 Recovery for whom? Findings from post-earthquake Christchurch, New Zealand — 115

Box 5.6 Business vulnerabilities in small developing island states: Evidence from Vanuatu — 125

Box 5.7 Toolkit for community-led destination resilience: The UNEP Disaster Risk Management for Coastal Tourism Destinations Responding to Climate Change — 127

Box 5.8 Residents' role in a resilient destination: Evidence from Whistler, Canada — 128

Box 5.9 Planning a resilient destination: England's Wise Growth Action Plan — 129

Box 6.1 Policy change, public management and resilience — 139

Acknowledgements

This book has a significant backdrop in the form of the 2010–2011 Christchurch earthquake sequence and subsequent South Island earthquakes which we all either directly experienced or experienced the aftermath of. It has been a feature of a number of elements of our research in recent years. Direct experience and observation of individual, organisational, governmental, community and, of course, tourism responses to the earthquakes and their impacts laid the foundations for the present work. Extollation and praise from prime ministers, politicians, university leadership and the media to either being or needing to be resilient – at the same time as some interests benefited from the rebuild and recovery of Christchurch and others didn't – created a tension between academic discussion on resilience and on-the-ground experience. It is with this tension in mind, and the need to better clarify the term and its utility, that this book has been written.

Michael would like to thank a number of colleagues with whom he has undertaken related research over the years. In particular, thanks go to Duan Biggs, Dorothee Bohn, Tim Coles, David Duval, Alexandra Gillespie, Martin Gren, Stefan Gössling, Johan Hultman, Dieter Müller, Paul Peeters, Yael Ram, Jarkko Saarinen, Dan Scott, Anna Dóra Sæþórsdóttir and Allan Williams for their thoughts (and resilience), as well as for the stimulation of Agnes Obel, A Long Walk, Ann Brun, Beirut, Paul Buchanan, Nick Cave, Bruce Cockburn, Elvis Costello, Stephen Cummings, Chris Difford and Glenn Tilbrook, David Bowie, Ebba Fosberg, Aldous Harding, Father John Misty, Mark Hollis, Hoodoo Gurus, Margaret Glaspy, Aimee Mann, Larkin Poe, Vinnie Reilly, Susanne Sundfør, Matthew Sweet, David Sylvian, and *The Guardian*, BBC6 and KCRW – without whom the four walls of a hotel room would be much more confining. Michael would like to thank the many people who have supported his work over the years, and especially the Js and the Cs who stay at home and mind the farm. Girish would like to thank his parents, Ansoomatee and Jayduth, for their continuous love and support and would especially like to offer grateful thanks to Lyndon, Chris and Emma for putting up with him throughout the process of writing this book. Alberto would like to acknowledge the role of John and Jörg in advancing the understanding of resilience with respect to tourism and the service sector at large. Special thanks go to the staff at the University of Canterbury, particularly Irene and Donna. Finally, yet most importantly, Alberto would like to thank Bailey for her love and support throughout the drafting and edits of the book.

We are indebted to the support of several people at the University of Canterbury, but particularly Irene Joseph. In addition, we would like to note our thanks for the support of all at Channel View, and the comments of Dallen and Chris.

List of Acronyms

AGO	Australian Greenhouse Office
CAS	complex adaptive system
COR	Conservation of Resources
CRED	Centre for Research on the Epidemiology of Disasters
DVA	Destination Vulnerability Assessment
EAP	Employee Assistance Programme
EM-DAT	a global database on natural and technological disasters maintained by the Centre for Research on the Epidemiology of Disasters (CRED) at the School of Public Health of the Université Catholique de Louvain, Brussels, Belgium; www.emdat.be.
ENE	Extreme natural event
GBRMA	Great Barrier Reef Marine Authority
GFC	global financial crisis
HRD	human resource development
HRM	human resource management
OECD	Organization for Economic Co-operation and Development
OFDA	Office of US Foreign Disaster Assistance
ROR	Relative Overall Resilience model
RTAF	Regional Tourism Adaptation Framework
RTSAF	Regional Tourism Sustainable Adaptation Framework
SEI	Stockholm Environment Institute
SES	social ecological system
SLR	sea level rise
UNCTAD	United Nations Conference on Trade and Development
UNEP	United Nations Environment Programme
UNISDR	United Nations Office for Disaster Risk Reduction
UNWTO	United Nations World Tourism Organisation
USAID	United States Agency for International Development
V2R	vulnerability to resilience framework
WLB	work life balance
WMO	World Meteorological Organization

1 Disturbance and Change in the Tourism System

Introduction: From Stability to Change

Complex systems such as economies, ecosystems, societies or, as is the focus of this book, the tourism industry sectors, destinations and international travel networks, consist of autonomous agents such as organisms, humans, businesses, organisations and institutions that pursue their own objectives and interact with one another and their environment (Grimm *et al.*, 2005). Fundamental questions exist with respect to the stability of such systems. How long will these systems exist? How much do their characteristic features vary over time and space/jurisdictions? Are they sensitive to disturbances and change? If so, will they recover to their original state and, if that is the case, why, from what set of states and how fast? (Grimm & Calabrese, 2011). These are questions of resilience.

The building blocks of these systems – the organisations, organisms and people – usually do not have a blueprint of the entire system in mind, and instead follow their own aims, goals and objectives. Nevertheless, system-level properties emerge over time that allow for the identification of such systems and their behaviours (Grimm & Calabrese, 2011). Coral reefs and tropical rainforests, for example, can be self-similar over thousands of years and reliably provide functions and services that are important for the tourism industry. Systems can, however, also collapse and lose their identity and functions; for example: a stock market can crash; a coral reef can be exposed to agricultural runoff, overfishing or a bleaching event and be replaced by seagrass; a destination may experience a dramatic fall in visitation as a result of a disaster; or a savannah can turn into a scrubland due to overgrazing, rendering it virtually useless as rangeland and as a safari tourism location (Scheffer *et al.*, 2001, 2009).

In one of the most widely cited socio-ecological definitions, resilience is 'the capacity of a system to absorb disturbance and reorganise while undergoing change so as to retain essentially the same function, structure, identity and feedbacks' (Walker *et al.*, 2004: 6) that existed before the disturbance began. If resilience is a term that finds its meaning in relation to change, then we are at a stage in the Earth's history, and in human history, that has rarely been marked by so much change in such a short space of time – so much so that that the amount of change and 'markers' (its permanent effects that will show in the geological record) has even been given its own term: 'the Anthropocene'.

This chapter begins by highlighting some of the major forms of change that are affecting tourism and our understanding of resilience today. These include socio-economic change, technological change and environmental change. One form of rapid change is disaster and considerable attention has been given in the tourism literature to understanding how resilience concepts may assist in better mitigation and adaptation to the effects of disasters. The chapter then discusses the notion of a tourism system and the emphasis given in the literature to tourism being conceptualised as a complex rather than a complicated system. This then provides a context for the next chapter in which the concept of resilience is outlined and the ways in which it is used in the wider science and social science literature are discussed. The chapter concludes with a brief outline of the book.

All Change?

In human terms change is marked by the contemporary phase of globalisation – marked as it is by greater international trade, telecommunications, transport and movement of financial and economic capital than at any time in history. Of course, it is not just the size of such movement, but also the speed at which movement occurs. Events can be simultaneously seen on personal phones anywhere around the world, where digital controls allow, and video messaging via programmes such as Skype is something that only a generation earlier was regarded as close to science fiction and where the fax was still regarded as a very cool thing! However, another major socio-economic change is coming. Advances in artificial intelligence (AI) mean that a 'second wave' of robotic/AI technological change is approaching as part of the 'fourth industrial revolution': the first wave meant job losses in manufacturing; in the second wave the jobs at risk from the machines are going to be jobs in the service sector (Elliot, 2017).

This fourth industrial revolution, just like all the others, is expected to lead to a spurt in economic growth. 'Automation could raise productivity growth on a global basis by as much as 0.8 to 1.4 percent annually' (McKinsey Global Institute, 2017: 1). But the last major epoch of technological change was accompanied by political change which ensured that those making the cars, the washing machines and the televisions could also afford to purchase them. Full employment policies, capital controls, progressive income tax and strong trade unions helped ensure that this was the case (Elliot, 2017). However, technological change, global integration, domestic labour and economic market deregulation and increased immigration – the very 'stuff' of globalisation – have meant that economic inclusivity has declined. For example, the World Economic Forum (WEF, 2017) reported that median incomes in 26 advanced countries fell by 2.4% between 2008 and 2013.

The impact of the next wave of automation will be startling. Bowler (2017) observes that a typical industrial robot can cost about £4 an hour to operate, compared to average total European labour costs of about £40 an hour or £9 an hour in China. The McKinsey Global Institute (2017) suggests that while few occupations are fully automatable, 60% of all occupations have at least 30% technically automatable activities. In terms of specific sectors, their analysis showed that the accommodation and food services sector had a 73% automation potential – the highest of the sectors it examined, while the sector with the lowest potential was educational services (27%). In the case of the accommodation and food services sector, one of the main reasons for the high automation potential was because many jobs involve physical activities in highly structured and predictable environments, e.g. room cleaning and food preparation, while interface with customers is also quite predictable, e.g. front of house. Even where more optimistic studies are conducted, it is mostly low-skilled and low-income individuals who face a high risk of being automatable (Arntz *et al.*, 2016). Undoubtedly, 'some human services will probably continue to command a premium compared to robotically produced ones' (Pratt, 2015: 58). However, the extent to which such positions will exist in tourism and hospitality remains debatable, given the extent to which even highly tailored activities such as tour guiding may potentially be replaceable by apps and language applications. Similarly, many jobs in the tourism transport sector, such as taxis and buses, are also greatly at risk from the development of automated transport (Hall *et al.*, 2017). Baldwin (2016) even argues that advances in technology will allow virtual migration, thanks to telerobotics and telepresence, meaning that someone located in one country can underwork in another location – noting, for example, that hotel cleaners in Europe could be replaced by robots driven by staff based in the Philippines.

A number of factors are affecting the pace and extent of technological adoption:

- *Technical feasibility.* Technology has to be invented, integrated and adapted into solutions for specific case use.
- *Cost of developing and deploying solutions.* Hardware and software costs.
- *Labour market dynamics.* The supply, demand, and costs of human labour affect which activities will be automated.
- *Economic benefits.* These include higher throughput and increased quality, alongside labour cost savings.
- *Regulatory and social acceptance.* Even when automation makes business sense, adoption can take time.

Nevertheless, it is not just social and economic change that is affecting tourism and the viability of businesses and destinations, as well as the jobs of people within the industry, but also the rapidly changing global environment. This change is so substantial that it has even been given a term to describe the current period of geological history which a future intelligent species would be able to identify in the Earth's rock layers – the Anthropocene.

Humans are the principle factor in processes of contemporary environmental change. Their impacts provide the markers of the Anthropocene. The sudden and global arrival of radionuclides (e.g. plutonium, caesium, strontium) following the atmospheric atomic bomb explosions from the 1940s through to the 1970s, the widespread dispersal of plastics in the environment from alpine ranges through to deep ocean trenches, and the release of polyaromatic hydrocarbons from the burning of fossil fuels all provide a clear line in the rock that suggests that this is not just another interglacial period of the Holocene but potentially marks a new geological epoch. Indeed, the extensive release of carbon and other emissions into the atmosphere have the potential to change the very nature of the interglacial period. Although many of the Global Stratigraphic Section and Point ('golden spike') markers of the Anthropocene rest on chemical signals, other markers exist in the form of a distinct lithostratigraphic signal as a result of human-induced changes to physical sedimentation, and a biostratigraphic signal that is the legacy of a combination of human-induced extinctions, global species introductions and migrations, and the widespread replacement of indigenous natural vegetation with agricultural monocultures (Cox, 2004; Zalasiewicz *et al.*, 2008). These environmental signals are not just of interest to geologists and geographers but are also important for tourism both now and in the foreseeable future because they highlight how rapid and how impactful change can be to the very resources that tourism often depends on to attract visitors. Clearly, resilience may be an extremely important asset to possess given the changes occurring in the Anthropocene.

Tourism: Welcome to the Anthropocene

Tourism, as a socio-economic activity, is a major contributor to some of the markers of the Anthropocene (Table 1.1 outlines some of different resource use intensities identified with respect to global tourism). For example, tourism is a significant contributor to climate change which directly impacts various chemical, geomorphological and biological markers. Tourism and travel contribute to climate change through emissions of greenhouse gases (GHGs), including carbon dioxide (CO_2), methane (CH_4), nitrous oxides (NO_x), hydrofluorocarbons (HFCs), perfluorocarbons (PFCs) and sulfur hexafluoride (SF_6). There are also various short-lived GHGs that are important in

Table 1.1 Resource use intensities in global tourism

Aspect	Range of estimates	Global average	Reference
Energy			
per guest night	1.4–3717 MJ	n.a.	Gössling (2010)
per activity/tourist	7–1300 MJ per activity	n.a.	Becken (2001)
Emissions			
per trip (domestic and international)	0.2–9.00 t CO_2	0.25 tCO_2	UNWTO-UNEP-WMO (2008); Eijgelaar et al. (2010); Gössling et al. (2013)
per international arrival (air transport)	0.37–1.83 t CO_2	n.a.	Gössling et al. (2013)
per night (accommodation)	0.1–260 kg CO_2	16 kg CO_2/night	Gössling (2002, 2010)
Fresh water			
direct (accommodation)	87–2000 L/day/tourist	300 L/day/tourist	Gössling et al. (2011)
indirect (fuels, food)	2000–5000 L/day/tourist	n.a.	Gössling et al. (2011)
Land use			
direct, per bed	30–4580 m²/bed	40 m²/bed	Gössling (2002)

Source: OECD (2013); Rutty et al. (2015).

the context of aviation and, to a lesser extent, cruise ships (Scott *et al.*, 2012). There is a further, although unquantified contribution to climate change as a result of tourism-related land use changes, which may be significant in some areas of tourism-related urbanisation (Hall, 2006).

Without taking radiative forcing into account, tourism is estimated to have contributed approximately 5% to global anthropogenic emissions of CO_2 in 2005 (UNWTO-UNEP-WMO, 2008). The majority of CO_2 emissions are associated with transport, with aviation accounting for 40% of tourism's overall carbon footprint, followed by car transport (32%). Accommodation accounted for 21% of emissions in 2005 (UNWTO-UNEP-WMO, 2008). Not included in the original UNWTO-UNEP-WMO (2008) research, cruise ships provide an estimated 19.2 Mt CO_2, and account for around 1.5% of global tourism emissions (Eijgelaar *et al.*, 2010). However, with radiative forcing considered, which is a particularly important uncertainty of aviation emissions, it has been estimated that tourism contributed 5.2–12.5% of all anthropogenic forcing in 2005, with a best estimate of approximately 8% (Gössling *et al.*, 2013). Significantly, the emissions from tourism are predicted to increase in the foreseeable future in absolute terms as the continued growth of international and domestic travel and tourism and aviation substantially exceeds any expected efficiency gains (Gössling *et al.*, 2013). The IPCC (2014) identified five reasons for concern (RFCs) critical to human, economic and environmental wellbeing:

(1) *Unique and threatened systems.* Climate change will affect already threatened ecosystems and cultures with warming of 2°C. Arctic sea ice and coral reef systems that have particularly low adaptive capacities will be in severe danger.
(2) *Extreme weather events.* Risks from extreme events are already moderate and are expected to rise with increasing temperatures. Higher levels of warming may exacerbate risks from certain types of events such as heat waves.
(3) *Distribution of impacts.* Unevenly distributed risks generally affect disadvantaged communities the most. Climate change impacts are already known to be regionally differentiated, with high risks of unevenly distributed impacts for warming above 2°C.
(4) *Global aggregate impacts.* The risks of global aggregate impacts encompassing both biodiversity and the global economy are moderate with warming of 1–2°C. Aggregate impacts increase with rising temperatures, leading to high risks associated with warming of 3°C or more.
(5) *Large-scale singular events.* The risks associated with abrupt and irreversible changes in some physical systems and ecosystems are moderate for

warming between 0°C and 1°C, with Arctic ecosystems and coral reef systems already experiencing irreversible changes. Disproportionate increases in risks are expected as temperatures change between 1°C and 2°C, with high risks associated with warming of 3°C or more due to the potential of sea level rise from ice sheet loss. (IPCC, 2014)

The impact of climate change on tourism is also becoming increasingly recognised. Sea level rise (SLR) is clearly a major concern in coastal resort regions, where much tourism is concentrated, while changes to the snow regime affect winter tourism, as do water availability and cold enough temperatures to make artificial snow. Temperature change scenarios have also been connected to possible future shifts in tourism as a result of some places being 'too hot' for tourism. While such deterministic models often do not take into account the capacity for behavioural change by consumers as well as institutional change, i.e. changing school holidays, as adaptive responses to climate change they do at least often grab the attention of government and industry with respect to longer term infrastructure and strategic planning. However, more concerning for many stakeholders in tourism are the impacts of extreme events, such as cold waves or heat waves, along with storms with a higher level of intensity, as these can have major impacts on tourism infrastructure and destination image as well as direct effects on tourist markets. Significantly, such 'sudden' changes or crisis events, e.g. coral bleaching, interact with and are related to the longer term changes in the environmental system, e.g. increases in water temperature and ocean acidification. The interplay between 'sudden' and 'slow' change is a major issue in understanding the resilience of natural systems and the socio-economic systems that rely on them.

Box 1.1 The Great Barrier Reef Climate Change Action Plan 2007–2011 and beyond

The Great Barrier Reef is a renowned attraction inserted in the UNESCO World Heritage List in 1981 and contains the largest collection of corals worldwide (UNESCO, 2016). Over the years, however, climate-related events along with unsustainable fisheries have substantially influenced the fragile ecosystem. In 2007 the Great Barrier Reef Marine Authority (GBRMA) and the Australian Greenhouse Office (AGO) released the Great Barrier Reef Climate Change Action Plan to identify 'specific measures to enhance resilience of the Great Barrier Reef ecosystem and support adaptation by regional communities and industries that depend on it' (GBRMA, 2007: 2). The Plan acknowledged that the survival of the local tourism economy, estimated to be worth around AU$7bn annually, depended highly on the resilience of the Great Barrier Reef ecosystem.

While acknowledging the likely decline of the Great Barrier Reef ecosystem over a long period, the Plan's primary focus is on the resilience of the Great Barrier Reef, to be achieved through effective local management strategies. In particular, the actions of the Plan 'aim to reduce stresses on the ecosystem, facilitate natural adaptation and minimize ecological impacts' (GBRMA, 2007: 7) through a range of actions of relevance to reef tourism, including:

- identification of the principal water quality threats;
- identification and protection of those habitats that can provide for shifts in the distribution and abundance of species;
- promotion of sustainable fishing practices to ensure protection of habitats and species;
- development of sustainable management guidelines to reduce the vulnerability of ecosystems; and
- minimisation of climate change related impacts with targeted actions to enhance the resilience of the Great Barrier Reef and its ecosystems.

Crucial to the achievement of ecological resilience is the adaptation of communities and industries in the context of climate and environmental change. Particularly in the case of agriculture (which is responsible for much of the nutrients that run off onto the reef) and tourism, local authorities are expected to assist businesses in preparing adaptation responses. However, this was far from being achieved. Furthermore, there was little effort from national and local governments in undertaking mitigation strategies. Eventually, international non-governmental organisations (NGOs) such as Greenpeace launched an international plea to list the Great Barrier Reef in the List of World Heritage in Danger in 2014 (Greenpeace, 2014). In response, the UNESCO World Heritage Committee declared that the Australian Government had to report back a long-term recovery plan for the Great Barrier Reef by the end of 2015 as a *sine qua non* condition to keep the site on the World Heritage List (Milman, 2015). Nevertheless, subsequent events have continued to show the fragility of the reef and of its continued World Heritage status.

> In 2016 and 2017 the reef experienced consecutive bleaching events that affected two-thirds of the reef, a 1500 km stretch, leaving only the reef's southern third unscathed. The 2016 bleaching was concentrated in the reef's northern third; the 2017 event spread further south and was most intense in the middle section of the Great Barrier Reef. The 2017 mass bleaching, second in severity only to the previous year's event, also occurred even in the absence of an El Niño event. The 2017 bleaching is likely to be compounded by other stresses on the reef, including the destructive crown-of-thorns starfish and poor water quality as a result of agricultural runoff and cyclone-fed river waters carrying sediment onto the reef. The Category 4 tropical cyclone Debbie not only came too late and too far south for its cooling effect to alleviate bleaching but also served to reduce water quality (Knaus & Evershed, 2017).
>
> In an interview with *The Guardian*, water quality expert Jon Brodie stated that the reef was now in a 'terminal stage'. He said measures to improve water quality, which were a central tenet of the Australian government's rescue effort, were failing. 'Last year was bad enough, this year is a disaster year … The federal government is doing nothing really, and the current programs, the water quality management is having very limited success. It's unsuccessful' (Jon Brodie, in Knaus & Evershed, 2017). Former director of the Great Barrier Reef Marine Park Authority Jon Day said that the Australian federal government was taking too relaxed an approach to fishing, runoff and pollution from farming and the dumping of maintenance dredge spoil, with funding far short of the money needed to meet water quality targets. 'You've got to be optimistic, I think we have to be … But every moment we waste, and every dollar we waste, isn't helping the issue. We've been denying it for so long, and now we're starting to accept it. But we're spending insufficient amounts addressing the problem' (Jon Day, in Knaus & Evershed, 2017).

Arguably, for many readers, tourism's contribution to climate change may well be regarded as its only significant role in the Anthropocene, particularly given the supposed virtues of ecotourism and other forms of nature-based tourism to help conserve biodiversity (e.g. Christ *et al.*, 2003). However, despite the very good intentions of those who seek to use tourism as a conservation tool, for example with regard to creating protected areas and providing an economic justification for conservation, tourism is also deeply embedded within processes of anthropogenic-driven species loss that are part of the Earth's sixth great extinction event (Anderson *et al.*, 2015; Ceballos *et al.*, 2010; Chapin *et al.*, 2000; Hall, 2010a, 2010b).

The extinction of species is a natural process (Lande, 1998). According to the Secretariat of the Convention on Biological Diversity (CBD) (2010: 9), 'There are multiple indications of continuing decline in biodiversity in all three of its main components – genes, species and ecosystems', the loss of which has accelerated as a result of human activity. Biological diversity (biodiversity) refers to the total sum of biotic variation, ranging from the genetic level, through the species level and on to the ecosystem level. The concept indicates diversity within and between species as well as the diversity of ecosystems. The extent or quantity of diversity can be expressed in terms of the size of a population, the abundance of different species, as well as the size of an ecosystem (area) and the number of ecosystems in a given area. The integrity or quality of biodiversity can be expressed in terms of the extent of diversity at the genetic level, and resilience at the species and ecosystem level (Martens *et al.*, 2003).

In October 2014 it was reported that the global wild animal populations had declined by 52% in the previous 40 years with populations of freshwater species suffering an even worse fall of 76%. The figure came from a Zoological Society of London and World Wildlife Fund (ZSL and WWF, 2014) study that found that there were half as many mammals, birds, reptiles, amphibians and fish in 2010 as there were in 1970. The report's Living Planet Index tracks more than 10,000 vertebrate species populations from 1970 to 2010. Although the finding was based on incomplete data, only 181 of the 3038 species investigated came from low-income countries. What was notable was that 'while there are those who argue about whether the precise figure is accurate, there seem to be few who doubt the general trend' (BBC, 2014). Similarly, the fourth iteration of the Global Biodiversity Outlook of the Secretariat of the CBD, also published in October 2014, reported that progress with respect to government implementation of measures to reduce biodiversity loss was poor.

> Extrapolations for a range of indicators suggest that based on current trends, pressures on biodiversity will continue to increase at least until 2020, and that the status of biodiversity will continue to decline.
>
> Despite individual success stories, the average risk of extinction for birds, mammals and amphibians is still increasing ... Genetic diversity of domesticated livestock is eroding, with more than one-fifth of breeds at risk of extinction and the wild relatives of domesticated crop species are increasingly threatened by habitat fragmentation and climate change. (Secretariat of the CBD, 2014: 10, 14)

Major transformations have also occurred at biome scale. Ellis *et al.* (2010) identified that in 1700 nearly half of the terrestrial biosphere was wild, without permanent human settlements or substantial land use; most of the remainder (45%) was in a semi-natural state with limited agricultural use and settlements. By 2000 the opposite was true, with the majority of the biosphere utilised by agriculture and settlements; less than 20% was semi-natural and only 25% left as wilderness. According to Ellis *et al.* (2010), anthropogenic transformation of the biosphere during the Industrial Revolution resulted about equally from land-use expansion into wilderness areas and intensification of land use within semi-natural biomes (see also Goldewijk *et al.*, 2011).

Current estimates put the extinction rate at 100–1000 times greater than the natural background level (Mace *et al.*, 2005; Pimm *et al.*, 1995, 2014), and the rate is projected to increase by a further tenfold this century (Barnosky *et al.*, 2011; Ceballos *et al.*, 2010; Mace *et al.*, 2005; Pimm *et al.*, 2014). The five principal pressures directly driving biodiversity loss – habitat change, overexploitation, pollution, invasive alien species and climate change – are all factors to which tourism is a significant contributor and 'are either constant or increasing in intensity' (Secretariat of the CBD, 2010: 9). Tourism contributes to habitat change via development of specific infrastructure, such as resort and accommodation complexes, second home developments and also providing a market for facilities such as golf courses. One of the most significant aspects of such developments is that they are often spatially concentrated along coastal strips or in high-amenity alpine and lake areas, while providing competition for water resources in some locations. Of course, tourism can provide a justification for habitat protection, especially national parks and reserves, and a having a market that watches wild animals rather than shooting them is clearly preferable. However, a significant issue is to try and ensure that habitats as well as charismatic species are not overexploited in such a way that their behaviour changes or they are otherwise affected by the presence of large numbers of humans. Poorly planned tourism development can generate substantial pollution, especially when sewerage facilities are inadequate to cope with seasonal demand, as with some coastal areas in the Mediterranean. Furthermore, pollution occurs not just at destinations but along all stages of the travel journey, an issue which is particularly important with respect to GHGs and other emissions. Finally, among its other main pressures, tourism is a significant pathway for the introduction of alien and invasive species (Anderson *et al.*, 2015).

Although all parts of the world will be affected by global environmental change, some parts will be more affected than others. This is important not just with respect to adapting to gradual change but in the need to respond to the likelihood of increased disasters. As the United Nations Office for Disaster Risk Reduction's *Global Assessment Report* highlighted:

> Through changing temperatures, precipitation and sea levels, among other factors, global climate change is already modifying hazard levels and exacerbating disaster risks. By 2050, it is estimated that 40% of the global population will be living in river basins that experience severe water stress, particularly in Africa and Asia. In the Caribbean basin, climate change will contribute an additional US$1.4bn to the expected annual losses from cyclone wind damage alone. (UNISDR, 2015a)

Table 1.2 highlights a number of significant tourism regions and the threats they face with regard to water security, loss of biodiversity hotspots and vulnerability to climate change.

Table 1.2 Important tourism regions facing biodiversity loss, water security threats

Region	Tourism importance (% GDP)	Water security threat	Threatened regional biodiversity hotspot	Climate change vulnerability
Caribbean	High	High	Caribbean	High
Mediterranean	High	Low–High	Mediterranean Basin	Medium–High
Southeast Asia	Medium–High	High	Sundaland, Wallacea, Philippines & Indo-Burma	Medium–High
New Zealand & SW Australia	High	Low	New Zealand & South West Australia	Low–Medium
East Africa	High	High	Eastern Arc Mountains and Coastal Forests of Tanzania & Kenya	High
West Coast USA	High	Low–High	California Floristic Province	Low–Medium
Coastal zone Brazil	Medium	Low–High	Atlantic Forest Region	Medium
Indian subcontinent	Low	High	Western Ghats & Sri Lanka	High
China	Low	High	Mountains of South-central China	Medium

Source: Derived from Christ *et al.* (2003); Gössling *et al.* (2012); Rutty *et al.* (2015); UNCTAD (2008); Vörösmarty *et al.* (2000).

Adaptation and vulnerability

One of the great difficulties in both understanding and responding to change is the rate at which change occurs. If the rate of change is slow then people may not perceive it as being particularly significant. However, if it is too fast, then they may not be able to adapt. Therefore, ideas of resilience are related not only to stability, change and response, but also to the capacity to adapt, referred to as adaptation and, where that capacity is limited, to the idea of vulnerability. Useful working definitions of adaptation and vulnerability are:

- *Adaptation*: the decision-making process and the set of actions undertaken to maintain the capacity to deal with current or future predicted change;
- *Vulnerability*: the susceptibility of a system to disturbances determined by exposure to perturbations, sensitivity to perturbations, and the capacity to adapt. (Nelson et al., 2007: 396)

One of the areas in which these concepts has become most pronounced is the area of disasters, not only because of their direct impacts, but also because many of them are part of some of the broader processes of environmental and global change.

Disasters

A disaster is 'a serious disruption of the functioning of a community or a society involving widespread human, material, economic or environmental losses and impacts, which exceeds the ability of the affected community or society to cope with its own resources' (UNISDR, 2009: 9). Economic losses from disasters such as earthquakes, tsunamis, cyclones and flooding are now reaching an average of US$250–300bn each year and are continuing to grow as a result of increased urbanisation, population growth and economic and environmental change (Swiss Re, 2014). Future expected annual losses are now estimated at US$314bn in the built environment alone, while global average annual loss is estimated to increase up to US$415bn by 2030 due to investment requirements in urban infrastructure (UNISDR, 2015a). However, one of the major issues in assessing the impacts of disasters is that the estimates of their affects can vary substantially as a result of different evaluation methods, definitions and jurisdictions (Petrucci, 2012). However, the notion of impact is broadly understood as including the direct, indirect and intangible economic, environmental and social losses caused by a disaster event (Lindell & Prater, 2003; Swiss Re, 2014). Direct losses include physical effects such as destruction and changes that reduce the functionality of an individual, system or structure. This includes damage to people (death/injury), buildings, contents, and clean-up and disposal costs. Indirect losses include: the effects of disrupted or damaged utility services and local businesses, including loss of revenue; cost increases; expenses connected to the provision of assistance, such as lodging, food and drinking water; and costs associated with the need to drive longer distances because of blocked or damaged transport systems. Intangible losses include psychological impairments caused by both direct and intangible losses that individuals personally suffer during the disaster and over the longer term (Hall *et al.*, 2016a; Petrucci, 2012).

Table 1.3 provides estimates of the economic and human impact of disasters over 2005–2014, while Table 1.4 gives a global breakdown of the human impacts for the period for different disaster types, together with definitions of the various categories of disaster. Floods and storms were the most significant with respect to occurrence, although earthquakes and tsunami led to the most deaths. In terms of the number of people affected, floods were the most significant. Table 1.5 indicates the top ten countries affected by disasters over the same decade. Importantly, while less developed countries may often be more vulnerable to disaster, developed countries can also be severely impacted. For example, the United States and Japan were the first and third most affected countries with respect to economic damage from disasters from 2005 to 2014.

Table 1.3 The economic and human impact of disasters 2005–2014

Year	Damage ($ billion)	People affected (million)	People killed
2005	214	160	93,075
2006	34	126	29,893
2007	74	211	22,422
2008	190	221	169,737
2009	46	201	15,989
2010	132	260	328,629
2011	364	212	30,083
2012	156	107	11,154
2013	119	96	21,118
2014	110	102	7000
Total	1439	1696	729,100

Source: Annual figures from EM-DAT database, Centre for Research on the Epidemiology of Disasters (CRED), Munich Re, in UNISDR (2015b).

Table 1.4 Global human impact by disaster types 2005–2014 (annual average)

Type of disaster	Occurrence	Deaths	Affected
Flood	171	5938	85,139,394
Storm	99	17,778	34,888,330
Earthquake & tsunami	25	42,381	8,401,843
Extreme temperature	24	7232	8,755,064
Landslide	17	923	299,127
Drought	15	2030	35,427,852
Wildfire	9	73	193,534
Volcanic activity	6	46	136,103
Mass movement (dry)	1	23	373
All	367	76,424	173,241,621

Source: EM-DAT (25 January 2016), OFDA/CRED, Université Catholique de Louvain, Brussels, Belgium, in UNISDR, USAID and CRED (2016).

Notes: *Explanation of EMDAT terminology*
Disaster: Situation or event which overwhelms local capacity, necessitating a request to national or international level for external assistance. Although often caused by nature, disasters can have human origins. For inclusion on the EM-DAT database disasters must conform to at least one of the following criteria:
- 10 or more people dead;
- 100 or more people affected;
- The declaration of a state of emergency; and
- A call for international assistance.

Death: Number of people who lost their lives because the event happened. Total deaths is the sum of deaths and missing.
Affected: People requiring immediate assistance during a period of emergency, i.e. requiring basic survival needs such as food, water, shelter, sanitation and immediate medical assistance. Total affected is the sum of the injured, affected and left homeless after a disaster.
Flood: A general term for the overflow of water from a stream channel onto normally dry land in the floodplain (riverine flooding), higher-than-normal levels along the coast and in lakes or reservoirs (coastal flooding) as well as ponding of water at or near the point where the rain fell (flash floods).
Earthquake: Sudden movement of a block of the Earth's crust along a geological fault and associated ground shaking.
Tsunami (Japanese: 'wave in the port'): A series of waves (with long wavelengths when traveling across the deep ocean) that are generated by a displacement of massive amounts of water through underwater earthquakes, volcanic eruptions or landslides. Tsunami waves travel at very high speed across the ocean but as they begin to reach shallow water they slow down and the wave grows steeper.

(*Continued*)

Table 1.4 (*Continued*)

Landslide: Any kind of moderate to rapid soil movement including lahar, mudslide, and debris flow. A landslide is the movement of soil or rock controlled by gravity and the speed of the movementusually ranges between slow and rapid, but not very slow. It can be superficial or deep, but the materials have to make up a mass that is a portion of the slope or the slope itself. The movement has to be downward and outward with a free face.

Drought: An extended period of unusually low precipitation that produces a shortage of water for people, animals and plants. Drought is different from most other hazards in that it develops slowly, sometimes even over years, and its onset is generally diffcult to detect. Drought is not solely a physical phenomenon because its impacts can be exacerbated by human activities and water supply demands. Drought is therefore often defined both conceptually and operationally. Operational definitions of drought, meaning the degree of precipitation reduction that constitutes a drought, vary by locality, climate and environmental sector.

Wildfire: Any uncontrolled and non-prescribed combustion or burning of plants in a natural setting such as a forest, grassland, brush land or tundra, which consumes the natural fuels and spreads based on environmental conditions (e.g. wind, topography). Wildfires can be triggered by lightning or human actions.

Volcanic activity: A type of volcanic event near an opening/vent in the Earth's surface including volcanic eruptions of lava, ash, hot vapour, gas and pyroclastic material.

Mass movement: Any type of downslope movement of earth materials.

EM-DAT explanations of terminology are available from the EMDAT glossary at http://www.emdat.be/Glossary and from the FAQ http://www.emdat.be/frequently-asked-questions.

Table 1.5 Top 10 countries most affected by disasters 2005–2014

Country	Number of disasters	Damage ($ billion)
China	286	265
United States	212	443
Philippines	181	16
India	147	167
Indonesia	141	11
Vietnam	73	7
Afghanistan	72	16
Mexico	64	26
Japan	62	239
Pakistan	59	25

Source: Annual figures from EM-DAT database, Centre for Research on the Epidemiology of Disasters (CRED), Munich Re, in UNISDR (2015b).

Natural hazards, vulnerability and crisis events

Natural hazards are an integral part of life on Earth (Leroy, 2006). A *natural hazard* is a geophysical, atmospheric or hydrological event (e.g. earthquake, landslide, tsunami, flood or drought) that has the potential to cause loss or harm. In comparison, a disaster is 'the occurrence of an extreme hazard event that impacts on communities causing damage, disruption and casualties, and leaving the affected communities unable to function normally without outside assistance' (Benson & Twig, 2007: 126). A disaster is therefore a product of social, economic and environmental vulnerabilities as well as natural hazards (Blaikie *et al.*, 1994), a situation that reflects the argument that 'there is no such thing as a natural disaster' (Hartman & Squires, 2006; Mora, 2009: 101). The focus on vulnerability emphasises that disasters, which include measurable human and economic costs (e.g. death, infrastructure destruction, cultural impact, financial loss), are more a function of vulnerable people and systems than the severity of the natural hazard.

A related concept to disaster, but one which is usually more associated with a rapid change in the socio-economic environment for business and government than the effects of a natural hazard, is the notion of crisis and crisis events in particular. Many of the crises that affect tourism, for example, are crisis events that are of a specific duration and occur in an identifiable time and space, although their impacts may be longer lasting (Ren, 2000). The notion of an event is also significant because, as Hall (2010c) noted with respect to tourism, the limited duration of a high-impact crisis event serves to enhance the attention a crisis may receive in the media and enhance the perception that the event is of concern and should be responded to.

A key issue with respect to understanding change, whether slow or rapid, is the scale at which affects are described. This is extremely important when it comes to trying to understand response to change in the context of tourism and, as we shall see, the notion of resilience. One of the most common ways of describing and understanding scale is in terms of spatial characteristics, i.e. from a global scale through to a specific site (Figure 1.1). However, it is important to recognise that change does not just occur in a top-down fashion, as significant as this might be. Rather, changes occur both 'down' and 'up' between scales. Although what happens at the national level will influence change at specific sites, regions and countries are themselves comprised of a multitude of sites. This is an important observation both practically and conceptually as it begins to raise questions about how we perceive change and the connections between different influences on change. From a tourism perspective it also means that we need to understand how the tourism system operates.

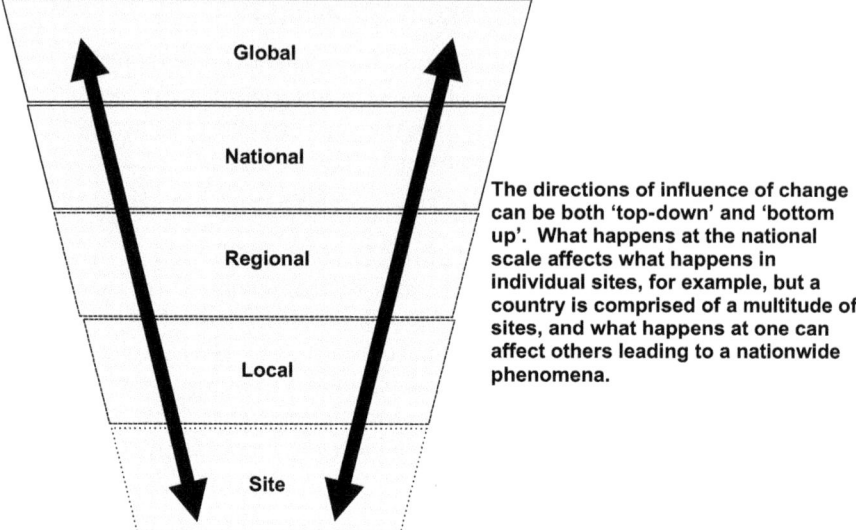

Figure 1.1 Spatial scales of change

The directions of influence of change can be both 'top-down' and 'bottom up'. What happens at the national scale affects what happens in individual sites, for example, but a country is comprised of a multitude of sites, and what happens at one can affect others leading to a nationwide phenomena.

Box 1.2 Dealing with weather and climate stressors in southern Florida

Along with major disasters like the BP Deepwater Horizon spill in 2010, the southern coast of Florida is vulnerable to long-lasting weather and climate stressors that are likely to have a negative impact on the state's multibillion-dollar tourism sector. In March 2014 local Senator Bill Nelson argued for an adaptation strategy for the destinations located on the southern coast of Florida, possibly the most threatened area by SLR in the continental United States (Gallucci, 2014). Projections up to 2060 expect sea levels to rise by at least 60 cm (Compact, 2015), with important repercussions for the state tourism oriented economy and nearly two-thirds of its population.

Despite the implementation of adaptation measures by some local government areas with respect to infrastructure adaptation and emissions mitigation strategies, climate expert Len Berry asserted that 'the tourism industry has done very little to prepare itself for the future' (quoted in Gallucci, 2014), and argued that the adoption of short-sighted strategies hinders destination resilience and climate-ready tourism.

> In response, the US Senate Subcommittee on Science and Space held a hearing in Miami to provide an overview of climate science analyses conducted by federal agencies and Florida universities, which informed state and local government adaptation plans to cope with climate change and SLR (US Senate, 2014). Particularly with respect to tourism, the hearing highlighted the need for a long-term planning vision and the necessity to divert tourism development away from low-lying areas at risk of SLR. Nevertheless, the response from the tourism stakeholders diverged substantially from the pleas of major public authorities like the Mayor of Miami Beach, which acknowledged that planning for climate change is pivotal for the resilience of the city as a major tourist destination (Levine, 2014).

Systems Thinking and the Tourism System

'Systems' approaches are integral to conceptualising the relationships that exist between external factors and the subject of any study of change and the relative direction of change (Glasson *et al.*, 2005). The notion of a tourism system is found throughout the tourism literature. Although often associated with the work of Leiper (1989), the concept of a tourism system is one that has existed since the late 1960s in various forms (Hall, 2008). A system is a group of elements organised such that each element is, in some way, either directly or indirectly interdependent with every other element and is usually regarded as being comprised of five elements:

- a set of elements (also called entities);
- the set of relationships between the elements;
- the set of relationships between those elements and their larger environment;
- a definition or identification of the system's boundaries; and
- identification of the system's function, goal or purpose, even if that only refers to the ongoing maintenance and survival of the system.

In the case of the geographical model of a tourism system popularised by Leiper (see Figure 1.2), three main spatial elements are identified: the tourist-generating region (the home or usual environment); the transit region; and the tourist-receiving region (the destination). The set of relationships between these elements is the flow of tourists. The three spatial elements and the flow

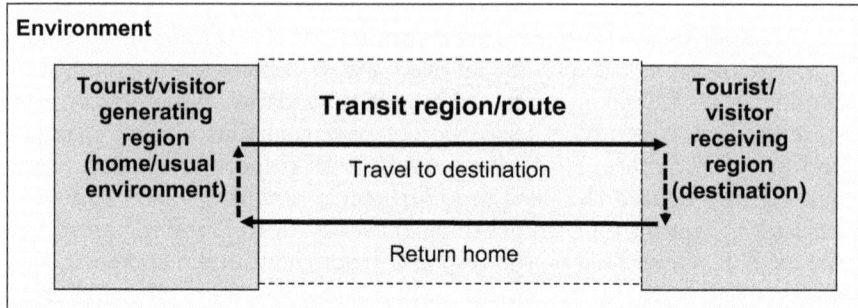

Figure 1.2 Elements of a geographical tourism system

of tourists are embedded in a larger environment, the boundaries of which are also often defined on a spatial basis. The tourism system is dynamic, reflecting the system's function of facilitating the flow of tourists.

Other types of tourism systems that could be used include: a tourist attraction system (Leiper, 1990; Lew, 1987) which is the relationship between tourists, a site to be viewed and the image or marker that makes the site significant; and a tourism production system, which is 'the mix of businesses and other organizations that provide tourism services' (Roehl, 1998: 53–4);

System-specific studies have four main issues to address (Hall & Lew, 2009):

- *Whether the system is open or closed.* A closed system has no links to or from any environment that is external to it. Open systems interact with elements or environments outside their system boundary. In reality, socio-economic systems such as tourism must have a degree of openness, although for ease of assessment the tourism system boundary is often set by selection of one of the spatial scales noted in Figure 1.1 as a governance jurisdiction. Very importantly, and depending on how it is defined, tourism is itself a specific sectoral sub-system of a larger societal and economic system.
- *Whether the system can be divided into sub-systems or interdependent elements* that are relatively weakly linked to the remainder of the system. In the case of tourism, each of the different geographical elements could potentially be treated as sub-systems if the focus was on firm interrelationships. For example, destinations are often examined in relative isolation from the rest of the system, while the destination itself can be further broken down into its various constituent elements, such as particular firm networks. Different sub-systems also have different sets of relations with other elements of the system.

- *Whether the links demonstrate flows, causal relationships or 'black-box' relationships*, the latter referring to a situation when the consequences of a linkage are known but the causal factors are not. In a tourism system, the flows of tourists can clearly be identified, along with, in some cases, the flows of capital, energy and even water – for example, embedded water and energy in the food that tourists may eat (Gössling et al., 2011, 2015). However, the exact nature of many of the relationships that result from these flows and the directions and strength of causality are often not well understood, as in the case of the tourist area cycle of evolution (Butler, 1980), where there is a suggested relationship between the number and nature of the tourist market and the characteristics of the destination over time.
- *Whether there is feedback in the system*, such that a change in x may stimulate a change in y, and this in turn will have either a positive or negative impact on x. Tourism has a number of examples of feedbacks that have a substantial impact on understandings of change and resilience, for example the notion that tourists in a tourism-generating region travel to a destination and return to the generating region with perceptions and understandings of the destination that can change future travel behaviours to that destination. Another example is the so-called 'rebound effect', which is the reduction in expected gains from new technologies that increase the efficiency of resource use, because of behavioural or other systemic responses. For instance, if a 5% improvement in vehicle fuel efficiency results in only a 2% drop in fuel use, there is a 60% rebound effect (since $(5 - 2)/5 = 60\%$). The 'missing' 3% might have been consumed by individuals driving faster or further than before because of the assumptions they had made regarding the fuel efficiency of their car. These two examples of the importance of feedback in systems, and therefore the need to gain a better understanding of system change, can be brought together in a third example, which would be the case of an ecotourism attraction or destination which is successful in attracting tourists who then generate positive 'buzz' and word of mouth which then attract so many tourists that the environmental integrity of the attraction begins to be affected.

Nevertheless, a critical factor which illustrates the difficulty in understanding feedback and the relationships between elements in a system is the length of time it takes for a feedback to be recognised as having occurred. Different effects within a tourism system will occur at different rates of time. An example of fast feedback is the well-publicised event in April 2017 on news and social media when a passenger was forcibly removed from a United Airlines flight from Chicago to Louisville, KT. Two days later, amid widespread coverage of the incident, the value of the carrier's holding company, United Continental Holdings, had fallen over 4% before noon, knocking almost a billion dollars off its value. It rallied slightly, leaving the share price down 2.8%, close to US$600m less than the company's US$22.5bn value as of the previous day's close (Rushe & Smith, 2017). Indeed, social media as a whole, and websites such as TripAdvisor, have become a significant fast feedback mechanism in tourism. An example of longer term feedback mechanisms in the aviation sector would include the impact of new technologies, whereby the introduction of a new plane or even the introduction of a new route serves to generate changes in the market which then lead to a gradual shift in transport mode shares as well as increases in people travelling by plane over time, as in the case of the introduction of budget airline carriers. Other examples of feedback mechanisms that affect tourism are discussed in Box 1.3.

Box 1.3 Feedback mechanisms in the High Arctic

An example of a prominent feedback mechanism that is receiving wide publicity at the moment is the changes occurring in the High Arctic as a result of anthropogenic climate change. In the case of both the Greenland Ice Sheet and the loss of permanent sea ice in summer in the Arctic Ocean, researchers are concerned that 'positive feedback loops' are occurring, meaning that a trend already underway is reinforcing itself. Two potential feedback mechanisms can be identified. The first is the albedo effect. When incoming sunlight strikes the ice in the Arctic Ocean, up to 70% of it is reflected back into space with the rest being absorbed as heat. However, as the Arctic sea ice melts and the incoming sunlight hits the much darker open water, only 6% is reflected back into space and 94% is converted into heat. This influences the accelerating shrinkage of Arctic sea ice and the rising regional temperature which directly affects the Greenland ice sheet (Brown, 2008).

The second positive feedback mechanism, which also highlights the complexities of such processes, is the melting of ice sheets. Rather than being a fairly simple linear process – in other words, a certain amount of the surface of an ice sheet melts each year, depending on the temperature – this is now regarded as being much more complicated. As the surface ice begins to melt, some of the water filters down through cracks in the ice sheet, lubricating the surface between the sheet and the rock beneath it. This accelerates movement of the ice sheet and glacial flow and the calving of icebergs into the surrounding ocean. The relatively warm water flowing through the glacier carries surface heat deep inside the ice sheet far faster than it would otherwise penetrate by simple conduction (Brown, 2008).

Such 'natural' changes also have a substantial influence on the tourism system, with the two going hand in hand over the long term. For example, in late March/early April 2017 more than 400 icebergs drifted into the North Atlantic shipping lanes in an unusually large swarm for so early in the season, forcing vessels to slow to a crawl or take detours of hundreds of kilometres. As of 5 April 2017, there were about 450 icebergs near the Grand Banks of Newfoundland (the waters where the Titanic was sunk), up from 37 a week earlier, according to the US Coast Guard's international ice patrol. Those kinds of numbers are usually not seen until late May or early June with the average for this time of year being about 80 (Associated Press, 2017). Clearly, so many icebergs can have significant implications for cruise ships, although the opportunity to see icebergs is more likely an attraction for tourists rather than a negative! Similarly, the loss of permanent ice in the Arctic means that cruise tourism is growing as ships can travel further north than ever before, although the carbon emissions from such travel do still contribute to climate change and hence potentially to further loss of ice (Hall & Saarinen, 2010).

The conceptualisation of the relationships and feedbacks that occur within socio-economic and environmental systems are critical to how we come to understand tourism systems and, as we shall see, resilience. The system shown in Figure 1.2 is an extremely simple portrayal of the tourism system. In reality, as readers will be aware, it is much more complex with multiple relationships and connections between different firms, organisations and suppliers, let alone the tourists as well. Such notions can make it extremely difficult to understand how systems operate. McKercher (1999), for example, argued that tourism essentially functions as a chaotic, nonlinear, non-deterministic system.

Tourism has often been described as a *complex system* (Farrell & Twining-Ward, 2005; Hall & Lew, 2009; Ndou & Petti, 2006; Walker *et al.*, 1998). A system is regarded as complex 'if its parts interact in a non-linear manner. Simple cause and effect relationships among the elements rarely exist and instead a very little stimulus may cause unpredictably large effects or no effect at all' (Baggio, 2007: 5). Complex systems exhibit several kinds of behaviours (Holland, 2014):

- *self-organisation into patterns*, e.g. a school of fish or a flock of birds;
- *chaotic behaviour* in which small changes in an initial condition ('the flapping of a butterfly's wings in Argentina') produce large later changes ('a hurricane in the Caribbean');
- *fat-tailed behaviour*, where rare events, e.g. stock market crashes, occur more frequently than would be predicted using a normal (bell-curve) distribution;
- *adaptive interaction*, where interacting agents (as in a market) modify their strategies in diverse ways as experience accumulates;
- *emergent behaviour*, where 'the sum of the parts is greater than the sum of the whole'.

Table 1.6 outlines four properties of complex systems. A complex system is therefore 'a system for which it is difficult, if not impossible to reduce the number of parameters or characterising variables without losing its essential global functional properties' (Baggio, 2007: 6). This means that a complex system needs to be understood by considering it as a whole, almost independently of the number of parts composing it (Baggio, 2008). In contrast, a *complicated system* is a collection of an, often high, number of elements whose collective action is simply the cumulative sum of the component parts. This

Table 1.6 Properties of complex systems

Property	Characteristic
Non-determinism	A complex system is fundamentally non-deterministic. It is impossible to anticipate precisely the behaviour of such a system even if we completely know the function of its constituents.
Limited functional decomposability	A complex system has a dynamic structure. It is therefore difficult, if not impossible, to study its properties by decomposing it into functionally stable parts. Its permanent interaction with its environment and its properties of self-organisation allow it to functionally restructure itself.
Distributed nature of information and representation	A complex system possesses properties comparable to distributed systems, i.e. some of its functions cannot be precisely localised.
Emergence and self-organisation	A complex system comprises emergent properties that are not directly accessible (identifiable or anticipatory) from an understanding of its components.

Source: Pavard and Dugdale (2006).

means that a complicated system needs to be understood by close consideration of its constituent elements.

A particular type of complex system is a complex adaptive system (CAS), which is 'a complex, self-organizing and self-similar (it will look like itself at different scales) collection of interacting adaptive agents (also referred to as elements)' (Hall & Lew, 2009: 69). In a CAS the parts 'interact with each other according to sets of rules that require them to examine and respond to each other's behaviour in order to improve their behaviour and thus the behaviour of the system they comprise' (Stacey, 1996: 10). A CAS has been defined as:

> a dynamic network of many agents (which may represent cells, species, individuals, firms, nations) acting in parallel, constantly acting and reacting to what the other agents are doing. The control of a CAS tends to be highly dispersed and decentralized. If there is to be any coherent behavior in the system, it has to arise from competition and cooperation among the agents themselves. The overall behavior of the system is the result of a huge number of decisions made every moment by many individual agents. (Waldrop, 1992: 144)

The main properties of a CAS (Baggio, 2008; Hall & Lew, 2009) include the following.

- A large number of elements form the system.
- Interactions among the elements are nonlinear and usually have a somewhat short range.
- There are feedback loops in the interactions.
- Complex systems are usually open and their state is far from equilibrium.
- Order is emergent and self-organised, as opposed to predetermined.
- Complex systems have a history; the 'future' behaviour depends on the past one. This means that the system's history is irreversible, as the future behaviour of a system depends on previous behaviour. Nevertheless, the system's future is sometimes unpredictable.
- Each element is unaware of the behaviour of the system as a whole; they follow their own micromotivated rule-sets and interact with local network neighbours. Such behaviour allows the system to process information, and thus to learn. Microscale networks – the set of interactions between agents – are an essential feature of CAS. Networks allow the system to solve problems using the large numbers of individual agents that have local interactions with other agents.

The concepts of tourism systems and CAS clearly have implications for how we understand tourism and how the tourism system responds to change (Farrell & Twining-Ward, 2004; Hall & Lew, 2009). Tourism, as a socio-economic activity, is regarded as sharing many of the characteristics a CAS with, for example, a destination comprising many different agents in the form of the environment, firms and organisations, and individual decision-makers (Baggio, 2008; Farrell & Twining-Ward, 2004). There are a wide diversity of relationships between the various agents and elements in a destination and they have been described in many different ways, but they usually 'do not have any *linear* characteristic nor have they any *static* trait. The reaction of the different stakeholders to inputs that may come from the external world or from what happens inside the destination may be largely unpredictable as the outcomes of their conducts. Nonetheless, the system as a whole looks to follow some general "laws"' (Baggio, 2007: 8; emphasis in the original).

From stable to turbulent systems

Farrell and Twining-Ward (2005) emphasise that as a result of field observation and global change research it is clear that CAS exist and are not just humanly devised frameworks. They also contrast greatly with complicated systems in that 'they are dynamic, operational realities, being changeable, largely unpredictable, and only minimally explainable by linear cause and effect science' (Farrell & Twining-Ward, 2005: 113). Nevertheless, they are important for our understanding of resilience given that:

> Their stability states can range from stable to turbulent, and if their resilience is insufficient, then they can cross a threshold, brought about, for example, by the onset of hostilities, the over-stressing of the local environment or the aggressive and successful competition of a more attractive destination. Once the threshold is crossed they flip from an existing condition to one that is less productive or rewarding, perhaps with unpredictable and possibly irreversible, cascading results. (Farrell & Twining-Ward, 2005: 113)

However, stability itself is a multi-layered concept that includes a number of essential properties (Table 1.7), all of which add to our understanding of the term (Grimm & Calabrese, 2011; Grimm & Wissel, 1997). Importantly, the notion of stability 'is ambiguous by itself and cannot be narrowed down to one of the properties' (Grimm & Calabrese, 2011: 5). In addition, stability concepts should, with the exception of 'persistence', not be applied to entire systems but only to the specific state variables that characterise these

Table 1.7 Basic stability concepts in socio-ecological systems

Stability concept	Definition	Comment
Constancy	The system stays essentially unchanged after perturbation	The inverse property 'variability', degree to which a variable varies over time, is also often considered
Resilience	Returning to the reference state (or dynamics) after a temporary disturbance	In theoretical ecology, this property is often simply referred to as 'stability'
Persistence	Persistence through time of a system	This concept refers to entire systems, whereas the other concepts refer to one or more specific state variables. Pahl-Wostl (2000) uses the term to refer to how long a variable lasts before it is changed into a new value
Resistance	System or variable stays essentially unchanged despite the presence of disturbances	This is an interpretation of 'constancy'
Elasticity	Speed of return to the reference state (or dynamics)	This has often been referred to as 'resilience' or 'engineering resilience'
Domain of attraction	The whole of states from which the reference state (or dynamics) can be reached after a temporary disturbance	Related to 'persistence' since the 'domain' quantitatively defines the states a system can achieve without losing its identity

Source: Grimm and Calabrese (2011); Grimm and Wissel (1997); Pahl-Wostl (2000).

systems, for example in ecological system terms to such variables as total biomass, number of species, fixation of CO_2, or spatial patterns. In a tourism system context, we could use such variables as the total number of tourists, the temporal-spatial patterns of tourists, the expenditure of tourists, the number of bed nights or the number of accommodation providers in a destination (for an early and extremely influential observation on the stability of tourism systems, see Williams & Zelinsky, 1970). Moreover, statements about the stability properties of a system also depend 'on the specific type of disturbance considered, on the temporal and spatial scales involved, and on how, precisely, the reference state or dynamics are defined' (Grimm & Calabrese, 2011: 5–6).

Resilience, therefore, is an essential property of the relative stability of a system, but it is one of several related properties. Furthermore, systems can be conceptualised in different ways with corresponding implications for how they are understood and, especially important for the present book, how actors in the wider system seek to either maintain stability in the tourism system or intervene so that they continue on a trajectory of growth. The next chapter therefore specifically discusses the concept of resilience and its evolution and use, before the following chapters examine its relevance to different parts of the tourism system.

Chapter Summary and Outline of the Book

This chapter has provided an overview of some of the factors that are driving change in tourism and which are acting to stress the tourism system at various levels – the change environment within which the tourism system is operating. The chapter has provided an introduction to tourism system concepts which are essential, as we will see, to understanding the concept of resilience and its different interpretations, because resilience thinking emerges from systems thinking.

The next chapter focuses on the concept of resilience and some of the core approaches, and highlights the importance of systems thinking for engineering and ecological formulations of resilience, of which socio-ecological approaches are a development. It also discusses some of the influential concepts that have emerged from ecological resilience including adaptive cycles and panarchy, and relates these to ideas surrounding the elements of tourism systems which then frame the remaining chapters of the book, examining particular system elements – individuals, organisations and destinations – that function at different scales. Chapter 3 focuses on resilience and the individual. The chapter draws on the wider literature before reviewing specific tourism-related research. Chapter 4 discusses resilience and organisations. The growing literature on organisational resilience is used to highlight understanding of tourism businesses' responses to change and disaster. Chapter 5 takes a destination-level analysis although it also notes the significance of cross-scale linkages for destination resilience. The chapter highlights the way in which resilience is often used as a normative concept for political purposes, particularly with respect to destinations where response to disaster and crisis is often framed by broader issues of regeneration. The final chapter then provides a reassessment of the value of resilience as a concept and what we can learn from it in a tourism context. Attention is also given to its wider potential role in planning and policy.

Table 1.8 Types of change in the tourism environment

Type of change	Examples	Frequency (number of disturbances per unit time)	Amplitude (magnitude of deviation from initial conditions caused by a disturbance)	Speed (rate of change of disturbance)	Scope (number of environmental dimensions that are affected by simultaneous disturbances)	Predictability
Regular (low intensity, gradual change)	Business cycle; election cycle; seasonality	Low–medium	Low	Low	Low	High
Hyper-turbulence (high frequency of change in one dimension)	Hyper-competition in rapidly changing markets; social fashion; increase in coral bleaching and high magnitude storm events under climate change	High	Low	High	Low	Low–medium
Specific shock (rare, rapid and high intensity environmental changes)	Industry deregulation/nationalisation; oil/energy crises; political revolution; technological substitution	Low	High	High	Low	Low
Disruptive (Infrequent gradual change in one dimension but with a high-intensity effect)	Disruptive technologies, e.g. mobile technologies, automated transport; peak oil; sea level rise; ocean acidification	Low	High	Low	Low–medium	Medium
Avalanche/institutional upheaval (Infrequent but high intensity and fast change in multiple dimensions)	Neoliberal economic reforms; biodiversity loss; deforestation	Low	High	High	High	Low

Source: After Wholey and Brittain (1989); Suarez and Oliva (2005); Geels and Schot (2007); Hall (2010c, 2017).

The circulation of individuals, and to a lesser extent firms, while being one of the defining elements of the tourism system, also means that it is extremely dynamic and stretched out over time and space between generating regions and the destination, potentially making it very susceptible to disturbance at lower levels even though the global system is characterised by relative inertia. Such an observation reinforces the extent to which larger and slower structures, i.e. the global tourism system, tend to set the conditions in which faster ones, i.e. individual destinations, function. Nevertheless, as discussed further in the next chapter, such metaphorical descriptions require further interrogation as to their validity. But what we do know is that many destinations, generating regions, tourism businesses and the people within them are susceptible to disturbance and change with unwanted and undesirable economic, environmental and social consequences (Table 1.8). Rapid socio-economic and technological change, climate change and other forms of environmental change and disasters provide existential risks to tourism destinations and businesses and the people within them. Therefore, there is growing interest from governments and the tourism industry in the capacities to adapt to and sometimes mitigate change and disturbance. We hope that this book makes a small contribution to understanding both change and tourism's response.

Further reading

On the global effects of tourism see:

Rutty, M., Gössling, S., Scott, D. and Hall, C.M. (2015) The global effects and impacts of tourism: An overview. In C.M. Hall, S. Gössling and D. Scott (eds) *The Routledge Handbook of Tourism and Sustainability* (pp. 36–63). Abingdon: Routledge.

A number of books in tourism studies discuss the application of systems models to understanding both the concept of a tourism system as well as the notion of impacts. See:

Hall, C.M. (2008) *Tourism Planning: Policies, Processes and Relationships*. New York: Pearson/Prentice Hall (discusses systems approaches as well as notions of panarchy and their application to planning and sustainability).
Hall, C.M. and Lew, A. (2009) *Understanding and Managing Tourism Impacts: An Integrated Approach*. Abingdon: Routledge.

Useful articles on particular aspects of systems thinking in tourism and tourism systems include:

Baggio, R. (2008) Symptoms of complexity in a tourism system. *Tourism Analysis* 13 (1), 1–20.
Farrell, B. and Twining-Ward, L. (2005) Seven steps towards sustainability: Tourism in the context of new knowledge. *Journal of Sustainable Tourism* 13 (2), 109–122.

Leiper, N. (1989) *Tourism and tourism systems*. Occasional Paper No. 1, Department of Management Systems, Massey University, New Zealand (an extremely influential publication but was not the first model of a tourism system. For a discussion of Leiper's work see Hall, C.M. and Page, S.J. (2010) The contribution of Neil Leiper to Tourism Studies. *Current Issues in Tourism* 13 (4), 299–309).

On systems thinking in general and its value with respect to sustainability and resilience see:

Fiksel, J. (2006) Sustainability and resilience: Toward a systems approach. *Sustainability: Science, Practice, & Policy* 2 (2), 14–21.

2 Resilience: Responding to Change

Introduction: Responding to Change

Resilience has become a core term in the natural and social sciences which is being increasingly adopted as a way to describe the capacity of a 'thing' to respond to or withstand change, especially rapid change such as that which occurs in a crisis event like an economic or financial crisis, or a disaster such as the impact of an earthquake or flood. Although the concept has a rich history in engineering and materials science, since the late 1980s the term has been picked up and utilised in a wide variety of fields such as medicine, psychology, ecology and the environmental sciences, computer systems and, of course, the social sciences, business studies and tourism (Hall *et al.*, 2016b; Janssen, 2007; Janssen *et al.*, 2006; Meerow & Newell, 2015). This growth should not really come as a surprise given how we seek to understand the rapidly changing world in which we live.

This chapter provides a discussion of the concept of resilience and the ways in which it is used in the wider science and social science literature discussed. Considerable attention is given to differentiating between engineering and ecological conceptualisations of resilience and this is then used to outline and describe further central concepts promoted by the Resilience Alliance, an international multidisciplinary network, to improve the sustainable management of socio-ecological systems (Folke, 2006). The advantages and disadvantages of the various approaches are then discussed together with a brief outline of the book.

Resilience

The etymological origins of the resilience concept date back to the late 16th and early 17th centuries and stem from the Latin term *resilio*, which literally means 'to spring back' (Klein *et al.*, 2003). Although widely used in the sciences and social sciences as well as in organisational and policy settings, there is no single accepted definition of resilience. Indeed, as an academic concept, the meaning and origins of the term are much more ambiguous (Meerow *et al.*, 2016). Nevertheless there has been phenomenal growth in its use.

Table 2.1 illustrates the use of 'resilience' in journal article titles, abstracts or keywords in the Scopus bibliographic database (Hall, 2016b). The table covers all use up to August 2016. The term was initially primarily used in engineering and material science mainly to refer to the capacity of materials and structures to withstand physical stress. Work in engineering has also been influential in computer science and infrastructure related research, i.e. power systems, where resilience is regarded as a capacity or measure of network fault tolerance, including when placed under stress. Research on personal resilience had its origins in the medical and psychology literature, which is now the single largest field of writing on resilience, and which has also been influential in organisation studies and human resources (HR) management aspects of resilience. In the social sciences, the first wave of research referring to resilience as a significant concept was initially influenced by engineering and psychological research. However, over time, ecological notions of resilience have become more important, especially as the social sciences are increasingly utilised in natural resource management and environmental change studies (Adger, 2000; Adger *et al.*, 2005). Even though Holling's (1973) seminal paper on ecological resilience underlies the great majority of publications on resilience in environmental science, it is significant to note that it was not until the late 1980s and 1990s that there was substantial growth in papers published in the area. The reasons for this are arguably related to the growth of sustainability science and the scientific response to environmental change (Janssen, 2007; Janssen *et al.*, 2006; Nelson *et al.*, 2007), especially climate change (Leichenko, 2011), emphasising, of course, that the academic research and publishing system also responds to changes in its own environment.

Nevertheless, the broad application of the concept of resilience has led to issues as to its definition and meaning (Hall, 2018). Pendall *et al.* (2010) note the 'fuzziness' of the idea of resilience in social science and urge considerable caution with regard to the rapid and simplistic transfer of an ecological systems concept into social science research and public policy applications (Hall, 2016a). For example, in social policy resilience is usually characterised as

Table 2.1 Use of 'resilience' in journal article titles, abstracts or keywords (as of August 2016)

Years	Engin.	Materials Science	Med.	Physics & Astronomy	Chem.	Social Sciences	Agriculture	Business	Energy	Environ. Sci.	Psych.	Arts	Biochem.	Earth	Comp. Sci.	Other	Total
>2015	1939	325	3514	242	190	3000	1889	1182	323	2307	1627	510	657	815	1836	160	11,539
2010–2014	3893	640	6446	495	289	5067	3301	1781	416	3995	3273	997	1084	1344	4506	238	22,856
2005–2009	2146	343	2059	340	110	1559	1167	568	85	1445	1152	161	508	461	2386	93	9385
2000–2004	847	199	749	155	61	528	546	154	23	737	443	40	153	182	628	67	3673
1995–1999	356	122	329	55	38	256	279	103	6	361	170	18	45	133	230	31	1599
1990–1994	122	82	162	26	21	84	91	37	5	144	100	11	30	104	48	2	642
1985–1989	183	85	74	7	11	42	40	15	5	73	36	6	14	56	14	3	469
1980–1984	94	76	35	5	9	15	28	2	3	53	7	2	3	30	5	2	272
1975–1979	110	107	25	2	12	5	16	–	2	–	3	1	10	5	6	–	248
1970–1974	88	65	13	1	6	2	3	–	–	5	3	1	1	1	–	2	164
1965–1969	31	18	3	2	2	–	5	–	1	1	1	–	–	–	–	2	48
1960–1964	10	14	1	2	1	2	1	–	1	–	–	–	–	–	–	–	22
<1960	30	17	9	5	3	2	2	2	–	3	1	–	3	1	6	1	51
Total	9849	2103	13433	1337	753	10562	7368	3847	870	9133	6814	1750	2506	3132	9728	602	50,967

Notes: Analysis undertaken via Scopus, 21 August 2016.
Key: Chem. = Chemistry; Engin. = Engineering; Chemical Engineering; Med. = Medicine, Dentistry, Nursing, Health Professions, Immunology & Microbiology, Pharmacology, Toxicology & Pharmaceutics; Agriculture = Agricultural & Biological Science, Veterinary; Business = Business, Management & Accounting, Economics, Econometrics & Finance, Decision Science; Environ. Sci. = Environmental Science; Psych. = Psychology, Neuroscience, Arts = Arts & Humanities; Biochem. = Biochemistry, Genetics & Molecular Biology; Earth = Earth and Planetary Sciences; Comp. Sci. = Computer Science, Mathematics, Other = Undefined, Multidisciplinary
Source: Hall (2016b).

being successful adaptation in the presence of risk or adversity (Jenson & Fraser, 2015a; Luthar & Cicchetti, 2000; Luthar et al., 2000; Olsson et al., 2003), and resilience is regarded as

> ... the outcome of an interactive process involving risk, protection, and promotion. Thus, adaptation, which is expressed through individual behavior, is interpreted as an interactive product involving the presence or absence of specific risk; level of exposure to risk; and the strength of the specific risk, protective, and promotive factors present in a child's life. (Jenson & Fraser, 2015b: 15)

Positive thinking has come to be regarded as a well-accepted strategy for building personal resilience after traumatic experiences such as a bushfire (Gibbs et al., 2013). However, other authors, such as Hayward (2013: 37) suggest that 'the idea of resilience as a personal quality must be treated with caution':

> Given that human resilience is best understood as the interrelationships among the individuals and their community, environment, and social institutions, it has been disturbing to witness the plethora of consultancies that have sprung up in the wake of our local disaster to offer courses in personal resilience, aimed at helping employees to adapt to the 'new normal' of life lived in ongoing aftershocks. The implicit subtext of many of these self-help resilience courses appears to be to restore individuals to their roles as willing workers to aid an economic recovery as quickly as possible. (Hayward, 2013: 37)

In a community context, Sharifi and Yamagata (2016) suggest that resilience is widely understood in the context of the 'four abilities': the ability to prepare and plan for, absorb, recover from, and successfully adapt to adverse events. In business and organisational studies the notion of resilience is usually used with respect to organisational survival in the face of severe shocks (Davoudi et al., 2012; Shaw & Maythorne, 2013), if not thriving on change and the unexpected (Sheffi, 2015). Within organisation theory, the concept of resilience has attracted interest from research on positive organisational scholarship (Sutcliffe & Vogus, 2003) and high-reliability organisations (Roberts, 1990). Norris et al. (2008) view resilience as a process that links organisational resources to a positive trajectory of performance following a disaster. In this literature, resilience is defined as positive adjustment under challenging conditions such that the organisation is stronger after an adverse event (Vogus & Sutcliffe, 2007). Resilient organisations are regarded as being less likely to fail, have fewer negative consequences as a result of disaster, and are likely to recover more quickly compared to a vulnerable organisation (Bruneau *et al.*, 2003). Nevertheless, as Nilakant *et al.* (2016) point out, there is very little empirical evidence to support such conceptual arguments (see also Lengnick-Hall & Beck, 2005, 2009). Nilakant *et al.* (2014, 2016) argue that organisational resilience should perhaps best be regarded as a continuum, ranging from bouncing back to bouncing forward – that is, from surviving a crisis to thriving in the new environment following a crisis. They suggest that it is useful to view resilience as consisting of two aspects: (a) inherent resilience that enables an organisation to function well in the absence of any adverse events; and (b) adaptive resilience, which refers to flexibility in response during adverse events (Cutter *et al.*, 2008). 'Inherent resilience reduces the probability of failure and reduces negative consequences of failures, whereas adaptive resilience that enables the organization to recover quickly after an adverse event' (Nilakant *et al.*, 2016: 44).

The resilience of small business, which is often vital for tourism, is regarded as being relatively unexplored but vital (Herbane, 2010), as understanding the resilience of small business owners in the wake of disasters, for example, is important not only in terms of lost revenue but also in terms of the damage to services, local communities, supply chain capacity and business capability (de Vries & Hamilton, 2016). Biggs *et al.* (2015) define resilience as a business's ability to maintain and adapt in the face of disturbance while maintaining its identity. Doern (2016) analysed small business owners' resilience during the London riots of 2011. She considered the preparedness and immediate impact of a major crisis, and regarded small business resilience as a mindset that is both anticipatory and containment oriented.

In ecology, the seminal paper by Holling (1973) defined resilience as the ability of a system to maintain its functionality and behaviour after a disturbance. This was later built on by Walker *et al.* (2004) in one of the most widely cited socio-ecological definitions, as resilience being 'the capacity of a system to absorb disturbance and reorganise while undergoing change so as to retain essentially the same function, structure, identity and feedbacks' (Walker *et al.*, 2004: 6) that existed before the disturbance event.

An attempt at an integrative definition is to be found in the work of the highly influential Rockefeller Foundation, which defines resilience as

> The capacity of individuals, communities and systems to survive, adapt, and grow in the face of stress and shocks, and even transform when conditions require it. Building resilience is about making people, communities and systems better prepared to withstand catastrophic events – both natural and manmade – and able to bounce back more quickly and emerge stronger from these shocks and stresses. (Rockefeller Foundation, 2016)

Although there are clearly commonalities in these definitions there are also substantial differences, raising the prospect that resilience is a polysemic concept that has been defined differently in different disciplines and contexts (Hall, 2018; Sharifi & Yamagata, 2016). The implications of this situation are clearly substantial and are well described by Cutter *et al.* (2010: 1):

> Lingering concerns from the research community focus on disagreements as to the definition of resilience, whether resilience is an outcome or a process, what type of resilience is being addressed (economic systems, infrastructure systems, ecological systems, or community systems), and which policy realm (counterterrorism; climate change; emergency management; long-term disaster recovery; environmental restoration) it should target. (Cutter *et al.*, 2010: 1)

Order out of chaos? (Or why socio-ecological systems are not really the same as a building)

Different interpretations of resilience have implications not only for how systems are understood but also for how they are designed and managed (Folke, 2006). Critical to this, as discussed in the previous section on tourism systems, is how systems are conceptualised. A substantial division exists in the literature between so called 'engineering resilience' and 'ecological resilience' (Holling, 1996, 2001). Engineering resilience is the same as 'elasticity' as defined in Table 1.7. Engineering resilience is a measure of the speed at which a system can return to its previous equilibrium. But why 'engineering'? Because it can easily be calculated from simple dynamical models representing communities of interacting populations (Grimm & Calabrese, 2011; Otto & Day, 2007). Although this is a static conception of resilience linear stability analysis, the 'engineering resilience' approach dominated theoretical ecology in the 1980s and much of the 1990s. However, many ecologists felt that these approaches reflected a quite narrow notion of the stability properties of ecosystems and did not allow the study of entire systems and how their internal organisation and mechanisms promote persistence, despite disturbances which could cause ecosystems to lose their characteristic features and functions (Grimm & Calabrese, 2011; Gunderson & Holling, 2002). Instead, many such researchers focused on the holistic ideas of ecological resilience framed by the work of Holling (1973, 1996).

According to Holling (1973: 17), 'resilience determines the persistence of relationships within a system and is a measure of the ability of these systems to absorb changes of state variables, driving variables, and parameters, and still persist. In this definition resilience is the property of the system and persistence or probability of extinction is the result.' Holling (1973) suggested two measures of resilience:

> Since resilience is concerned with probabilities of extinction, firstly, the overall area of the domain of attraction will in part determine whether chance shifts in state variables will move trajectories outside the domain. Secondly, the height of the lowest point of the basin of attraction ... above equilibrium will be a measure of how much the forces have to be changed before all trajectories move to extinction of one or more of the state variables. (Holling, 1973: 20)

Holling's definition was later modified and adapted and laid the foundations for ecological resilience. Ecological resilience suggests that bouncing back to a previous equilibrium may be impossible in complex ecosystems because they can shift between multiple stable states (Gunderson, 2000; Gunderson & Holling, 2002; Walker *et al.*, 2004). But, significantly, Holling's (1973) and subsequent definitions are verbal and qualitative, not mathematical and quantitative, and comprise several stability properties simultaneously: persistence, resistance, resilience and domain of attraction (see also Table 1.7; Grimm & Calabrese, 2011) (Table 2.2).

Box 2.1 Disturbance ecology

Disturbance ecology refers to the disruption of the function of ecosystems by discrete events. One of the most widely used definitions of disturbance is that of Pickett and White (1985: 7): 'any relatively discrete event in time that disrupts ecosystem, community, or population structure and changes resources, substrate availability, or the physical environment'. Disturbance is an extremely important concept in ecology. Disturbance was once viewed largely as damaging the 'balance of nature' and seen as synonymous with habitat destruction (Hall, 2016a; Worster, 1990). This has meant, for example, that in colonial countries such as Australia, Canada, New Zealand, South Africa and the United States where colonists came from different understandings of the role of fire in the environment, some fire-adapted landscapes, which depend on fire for regeneration, have been severely affected by the suppression of fire under a cultural perspective that sees fire as 'unnatural' (Pyne, 1982, 1991). However, certain forms of ecosystem disturbance, including fire, floods, storms and other 'natural disasters', are now recognised as playing a fundamental and creative role in biodiversity conservation by maintaining 'the natural heterogeneity in environmental conditions that organisms experience through space, time, or both' (Brawn et al., 2001: 252).

As noted in Chapter 1, an important element in seeking to understand the role of disturbance in either ecosystems or socio-economic systems is the assumption of long-term stability in the system prior to disturbance. In ecology, the concept of succession has been extremely important with regard to such ideas. Ecological succession is 'an orderly unidirectional process of community change in which communities replace each other until a stable (self-reproducing) community is reached' (Johnson & Miyanishi, 2010: 1). This very influential concept has been part of the history of ecological ideas since the 19th century (Worster, 1990), and is based on the idea that, for each type of environment, species are adapted to different stages in a succession and in some way make the environment unsuitable for themselves and better suited for the species in the next stage until a stable 'climax' is reached, i.e. a representation of environmental histories and futures in which there is 'sequential invasion and replacement of dominants driven by facilitation' (Johnson & Miyanishi, 2010: 3) as the natural order of things (Hall, 2016a). In tourism studies an analogue is perhaps seen with respect to the ideas in the tourism area life cycle. As Hall noted:

> Despite substantial evidence that traditional ideas of succession are not well supported by research results, the concept of succession persists. Change does definitely occur of course, ecological communities are constantly changing, but species assemble and reassemble in different, and sometimes novel or unfamiliar, combinations, often as a result of the effects of change in the physical environment. (Hall, 2016a: 271)

The trajectories of ecological succession from one state to another are complex and problematic, especially as assumptions of long-term stability without disturbance usually do not hold (Prach & Walker, 2011). Community assembly is therefore neither entirely predictable nor completely random. As Johnson and Miyanishi (2010: 11) argue, 'All disturbances have differential impacts on different populations within communities and also on different ecological processes. Therefore, to advance our understanding of the ecological effects of disturbances, we must couple the disturbance process with ecological processes.'

Table 2.2 Modifications in the understandings of resilience at different levels of integration

Nature of comprehension	Definition	Source
Disturbance–focused	Measure of the persistence of systems and of their ability to absorb change and disturbance and still maintain the same relationships between populations or state variables.	Holling (1973)
Disturbance–focused	Magnitude of disturbance that can be absorbed before the system changes its structure by changing the variables and processes that control behaviour.	Holling and Gunderson (2002)
Ecological–functional	Capacity of a system to absorb disturbance and reorganise while undergoing change so as to still retain essentially the same function, structure, identity and feedbacks.	Gundersson and Holling (2002)
Ecological–systemic	(1) Capacity of a system to undergo disturbance and maintain its functions and controls, to be measured by the magnitude of disturbance that the system can tolerate and still persist; (2) Ability of the system to resist disturbance and the rate at which it returns to the pre-disturbance steady state (engineering resilience after Pimm (1984).	Carpenter et al. (2001)
Ecological–quantitative	(1) The amount of change (external pressure) the system can sustain without changing the domain of attraction; (2) The degree to which the system is capable of self-organisation; (3) The degree to which the system can build capacity to learn and adapt.	Walker et al. (2002)
Social–ecological: ecosystem services	The underlying capacity of an ecosystem to maintain ecosystem services in the face of a fluctuating environment and human perturbations.	Deutsch et al. (2003)
Social–ecological: societal progress	The capacity of ecosystems to sustain societal development and progress with essential ecosystem services.	Folke et al. (2003)
Social–ecological: functions and services	Resilience refers to the magnitude of change or disturbance that a system can experience without shifting into an alternate state which has different structural and functional properties and supplies different bundles of ecosystem services.	Resilience Alliance (2010)
Explicitly normative	Maintenance of natural capital.	Tot (2001)
Dynamic: development	Resilience is the capacity of a system, be it an individual, a forest, a city or an economy, to deal with change and continue to develop. It is about how humans and nature can use shocks and disturbances like a financial crisis or climate change to spur renewal and innovative thinking.	Stockholm Resilience Center (2015)
Sociopolitical: transformation	Resilient systems in agricultural landscapes are able to recover their fundamental structure and functionality in the face of change or to transform into new regimes where this has desirable environmental and social outcomes.	CGIAR (2014)

Source: After Brand (2005); Müller et al. (2016).

The extremely dynamic conception of ecological resilience is now widely acknowledged within the ecological community, especially in relation to addressing issues of sustainability (Ahern, 2011), although 'it has not been adopted by theoretical ecologists and modellers, because there is no simple way to quantify ecological resilience' (Grimm & Calabrese, 2011: 8). Furthermore, although the work of Holling and the Resilience Alliance on ecological resilience is increasingly widely cited, it has not yet been adopted throughout the social sciences beyond its role as a metaphor, suggesting that Meerow and Newell's (2015: 2) comment that 'It follows that as complexity science expands, more fields will adopt a dynamic conceptualization of resilience' may be optimistic. Nevertheless, drawing comparisons between the two approaches can be highly informative with respect to understanding the different 'traditions' and approaches that exist with regard to resilience as well as the relative value of different approaches.

The engineering tradition of resilience (which could also arguably be described as the economic tradition) is a relatively *static* conceptualisation of resilience which focuses on core attributes of *efficiency, constancy* and *predictability*, which are all critical elements, as Holling (1996) acknowledged, of engineering's focus on fail-safe designs. The engineering resilience tradition is therefore based on *complicated systems*. Engineering resilience concentrates on stability near an equilibrium steady state, 'where resistance to disturbance and speed of return to the equilibrium are used to measure the property' (Holling, 2010: 53). In contrast, ecological resilience focuses on core attributes of *persistence, change* and *unpredictability*, and these are attributes embraced by those with an evolutionary perspective and who search for safe-fail designs. The *dynamic* conceptualisation of the ecological resilience tradition is based on *complex systems*. The ecological resilience definition emphasises 'conditions far from any equilibrium steady state, where instabilities can flip a system into another regime of behavior' (another stability domain) (Holling, 2010: 53). The measurement of ecological resilience is the magnitude of disturbance that can be absorbed before the system changes its structure by changing the variables and processes that control behaviour.

As Holling himself noted, 'effective and sustainable development of technology, resources, and ecosystems requires ways to deal not only with near-equilibrium efficiency but with the reality of more than one equilibrium' (Holling, 2010: 54). This has enormous implications for evaluating, managing and understanding change and complexity. 'The two contrasting aspects of stability – essentially one that focuses on maintaining efficiency of function (engineering resilience) and one that focuses on maintaining

Table 2.3 Different foci of engineering versus ecological resilience

Engineering resilience	Ecological resilience
Equilibrium	Domain of attraction
Numerical values of state variables	Relationship between structure and function
Rate of recovery after perturbation (elasticity)	Ability to absorb the effect of disturbance
Maximising system performance	Preserving desirable system function
Optimal control	Monitoring and predicting

Source: After Grimm and Calabrese (2011); Song *et al.* (2015).

existence of function (ecological resilience) – are so fundamental that they can become alternative paradigms' (Holling, 2010: 54) and have different foci (Table 2.3). This also includes the mathematical focus that is applied. Engineering resilience is regarded as drawing more from deductive mathematical theory and an associated implicit assumption of global stability in which only one equilibrium steady state exists or, if other states exist, they should be avoided (Holling, 1996, 2010). In contrast, ecological resilience comes more from inductive theory formulation via traditions of applied mathematics and studies of the impacts of large-scale management disturbances to ecosystems.

According to Grimm and Calabrese (2011), the three main differences between ecological and engineering resilience are:

(1) A shift in focus from equilibria to domains of attraction, often also called 'regimes', where a certain characteristic network, or regime, of processes controls the system's properties and functions. In an ecological context this is important because ecosystems are usually not in equilibrium but can change within relatively wide margins, without losing their identity.
(2) A shift in focus from numerical values of state variables to 'relationships', i.e. to the internal organisation of systems which gives rise to their properties.
(3) A shift in focus from the ability to recover after disturbance (engineering resilience) to the ability to 'absorb' the effect of disturbances, i.e. not to change essentially in the first place (ecological resilience). Mechanisms are believed to be in place which buffer the effect of disturbances, the most important implication of which is that if this buffering ability is lost, it can lead to an abrupt regime shift.

Box 2.2 Social resilience and socio-ecological resilience

Influentially defined by Adger (2000: 361) as 'the ability of communities to withstand external shocks to their social infrastructure', social resilience has become a major separate area of research on resilience thinking especially because of its relevance to policy makers and planners. Social resilience is closely related to ideas of ecological resilience but also draws on research in disaster management, development studies, natural hazards and urban and regional planning. Coming in great part from the latter perspective, Hall and Lamont (2013: 2) use the notion of social resilience to 'refer to the capacity of groups of people bound together in an organization, class, racial group, community or nation to sustain and advance their wellbeing in the face of challenges to it' and regard it as an 'essential characteristic of ... successful societies – namely, societies that provide their members with the resources to live healthy, secure and fulfilling lives'. Significantly, in a manner which reflects something of the multi-scaled approach of ecological resilience, Hall and Lamont (2013) also believe that the understanding of social resilience requires making linkages between the micro, meso and macro levels of enquiry.

Over time, social dimensions, including economics and politics as well as social wellbeing, have increasingly become part of ecological resilience thinking (Brown, 2014; Folke, 2006). In many ways this should not be surprising given the extent to which humans are themselves major stresses of ecological systems as well as being part of 'natural' systems. The term social ecological system, the 'linked system of people and nature' (Walker & Salt, 2006: 164), is sometimes specifically used to highlight the ways in which ecological and social systems are interdependent, integrated and coupled systems that are co-evolving. By its very nature, resilience assumes disturbance (Hall, 2016a). When transferred to the social world, this means that uncertainty, variability in the environment, and surprise are 'part of the game and you need to be prepared for it and learn to live with it' (Folke, 2006: 255). Although subsumed under the overall ecological resilience approach, the particular 'twist' given by including social dimensions of resilience is the role of innovation, learning and transformability in the human system as part of the adaptive capacity of people, communities and places to disturbance and change (Folke, 2006). As Brown (2016: 79) observed, 'The broadening of resilience concepts ... to encompass a much wider social ecological systems perspective represents a shift not only in focus and from single and multiple and interdisciplinary analysis, it also integrates a new set of ideas around adaptation and adaptive capacity, learning and innovation'. Nevertheless, the explicit expansion of ecosystem resilience to socio-ecological resilience creates some fundamental shifts in thinking that are often not explicitly noted in discussions on resilience (Hall, 2016a).

'In ecology, resilience is neither a positive nor a negative: while longer-term survival may be appreciated by an individual of a species (if they are cognizant enough to appreciate such things), it may make no difference to the survival of a species or to ecosystem stability' (Hall, 2016a: 279). However, if the role of human agency is included in not only formulating notions of resilience but also their application and value, especially when the focus shifts from the resilience of a system to the resilience or survival of a firm, organisation or individual, then this suggests a move from a more stochastic understanding of change in ecology to one which is often much more deterministic and in which communities, organisations and individuals supposedly possess the attributes with which to adapt to external change (Hall, 2016a). 'This view of resilience is important because it acknowledges that people themselves are able to shape the trajectory of change ... and play a central role in the degree and type of impact caused by the change' (Maguire & Cartwright, 2008: 5).

If resilience is translated as a normative goal of being the capacity to generate ecosystem and/or economic services, it raises significant issues as to how resilience is to be maintained. For example, this means that resilience could be maintained through an inequitable social and economic system (Ernston, 2008). In incorporating human agency into notions of resilience, a more critically formulated definition of resilience would therefore suggest that resilience is the capacity of a system to sustain a certain set of services, in the face of disturbance, uncertainty and change, for a certain set of humans. Applying such an approach to research suggests that researchers need to analyse not only how systems are managed, but also which services are prioritised and for whom (Daily & Matson, 2008). As Hudson (2010) noted, questions of power in the determination of the role, agenda setting and interpretation of resilience in policy making are often unaddressed, as are the distributional effects of the promotion of particular interpretations of resilience (Cutter *et al.*, 2010; Vale, 2014). Indeed, following on from Lasswell's (1936) dictum of politics as the study of who gets what, where and how, it can also be suggested that the question of 'resilience for whom and for what' (Armitage & Johnson, 2006) needs to be asked (Hall, 2016a). Overly simplistic interpretations of resilience as equated to the survival of people or organisations, without appreciating the complex and heterogeneous nature of the regional systems they are embedded in (Hudson, 2010), only leads to policy fixes that 'exceed the capability of the research base to justify them' (Christopherson et al., 2010: 9).

Therefore, a key issue in determining policies is the development of a better understanding of the nature of the system that is meant to become resilient.

Regime shift

If environmental conditions change too much, for example due to environmental change, human impact or both, such as climate change, ecosystems can suddenly change to another regime (also known as a 'stability domain' or 'basin of attraction'). The system now behaves in a different way and has a different identity (Walker & Salt, 2012). For example, in coral reefs, which are a major attraction for tourism, there is a threshold (also called a tipping point) related to nutrient levels. If nutrient levels are too high, for example as a result of agricultural runoff, the nutrients stimulate the growth of algae which can then outcompete with coral polyps for bare space on the reef. Below the nutrient-load threshold, coral polyps outcompete algae. Therefore, when events such as coral bleaching or cyclones/hurricanes affect reefs that are exposed to high levels of nutrients and create new areas of bare space, this can provide the trigger for a regime shift from coral to algal reefs. Nevertheless, many regime shifts are reversible; for example, providing not all coral has been lost, it is possible that a subsequent drop in nutrient availability below the threshold at which coral polyps are outcompeted by algae may allow a coral reef to regenerate (Mumby & Steneck, 2008; Mumby et al., 2007, 2013).

According to Walker and Salt (2012: 6), 'you need to put the emphasis on thresholds because crossing them can come with huge consequences. Resilience practice is very much about thresholds'. Nevertheless, they go on to note:

> Thresholds are often not easy to identify. Most variables in a system don't even have them; that is, considered on their own, the variables show a simple linear response to the change in underlying controlling variables and at no point exhibit a dramatic change in behaviour ... For

the variables that do have thresholds, it's important to know about them because they cause regime shifts ...

So, for a number of reasons, thresholds are difficult things to deal with: they come in different forms and they're often difficult to spot (that is, until you've crossed them, and then it can be too late).

And if that weren't enough, some thresholds can move because of other changes in the system. This means that resilience (the distance your system is away from a threshold) can increase or decrease. (Walker & Salt, 2012: 6, 9)

Regime shifts have been demonstrated for a number of ecosystems, although the question of whether all systems, including ecosystems, show abrupt changes and are characterised by alternative states still remains open (Schroeder *et al.*, 2005). Nevertheless, as Grimm and Calabrese (2011: 9–10) suggest, 'regime shifts are the most important element of the resilience approach fostered by the Resilience Alliance. They make us focus on the risk of losing ecosystem functions that are vital to human wellbeing', leading them to conclude, 'management should not be concerned about equilibria and some kind of "balance of nature", but should instead focus on the key mechanisms that allow a system to persist, and on the fact that these mechanisms have only a certain capacity, which can be reduced by environmental change and human impact' (Grimm & Calabrese, 2011: 10).

Adaptive cycle and panarchy

The Resilience Alliance perspective on resilience is based on cyclic changes of two properties: potential and connectedness. According to Holling and Gunderson (2002: 51): 'Potential sets limits to what is possible – it determines the number of the alternative options for the future. Connectedness determines the degree to which a system can control its own destiny ... Resilience determines how vulnerable the system is to unexpected disturbances and surprises that can exceed or break that control.'

The adaptive cycle model is a way of describing the progression of a socio-ecological system over time in terms of its various stages of function and organisation over time. The four stages of the adaptive cycle are rapid growth, conservation, release and reorganisation, followed again by rapid growth (Holling, 2001) (Table 2.4; Figure 2.1a, b). Connectedness is assumed to increase over time, leading to a stage of high internal control and limited potential to cope with disturbances. When sufficient disturbance occurs then such overconnected systems collapse into a release period, where the system has the potential to reorganise, thereby better coping with disturbance.

Table 2.4 Stages of the adaptive cycle

Stage	Description	Resilience
Rapid growth and/or exploitation (r phase)	Resources/capital are readily available, and agents can exploit niches and opportunities	High
Conservation (K phase)	Resources are increasingly locked up and system becomes less flexible and responsive	Decreasing
Release (Ω[omega] phase)	A disturbance causes chaos/collapse and a consequent release of resources/capital	Low
Reorganisation/renewal (α[alpha] phase)	New actors and, in social systems, new ideas can take hold, leading to a recommencement of the cycle	Increasing

Source: After Gunderson and Holling (2002); Holling (2001).

Resilience, therefore, is assumed to change in tandem with the adaptive cycle. When connectedness is low, resilience is high because the system can therefore vary over a wide range of states and respond to disturbance in many different ways. In contrast, when connectedness is high, resilience is low because the system is more tightly organised and has fewer options for responding to disturbances. Interestingly, Grimm and Calabrese (2011) suggest that engineering resilience can also be high at the same time as ecological resilience is high, i.e. the effects of not too extreme disturbances may quickly disappear (Holling, 2001). Taken as a whole, the adaptive cycle has two opposing modes: a development loop (or fore loop) and a release and reorganisation loop (or back loop). The fore loop 'is characterized by the accumulation of capital, by stability and conservation, a mode that is essential for system (and therefore human) wellbeing to increase. The back loop is characterized by uncertainty, novelty and experimentation. The back loop is the time of greatest potential for the initiation of either destructive or creative change in the system' (Walker & Salt, 2006: 81–82; Figure 2.1c). Nevertheless, the four-phase model is not the only possible version of the adaptive cycle, as Walker and Salt (2006: 82) note, 'It is important to emphasize that the adaptive cycle is not an absolute, it is not a fixed cycle, and many variations exist in human and natural systems … Transitions are possible (and have been observed) between all phases except from the release or reorganization phases directly to the conservation phase' (see Figure 2.1d).

The different transitions in the cycle also raise substantial questions about the temporal and spatial units under which the adaptive cycle is being examined as, over time for example, it is possible that a specific system that is being studied will move between the different types of transitions

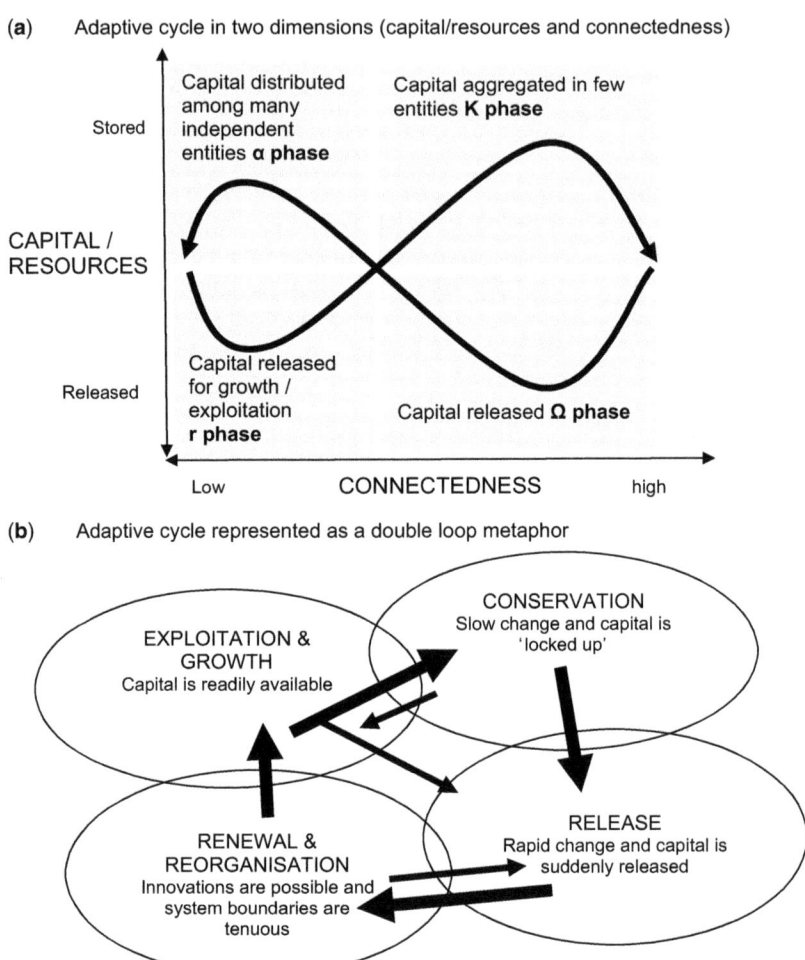

Figure 2.1 Metaphors of adaptive cycles

depending on the nature of the disturbance. In an ecological context, exergy (the opposite of entropy and the law that ecosystems tend towards maximum energy storage, maximum power and maximum ascendency as an emergent property; Jørgensen & Svirezhev, 2004) and adaptive cycles tend to apply to smaller spatial units, not an entire ecosystem (Grimm & Calabrese, 2011). However, this observation in itself is likely to be related to the length of the observational timespan, the spatial metric used (Renslow et al., 2016) and, possibly, the absence of anthropogenic disturbance.

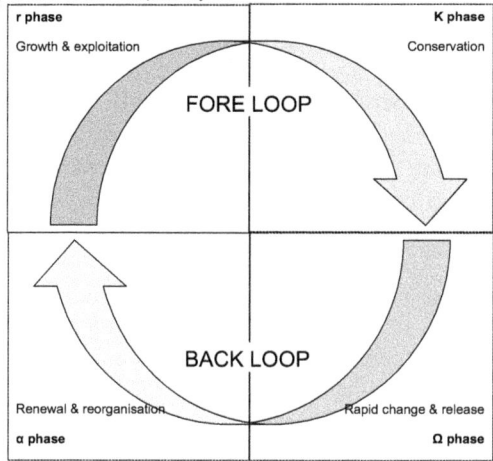
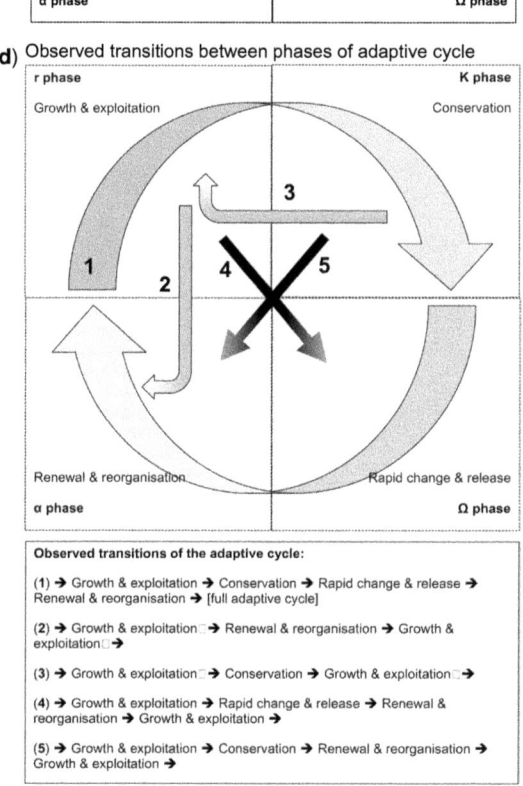

Figure 2.1 (*Continued*)

Social-ecological systems clearly have structures and functions that cover a wide range of spatial and temporal scales. Figure 2.2 illustrates the influence of temporal and spatial resolution on assessing tourism-related phenomena and change (adapted from Hall, 2004). However, processes and structures are linked – 'what happens at one scale can influence or even drive what's happening at other scales' (Walker & Salt, 2006: 90) – and these interactions can occur both bottom up and top down. This means that we cannot really understand the dynamics and stability and change at one scale without considering what happens at other scales, what are therefore described as 'cross-scale' interactions (Walker et al., 2004).

The ideas behind such cross-scale interactions are not new and relate strongly to systems thinking and seeking to understand the relationships and interactions between different levels of a system. However, Simon (1974), who described such structures as hierarchies, was one of the first to argue for their adaptive significance. 'As long as the transfer from one level to another is maintained, the interactions within the levels themselves can be transformed or the variables changed without the whole system losing its integrity' (Holling et al., 2002: 72). Rather than use the concept of hierarchy,

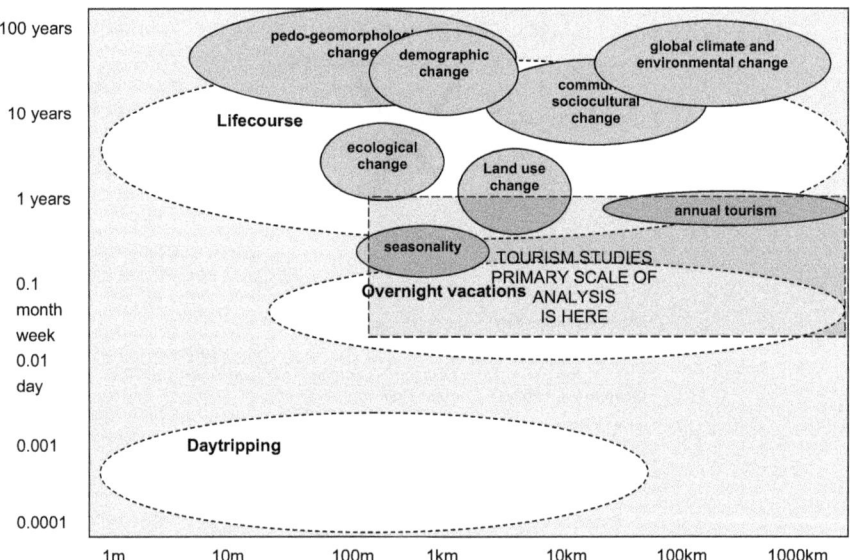

Figure 2.2 The influence of temporal and spatial resolution on assessing tourism-related phenomenon
Source: Adapted from Hall (2004).

which Holling et al. (2002) argued was burdened by the rigid, top-down nature of its common meeting, they invented the term panarchy (after the Greek god Pan, the god of nature) to describe 'the adaptive and evolutionary nature of adaptive cycles that are nested one within the other across space and time scales' (Holling et al., 2002: 74; see Figure 2.3). Larger and slower structures tend to set the conditions in which faster ones function. However, the structures and the relationships between them are not static. Ecological resilience thinking already argues that the adaptive cycle is highly dynamic but it also suggests that when an adaptive cycle at a particular level in a panarchy enters its omega rapid change and release phase then the corresponding collapse can cascade up to the next larger and slower level by triggering a crisis, especially if the larger level is in a K conservation phase. In its original formulation, this was termed 'revolt'. In contrast, the downward cross-scale interaction was termed 'remember' and was used to describe the

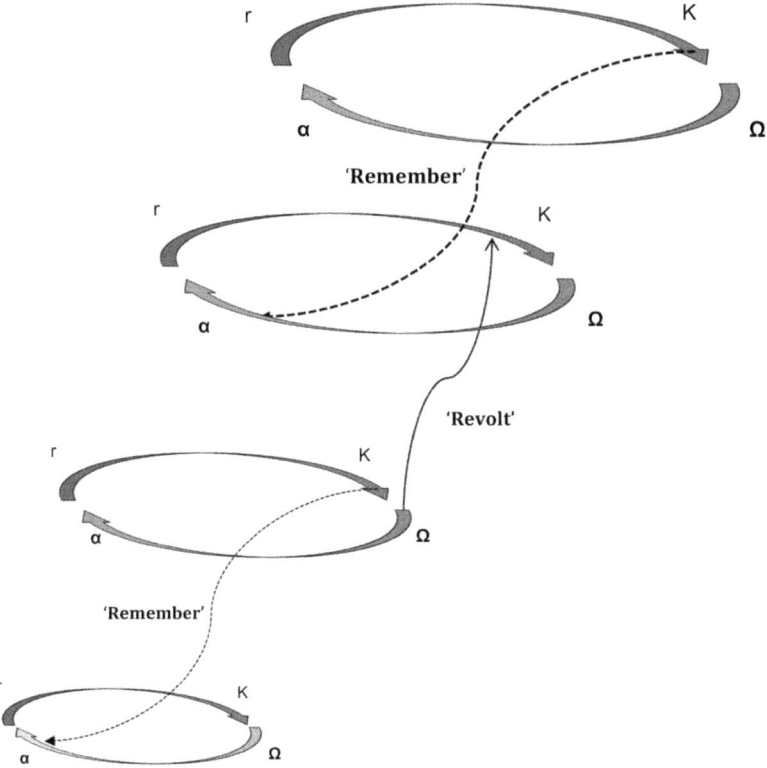

Figure 2.3 Panarchy: Linked adaptive scales

situation of when 'a catastrophe is triggered at a level. The opportunities and constraints for the renewal of the cycle are strongly organized by the K phase of the next and slower level' (Holling *et al.*, 2002: 76). Importantly, the notion of panarchy is regarded by Holling *et al.* as clarifying the meaning of sustainable development: 'Sustainability is the capacity to create, test, and maintain adaptive capability. Development is the process of creating, testing, and maintaining opportunity' (Holling *et al.*, 2002: 76). These relationships remain very clearly evidenced in the work of the Resilience Alliance:

> Adaptive cycles are nested in a hierarchy across time and space which helps explain how adaptive systems can, for brief moments, generate novel recombinations that are tested during longer periods of capital accumulation and storage. These windows of experimentation open briefly, but the results do not trigger cascading instabilities of the whole because of the stabilizing nature of nested hierarchies. In essence, larger and slower components of the hierarchy provide the memory of the past and of the distant to allow recovery of smaller and faster adaptive cycles. A nested hierarchy of adaptive cycles represents a panarchy. (http://www.resalliance.org/adaptive-cycle)

Figure 2.4 provides an example of a panarchy in terms of tourism and climate change (Scott *et al.*, 2012). The figure illustrates the various physical levels of

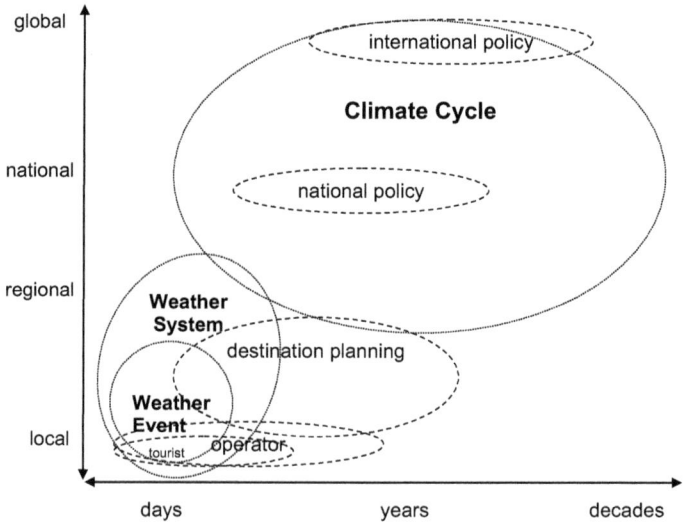

Figure 2.4 Panarchy: Tourism and climate change

climate and weather from a weather event, through to a weather system and then to climate, as well as the multiple tourism scales from the tourist and operator through to destination management and national and international policy. All of these levels are nested inside each other and interact across scales.

The concepts of the adaptive cycle and panarchy have proven to be attractive to both researchers and policy makers including, as the following chapters highlight, with respect to tourism. Nevertheless, while they are conceptually useful they are more metaphors than testable scientific theory (Grimm & Calabrese, 2011). However, ecological resilience, along with engineering resilience, generates significant contributions to the conceptual framing of resilience in tourism.

Resilience and Tourism

This final section of this introductory chapter seeks to provide a broad-scale overview of the themes and issues that have been covered in tourism-related research on resilience. Table 2.5 provides an overview of the use of the terms 'resilience' and 'tourism' in journal article titles, abstracts or keywords in the Scopus bibliometric database up to late 2016 (Hall, 2016b).

The concept of resilience came relatively late to tourism as a term with no significant growth in use of the term as a keyword until the 2000s. At the time of conducting the bibliometric survey more than half of all writing on resilience and tourism had been conducted post-2010. The majority of research related to tourism and resilience is in the environmental sciences, social sciences and business studies and, unlike the wider use of the concept in academic research, there is very limited research on the tourism-related dimensions of resilience in medical research. The most popular journals in which research had been published were *Journal of Sustainable Tourism* (18 papers), *Ecology and Society* (published by the Resilience Alliance) (12), *Tourism Geographies* (10), *Current Issues in Tourism* (8) and *Ocean and Coastal Management* (7). The range of journals is also significant as it highlights the importance of non-tourism studies outlets for relevant research on tourism and resilience.

The early writings on resilience were focused on its use in an economic context (Holder, 1980; O'Hare & Barrett, 1994; Rensel, 1993; Selya, 1978). Holder (1980), for example, used the term in a tourism context, employing the addition of using tourism as a means of economic diversification and therefore adding to the strength and resilience of the Caribbean economy. The first paper to draw on the ecological dimensions of resilience for tourism was Lovejoy (1994) in relation to the value of biodiversity as a tourism asset.

Table 2.5 Use of 'resilience' and 'tourism' in journal article titles, abstracts or keywords (as of August 2016)

Years	Engin.	Materials Science	Med.	Physics & Astronomy	Social Sciences	Agriculture	Business	Energy	Environ. Sci.	Psych.	Arts	Biochem.	Earth	Comp. Sci.	Other	Total
>2015	4	–	2	–	55	20	41	1	38	–	3	–	11	3	–	97
2010–2014	6	–	8	1	71	31	49	3	81	1	12	3	33	2	3	166
2005–2009	2	1	3	1	14	6	12	–	20	–	–	–	4	4	–	45
2000–2004	2	–	–	–	5	5	3	–	9	–	–	–	1	–	–	18
1995–1999	–	–	–	–	3	1	1	–	3	–	–	–	2	–	1	6
1990–1994	–	–	–	–	1	1	1	–	1	–	–	–	1	–	–	3
1985–1989	–	–	–	–	–	–	–	–	–	–	–	–	–	–	–	–
1980–1984	–	–	–	–	–	–	–	–	–	–	–	–	–	–	1	1
1975–1979	–	–	–	–	–	–	–	–	1	–	–	–	1	–	–	1
Total	14	1	13	2	149	64	107	4	153	1	15	3	53	9	5	337

Notes: Analysis undertaken via Scopus, 22 August 2016.
Key: Engin. = Engineering, Chemical Engineering; Med. = Medicine, Dentistry, Nursing, Health Professions, Immunology & Microbiology, Pharmacology, Toxicology & Pharmaceutics; Agriculture = Agricultural & Biological Science, Veterinary; Business = Business, Management & Accounting, Economics, Econometrics & Finance, Decision Science; Environ. Sci. = Environmental Science; Psych. = Psychology, Neuroscience; Arts = Arts & Humanities; Biochem. = Biochemistry, Genetics & Molecular Biology; Earth = Earth & Planetary Sciences; Comp. Sci. = Computer Science, Mathematics; Other = Undefined, Multidisciplinary.
Source: Hall (2016b).

Although this was arguably the first paper that strongly links tourism to ecosystem resilience, the first to suggest ecological resilience as a means of tourism-oriented resource management was Tyler and Dangerfield (1999) in an ecotourism context. However, as Hall (2018) noted, Tyler and Dangerfield's paper is also significant because it is one of the first to contribute to the substantial and ongoing confusion that exists in tourism studies with regard to the relationships between resilience and sustainable development (Lew et al., 2016).

Tables 2.6a and 2.6b highlight the thematic focus of journal articles that use 'resilience' and 'tourism' in titles, abstracts or keywords in Scopus. Almost half of the papers relating to tourism and resilience have been in relation to the economic aspects of tourism; this has been both specific to the resilience of tourism or of specific tourism destinations and to how tourism affects the resilience of economies and places. The next most significant areas are with respect to communities, policy and planning, and sustainable development. About a third of the papers relate to conservation and ecosystems while coastal regions and islands account for almost a quarter (Biggs et al., 2015; Hall, 2012). Perhaps surprisingly, and despite the broad significance of the theme, issues of crisis, disaster and security in tourism have not been well connected to the resilience literature, and have instead been better linked to more general studies of crisis, disaster management, security and vulnerability (Hall, 2010c). However, given the significance of vulnerability in ecological resilience studies (Janssen, 2007; Janssen et al., 2006) and natural hazards (Birkmann, 2006; Cutter & Finch, 2008; Cutter et al., 2014), research in this area is clearly an area in which much growth can be expected.

The dominant scales of analysis by far in the tourism papers identified in the Scopus search are those of communities and regions and a focus on organisations has only really developed post-2010 (Orchiston et al., 2016; Prayag & Orchiston, 2016). Given its centrality as a framing concept in tourism studies, there is also surprisingly limited overt research on destinations. Similarly, given the vulnerability of the tourism system to disturbance, there are extremely limited studies of tourism and supply chains. There is little direct analysis of individuals, whether as tourists, community members or entrepreneurs (Biggs et al., 2012). The citation analysis of the references for the journal articles suggests that approximately a quarter of publications are connected to the ecological and socio-ecological resilience approaches, at least with respect to citation of key authors and papers, e.g. the works of Carpenter, Folke, Holling or Walker (Hall, 2018). However, in the main, notions of resilience are not made clear, with often no attempt to delineate between the different approaches towards resilience and, in many cases, no

Table 2.6a Resilience and tourism in journal article titles, abstracts and keywords by key themes and foci as of August 2016

Year	Coastal	Rural	Urban	Island	Alpine/ mountain	Reef	Ecosystem	Protected area/ national park	World Heritage	Entrepreneur/ business	Community	Destination	Resort
2016	8	2	2	13	2	2	9	4	–	6	18	16	3
2015	12	4	10	3	3	4	14	7	2	12	15	7	1
2014	16	9	3	15	2	5	16	11	2	6	22	10	–
2013	9	4	3	9	2	4	10	5	–	10	10	9	2
2012	10	2	3	5	6	6	8	3	–	6	10	1	1
2011	6	1	2	2	–	4	8	5	1	3	7	2	2
2010	2	4	–	1	2	3	5	2	1	2	8	3	–
2009	2	–	–	–	1	2	4	1	–	2	4	2	–
2008	3	1	1	3	1	–	2	1	1	1	5	2	1
2007	2	1	1	1	–	–	5	1	–	1	3	4	2
2006	1	–	1	–	–	–	1	1	–	3	3	–	–
2005	–	–	–	–	–	–	1	1	1	1	3	–	–
2004	2	–	3	1	1	–	1	–	–	–	1	1	–
2003	1	–	–	–	–	–	2	–	–	–	1	1	–
2002	–	1	–	1	2	–	3	1	–	–	2	1	1
2001	1	–	–	–	–	1	–	–	–	–	1	–	–
2000	1	–	–	–	–	1	1	–	–	–	–	–	–
<2000	1	–	–	1	–	–	5	–	–	1	2	–	–
Total	77	31	29	55	22	32	95	43	8	54	115	59	13

Note: Analysis undertaken via Scopus, 23 August 2016.
Source: Hall (2016b).

Table 2.6b Resilience and tourism in journal article titles, abstracts and keywords by key themes and foci as of August 2016

Year	Adaptation	Conservation	Crisis	Culture	Disaster	Economy	Policy/ planning	Risk	Sustainability/ sust. dev	Vulnerability	Climate change	Biodiversity	Water	Supply chain
2016	11	6	4	3	6	21	16	9	19	10	14	1	6	3
2015	5	14	6	6	8	26	19	7	16	4	6	6	4	–
2014	7	14	9	5	5	34	20	10	20	11	15	8	8	1
2013	6	8	3	6	4	15	15	9	10	6	8	2	9	–
2012	4	4	2	2	6	14	16	7	6	7	10	5	5	1
2011	2	5	1	2	4	5	3	5	4	5	5	2	3	1
2010	3	7	1	3	–	9	8	2	8	4	6	4	1	–
2009	3	2	2	–	–	8	2	1	2	4	2	1	3	–
2008	–	3	2	1	3	8	5	2	6	2	1	2	1	–
2007	–	1	2	–	3	7	2	3	4	2	2	2	4	–
2006	–	1	–	–	2	7	1	1	2	–	–	–	–	3
2005	–	3	–	1	–	2	3	–	2	1	–	1	3	–
2004	–	–	–	–	–	2	1	–	2	–	–	1	1	–
2003	–	2	–	1	–	1	–	1	1	–	–	–	2	–
2002	–	1	–	–	–	1	2	1	1	–	–	–	2	–
2001	–	–	1	–	–	2	–	–	–	1	–	–	–	–
2000	–	1	–	–	–	–	–	–	–	–	–	–	–	–
>2000	–	1	–	1	–	5	2	–	4	–	–	2	1	–
Total	41	73	34	31	41	166	115	58	107	57	69	37	53	9

Note: Analysis undertaken via Scopus, 23 August 2016.
Source: Hall (2016b).

definition at all. Resilience is extremely important so it seems, but not so important for many authors that it should be clearly conceptualised. Instead, resilience appears to be becoming a positive normative statement often without an appreciation of issues of operationalisation beyond that of a metaphor – as useful as that might sometimes be.

Chapter Summary

Figure 2.5 provides an outline of the conceptual approach used to organise this book. Although we do not focus only on adaptive cycles, considerable attention is given in many models of the tourism system of its multi-scaled nature. This parallels much of the interest in panarchical relations in ecological resilience thinking, including socio-ecological resilience. In the book we present separate chapters on tourism-related resilience at the level of the individual (both as people within destinations and their communities as well as people as tourists) (Chapter 3), public and private

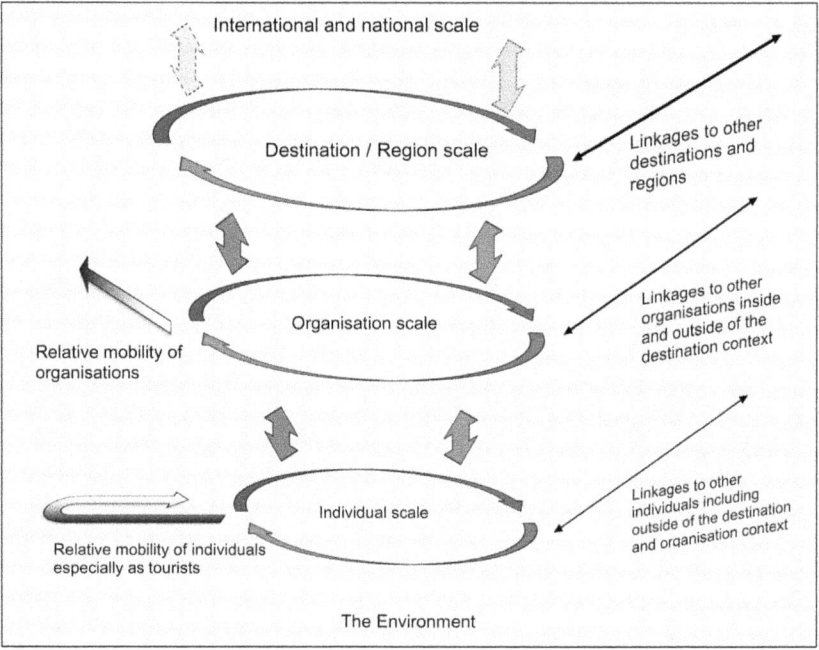

Figure 2.5 Linked adaptive scales in the tourism system

tourism organisations (Chapter 4), and the destination (Chapter 5). These divisions provide a useful means of dividing up the literature on tourism and resilience, as well as for discussing the interconnections between the different nested scales. However, in addition to the vertical nested relations, the tourism system is also characterised by horizontal linkages and relations to other destinations and regions, including at the organisational and individual level, as well as the inherent mobility of tourists and the potential mobility of organisations. Furthermore, given the contested nature of resilience thinking, the potential for different definitions and interpretations by stakeholders, and the need for clarity in its use and a management tool for each level of analysis, we ask the reader to consider significant questions of who?, what?, when?, where?, and why? with respect to resilience (Meerow & Newell, 2016; Vale, 2014).

This chapter has provided an overview of the concept of resilience, some of the core approaches, and the change environment within which the tourism system is operating. It has highlighted the importance of systems thinking both for tourism as well as engineering and ecological formulations of resilience. Influential concepts that have emerged from ecological resilience include adaptive cycles and panarchy but, as has been emphasised, these concepts primarily operate as metaphors. This constitutes a significant issue with regard to the use of resilience not only in terms of its use as a normative concept but also with regard to being able to measure resilience and therefore the effectiveness of any resilience policies that are developed by government or industry.

Further reading

The original influential article by Holling (1973) can be found at:

Holling, C.S. (1973) Resilience and stability of ecological systems. *Annual Review of Ecology and Systematics* 4 (1), 1–23.

while comparisons between ecological and engineering approaches to resilience are discussed by Holling at:

Holling, C.S. (1996) Engineering resilience versus ecological resilience. In P. Schulze (ed.) *Engineering within Ecological Constraints* (pp. 31–44). Washington, DC: National Academies Press.
On socio-ecological approaches to resilience, see:

Folke, C. (2006) Resilience: The emergence of a perspective for social – ecological systems analyses. *Global Environmental Change* 16 (3), 253–267.
Walker, B., Holling, C.S., Carpenter, S. and Kinzig, A. (2004) Resilience, adaptability and transformability in social-ecological systems. *Ecology and Society* 9 (2), 5.

On the concept of panarchy, see:

Gunderson, L.H. and Holling, C.S. (eds) (2002) *Panarchy: Understanding Transformations in Human and Natural Systems*. Washington, DC: Island Press.

The use of ecological resilience thinking as a resource management tool can be found at:

Walker, B. and Salt, D. (2006) *Resilience Thinking: Sustaining Ecosystems and People in a Changing World*. Washington, DC: Island Press.
Walker, B. and Salt, D. (2012) *Resilience Practice: Building Capacity to Absorb Disturbance and Maintain Function*. Washington, DC: Island Press.

The application of a range of different resilience approaches to a post-disaster situation, including with respect to tourism, as well as discussions of the different approaches, can be found in:

Hall, C.M., Malinen, S., Vosslamber, R. and Wordsworth, R. (eds) (2016) *Business and Post-Disaster Management: Business, Organisational and Consumer Resilience and the Christchurch Earthquakes*. Abingdon: Routledge.

3   Individual Resilience

Introduction

The notion of 'keep going on no matter what happens' often imbues much of what has been written about individual resilience. In the context of human beings, resilience is a phenomenon that results from the interaction between individuals and their environment (Rutter, 2006). With this notion in mind, the chapter explores the nexus of individual resilience and tourism. The chapter starts with definitional and conceptual issues with the term 'individual' resilience, followed by a review of the major theories on resilience from psychology and related fields. The chapter progresses to a discussion of the different methods and tools available to measure individual resilience. This is followed by a discussion of the role of individual resilience in a disaster context and the interface between individual and employee resilience. The chapter concludes with a discussion of the relevance of individual resilience to tourism, and particularly whether it impacts other aspects of resilience such as organisational, community and destination resilience.

It is clear that psychological aspects of resilience are not only about biological survival but also involve the ability of the individual to grow and prosper (Reich, 2006). The psychology and social sciences fields in general provide sufficient literature on the fundamental principles underlying human resilience in the face of adversity. Resilient individuals typically have a high level of positive emotionality such as optimism, enthusiasm and a positive attitude towards work and life (Tugade & Fredrickson, 2004). They also achieve growth and strength through facing difficult challenges (Harland *et al.*, 2005) and usually capitalise on these challenges and turn them into opportunities (Lengnick-Hall *et al.*, 2011). They tend to appraise stressful encounters as less threatening (Tugade & Fredrickson, 2004), and utilise more assertive or active problem-solving strategies (Moorhouse & Caltabiano, 2007). It is therefore of no surprise that resilient individuals have a sense of confidence and mastery in their ability to cope (Fredrickson *et al.*, 2003) and experience greater psychological wellbeing (Beasley *et al.*, 2003) and life satisfaction (Liu *et al.*, 2012). However, it is also important to note contrasting perspectives, such as those of Hall and Lamont (2013), whose approach to social resilience can be contrasted with influential perspectives that emphasise the psychological qualities needed to cope with various types of shocks. As they note, they place more emphasis on the social and cultural frameworks underpinning resilience rather than individual traits, and are sceptical about the efforts of some governments to find in individual resilience the solution to social problems.

Advocates of tourism have long argued that holidays contribute to psychological wellbeing and life satisfaction (Gilbert & Abdullah, 2004; McCabe & Johnson, 2013; Neal *et al.*, 1999). Are such tourists more resilient individuals or vice versa? Along with this question, several others remain unanswered. Given that tourists are also victims of adverse circumstances such as disasters, theft and crime, do such individuals become more resilient as a result of negative experiences at the destination or do they become more resilient tourists only? Do resilient individuals or tourists, or both, contribute to resilient communities and destinations? This chapter will attempt to provide some answers to these questions.

Definitions and Conceptualisations of Individual Resilience

Individual resilience, much like the original concept of resilience, has been defined in multiple ways. Three main perspectives on individual resilience have emerged in the psychology and related literature. The first perspective suggests that individual resilience can be conceptualised as a trait or capacity that allows individuals to deal with and adjust positively to adversity (Jackson *et al.*, 2007). The terms personal resilience and ego-resilience have been associated with trait-based resilience. Resilience is not something that individuals innately possess (Pangallo *et al.*, 2015). As such, others have treated resilience as a dynamic process consisting of disruption and reintegration in the environment that leads to an individual displaying positive adaptation despite experiencing adversity (Luthar *et al.*, 2000). This perspective suggests that resilience is a 'state' implying a phenomenon that can be developed and managed (King *et al.*, 2015). Often termed as a 'process' view of resilience, this perspective focuses on both internal and external resources which can be used by the individual to foster positive adaptation when faced with adversity. The term 'resiliency' should be used when referring to a trait and 'resilience' when referring to the process of positive adjustment despite adversity (Luthar *et al.*, 2000). The third view treats resilience as an outcome variable and refers to the ability to bounce back from physical and psychological stressors (Smith *et al.*, 2008). However, this view has not galvanised much attention given that the ability to bounce back is inherent to both trait and process views of resilience.

Given the coexistence of these three perspectives, it is not surprising that several terms such as individual resilience, human resilience, personal resilience, psychological resilience and social resilience have been used interchangeably to describe the ability of human beings to bounce back from adverse conditions or negative emotional experiences but also their ability to adapt to the changing demands of stressful experiences (Block & Kremen, 1996). Adaptability and bouncing back are two commonalities that imbue all the main perspectives on individual resilience, and debates as to their use at the individual level are similar to what has been written in the debate on resilience in ecosystems in general. For example, in an echo of the engineering versus ecological resilience perspective, Hall and Lamont (2013) note that they draw on the psychological literature but try and draw away from individual traits to focus more on the cultural and social context in which they are situated (a perspective akin to the notion of cross-scale interaction, i.e. between a collective such as a community or an organisation and the individual).

Hall and Lamont (2013) use the term 'social resilience' to denote an outcome in which the members of a group sustain their wellbeing, defined as physical and psychological health, material sustenance, and the sense of dignity and belonging that comes with being a recognised member of the community (Hall & Lamont 2009), in the face of external challenges to it, e.g. neoliberal policy settings. They use such an approach as they want to avoid specifying a precise hierarchy of needs or self-actualisation as the goal of resilience given that the values attached to these is culture specific. Hall and Lamont (2009, 2013) therefore see resilience in dynamic terms, not as the capacity to return to a prior state (what we can term engineering resilience), but as the achievement of wellbeing even when that entails significant modifications to behaviour or to the social frameworks that structure and give meaning to behaviour (an ecological or socio-ecological perspective). For Hall and Lamont (2009, 2013), what is at issue in discussions of social resilience is the capacity of individuals or groups (i.e. communities) to secure favourable outcomes (material, cultural, emotional) under new circumstances and, if needed, by new means. Hall and Lamont's approach is also significant because it reinforces O'Dougherty Wright *et al.*'s (2013) notion of there being four waves of research on resilience in human development (Table 3.1), which are grounded in seeing individual resilience in increasingly complex and dynamic terms. However, it must be emphasised that the four waves of

Table 3.1 Four waves of research on positive adaptation in the context of adversity

Waves	Focus	Exemplars
First	Person and variable focused. Sought to identify the correlates or predictors of positive adaptation of individuals against a background of risk or adversity. Investigators were also interested in assessing individual or situational differences that might account for differential outcomes among children sharing similar adversities or risk factors, e.g. family, community, and cultural or societal characteristics.	Masten et al. (1990); Masten (1999)
Second	Resilience as an outcome of relationships and social interaction. More contextualised in multiple ways, including both how the individual interacts with many other systems at many levels throughout life and greater care about generalising conclusions about risk and protective factors from one context to another or one period of development to another.	Schoon (2006)
Third	Focus on the influence of society as a means of fostering resilience including the development of behavioural interventions. Researchers recognised that experiments to promote positive adaptation and prevent problems among individuals at high risk for developing problems represented a strategy for testing theory and hypothesised adaptive processes that were targeted in the theory or logic model of the experimental intervention.	Luthar (2006); Obradović (2010)
Fourth	Resilience as the outcome of complex multiscale system dynamics. Focused on multilevel dynamics and the many processes linking genes, neurobiological adaptation, brain development, behaviour and context at multiple levels. It is predicated on the idea that development arises from probabilistic epigenesis, involving many processes of interaction across multiple levels of function, with gene–environment interplay and co-action playing key roles and explicit recognition that adaptation is inherently multilevel.	Hall and Lamont (2013); Masten (2007, 2010)

Source: After O'Dougherty Wright et al. (2013).

resilience research in human development do not mean that research in one wave stops once the next one comes along, but rather that what we see is a multiplicity of potential ways of framing resilience, each with their particular framing of resilience as an issue and an accompanying set of research strategies and required interventions for resilience (Figure 3.1).

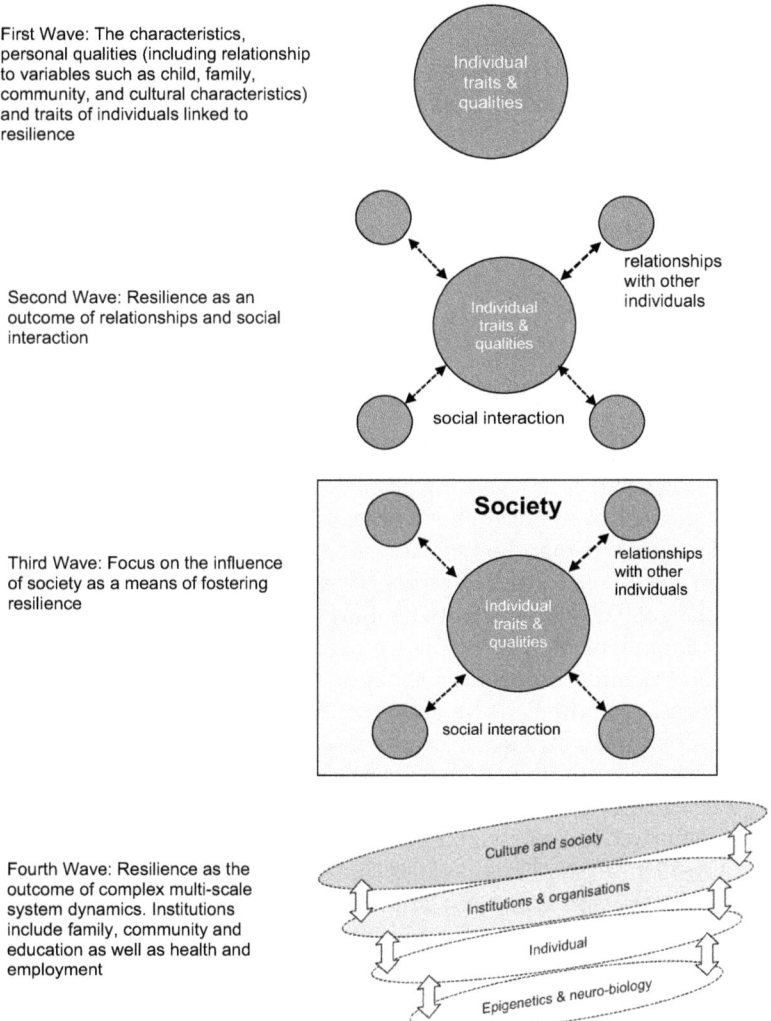

Figure 3.1 Diagrammatic representation of four waves of research on positive adaption in the context of adversity

One of the most synthetic definitions of resilience at the individual level was coined by Windle (2011) after a systematic review of the literature, concept analysis and stakeholder consultation. According to this author, resilience is 'the process of effectively negotiating, adapting to, or managing significant sources of stress or trauma using assets and resources within the individual, their life and environment that facilitate this capacity for adaptation and bouncing back in the face of adversity' (Windle, 2011: 152). This integrative definition in essence tries to capture the range of perspectives on individual resilience and dispels the notion of 'extraordinary' – one which is often associated with individuals' ability to cope in non-routine and non-normal circumstances, and where much of existing research has been carried out. In fact, individual resilience is now treated as 'ordinary magic' which emanates from individuals' ability to function with difficult life circumstances as part of a human being's adaptation to the environment (Masten, 2010; Masten & Powell, 2003). In Bonanno's (2004) words, resilience is not as rare as was once suggested.

Trait or Psychological and Process Resilience

At the core of trait or psychological resilience is the notion that individuals build resilience through gaining psychological resources when they experience a stressful event and that these psychological resources are then employed in future demanding situations to minimise the impact of stressful events (Berinsky et al., 2012). Resilience as a personal trait therefore helps individuals to cope better with challenging situations. Positive emotions are a crucial component of trait resilience (Tugade & Fredrickson, 2004). The experience of positive emotion is thought to have adaptive benefits in the coping process (Folkman & Moskowitz, 2004). Results have shown that resilient individuals can draw from positive emotion-eliciting coping strategies such as benefit finding and humour to resourcefully rebound from daily negative emotional encounters (Ong et al., 2006). For example, in a relationship the constructive expression of both positive and negative emotions is a source of resilience (Stephens et al., 2013). However, trait resilience does not capture within-person variations and fails to explain why some people are resilient in some situations and not in others (Gillespie et al., 2007). Pangallo et al. (2015) found a notable absence of socio-contextual and demographic factors that can predict resilience.

Research has also begun to assess the nature of process resilience, including how it may vary across contexts and unfold over time as well as the protective factors such as social support and personality traits that may account for individual differences in this process (Montpetit et al., 2010). The process view of resilience suggests that individuals who are more emotionally resistant to stress (stress resistance) and exhibit a higher capacity to recover from those stressors (stress recovery) are more likely to be resilient (Ong et al., 2006). The notions of stress resistance and stress recovery imply real-time and ongoing adaptation to life's challenges (Montpetit et al., 2010). Therefore understanding the coping strategies of individuals provides insights into their capacity to be resilient. Personal as well as social factors are thought to contribute to process resilience. Personal factors such as age, personality characteristics, education level and previous experience of stressful situations can all contribute to stress management and hence allow the individual to interpret and manage stressful experiences (Bergeman & Wallace, 1999; Bonanno et al., 2007). Bonanno et al. (2007) found that resilience could be predicted by gender, race/ethnicity, level of trauma exposure, income and social support. Thus, social factors such as affective ties between family members, support groups in the community, friends and socio-economic factors can also provide support in stressful times (Bergeman & Wallace, 1999; Montpetit et al., 2010). Thus, the capacity of an individual to be resilient can be nurtured and developed by enhancing coping strategies and stress management.

Measuring trait and process resilience

As noted in the psychology and mental health literature, the lack of a uniform operational definition of resilience and a corresponding methodology for studying it have hindered applications of the concept (Davydov et al., 2010). The lack of agreement on how to operationalise resilience is not surprising given that it is a common challenge associated with many latent psychological constructs (Luthar & Cicchetti, 2000). In a systematic review of how resilience has been operationalised, Pangallo et al. (2015) found that studies mainly measured either a multi-dimensional structure or a single dimension. Pangallo et al. (2015) also noted that items capturing resilience on existing scales tend to prioritise trait or process resilience but not their interaction. Such scales fail to capture different resilience outcome trajectories, the role of situational influences and the dynamic nature of the construct. That said, the variety of scales proposed in the literature offers researchers not only the opportunity to choose a scale that measure specific aspects of resilience that they are interested in but also 'macro'-level notions of resilience. Whether it is trait or process resilience, one key question that remains unanswered is whether it is better to conceptualise and thus measure the resilience of human beings as a loss-oriented resource that prevents resource loss and thus helps the individual to maintain status quo through assisting them in recovering from adverse events, or a gain-oriented resource that assists the individual in acquiring further resources (King *et al.*, 2015).

One of the earliest scales to measure trait resilience is the 25-item Resilience Scale (RS-25) developed by Wagnild and Young (1993). The RS-25 scale was developed on elderly people but has since been psychometrically validated through a number of studies across different age groups and ethnicities (see Ahern *et al.*, 2006). The 25 items tap into dimensions such as self-reliance, perseverance, equanimity and self-acceptance. The Ego-Resilience Scale (ERS or ER89) comprises a single dimension (14 items) aimed at capturing the stable personality characteristic of ego-resiliency. This scale assesses the individual's capacity to demonstrate control in terms of impulses and inhibition in response to environmental demands in order to safeguard or augment the ego equilibrium (Block & Kremen, 1996). The Resilience Scale for Adults (RSA) was developed by Hjemdal *et al.* (2001) and consists of 45 items that capture five core dimensions, namely personal competence, social competence, social support, family coherence and personal structure. The Connor–Davidson Resilience Scale (CD-RISC; Connor & Davidson, 2003) is also a multifactorial 25-item scale, which measures outcomes such as 'able to adapt to change' and 'prefer to take the lead in problem solving'. The scale has five dimensions, of which the first two dimensions reflect notions of personal competence, high standards, tenacity, trust in one's instincts, tolerance of negative affect and the strengthening effects of stress. The remaining two dimensions measure positive acceptance of change, secure relationships and control, while the last dimension refers to spiritual influences. The Brief Resilience Scale (BRS) comprises six items that are designed to measure a single component of resilience, that is, the ability to recover from adverse situations (Smith *et al.*, 2008). Wei and Taormina (2014) model personal resilience using 40 items that represent four dimensions of resilience (determination, endurance, adaptability and recuperability). The existing scales are diverse not only in terms of the dimensions measured but also in terms of the number of items used. While some of the scales are psychometrically sound (e.g. RS-25, CD-RISC and RAS), others such as Wei and Taormina's (2014) scale have not been developed using rigorous scale development procedures.

Individual Resilience during Disasters: The 3Cs

Reich (2006) argued that human resilience in the face of disasters can be summarised as what is known as the '3Cs' (control, coherence and connectedness). The first 'C' – personal control – refers to human beings' belief that they are able to secure the personal resources necessary to achieve personal goals. For example, one key lesson learnt from the 2004 Asian tsunami was that survivors placed a top priority on rebuilding their homes and businesses, getting jobs and starting their lives again. They showed remarkable resilience, and the psychological key to rebounding from the disaster could be seen in their effort to regain personal control (Reich, 2006). As such, disaster planning should provide pathways for survivors to re-establish personal control (Reich, 2006). Hence, the key to building resilience is to enable people to set their own goals by facilitating access to resources, empowering them to make their own decisions and guide the events of their own lives (Reich, 2006).

The second 'C' – coherence – relates to the need for human beings to 'know' and the desire to remove uncertainty. Disaster response should protect the drive of people for coherence through enhancing meaning, direction and understanding of what is happening around them. This arises from the need to maintain cognitive, emotional and behavioural capacities (Zautra, 2009; Zautra & Reich, 2010). Disaster response should thus focus on helping people mentally and behaviourally to create order and structure in their lives. Uncertainty undermines resilience and is the enemy of adaptation (Reich, 2006). The third 'C' – connectedness – is related to the fact that during disasters there is a need for people to band together, to seek out others, and to establish bonds with strangers (Reich, 2006). Providing instrumental, informational and emotional support is a key component of disaster response (Reich, 2006).

The Interface between Individual and Employee Resilience

Despite calls for a positive psychological approach to HR, few firms see resilience as a set of skills and attitudinal qualities that can be developed proactively as part of strategic human resource management (HRM) to improve individual and organisational performance and wellbeing (Cooke et al., 2016). Two theoretical approaches have so far underpinned research on the resilience of individuals in the organisational context: positive psychology and conservation of resources (COR) theory (Bardoel et al., 2014). Positive psychology conceptualises resilience as one of the four major positive dimensions of psychological capital (self-efficacy, hope, optimism and resilience). When developed and managed effectively, resilience has the ability to elicit positive individual and organisational outcomes (Youssef & Luthans, 2007). As such, resilience is perceived to be the most important positive resource for navigating through adversity and hence there is a need for organisations to adopt a more positive approach to managing HR (Avey et al., 2009). Using the COR theory, Shin et al. (2012) argue that resilience is an individual resource that can be enhanced. As such, resilience is a way to reduce the strain and stresses associated with organisational change and to increase employees' support and commitment to change. Resilience is seen as a precursor to employees' openness towards organisational change (Wanberg & Banas, 2000). COR theory thus provides an explanation for the value of proactive resilience-enhancing practices in organisations. However, Bardoel et al. (2014) argue that organisations should invest in resilience building irrespective of its use for organisational change. To this effect, HRM practices that can improve employee resilience (Bardoel et al., 2014) include work–life balance (WLB) practices that improve employee commitment and performance (Wood & de Menezes, 2010) and employee assistance programmes (EAPs) that, for example, provide counselling, coaching and change management (Kirk & Brown, 2003). Other aspects that can improve resilience of employees include flexible work arrangements, reward and benefit systems and diversity management (Bardoel et al., 2014).

Organisations that are capable of building and developing a resilient workforce will be more adaptive and successful (Luthans et al., 2006). However, there has been very limited integration of different theoretical perspectives to describe how resilience develops at the individual and collective level and the mechanisms through which it transmits its effects (King et al., 2015). To build resilience, Luthans et al. (2010) suggest that employees should be made aware of personal assets such as talents, skills and social networks. Self-development strategies in the workplace such as positive nurturing of professional relationships and networks, maintaining positivity, developing emotional insight, achieving life balance and spirituality and becoming more reflective on one's own life experiences can enhance personal resilience (Jackson et al., 2007). As such, an employee's resilience can be developed and maximised through HR interventions such as education, training and development to display the skills and behaviours relevant to the organisational context. Resilient individuals are better equipped to cope with a constantly changing workplace (Shin et al., 2012). With regard to human resource interventions that are perceived as nurturing resilience in employees, two main categories for human resource development (HRD) can be identified. Luthans et al. (2006) distinguished between reactive and proactive HRM practices that enhance psychological capital. The reactive approach focuses on the importance of reminding employees to think positively and find meaning in adversity, while the proactive approach involves structuring the organisation to anticipate the need for resiliency through reliance on strategies related to risk, asset and process within the organisation (Luthans et al., 2006).

Resilient individuals react to adverse circumstances by recognising and acknowledging the impact, and investing the time, energy and resources to bounce back to equilibrium (Youssef & Luthans, 2007). Resilient employees have the capacity to foster proactive learning and growth through conquering challenges (Youssef & Luthans, 2007). The notion of psychological capital has been used to describe organisations' investments in human capital to develop and promote resilience in employees (Bardoel et al., 2014). Resilient individuals are more emotionally stable when faced with adversity, more open to new experiences and more flexible to changing work circumstances (Tugade & Fredrickson, 2004). They use humour, relaxation techniques and optimistic thinking to boost their positive emotionality as effective strategies to cope with challenging events (Tugade & Frederickson, 2004). Contradictory findings exist on the effectiveness of resilience training in the workplace. For example, a systematic review of resilience training programmes from 2003 to 2014 by Robertson *et al.* (2015) concludes that such training can improve personal resilience and is a useful means of developing mental health and subjective wellbeing in employees. The authors also suggest that resilience training has wider benefits for the organisation including enhanced psychosocial functioning and improved employee performance. In another meta-analysis of resilience-building programmes by Vanhove *et al.* (2016), these authors found that the overall effects of such programmes on the organisation are small. Programmes employing a one-on-one delivery format (e.g. coaching) were most effective, while programmes using either train-the-trainer or computer-based delivery formats were the least effective. The authors conclude that resilience-building programmes have in general been as effective as, but no more effective than other primary intervention approaches to deal with employee stress in the workplace.

The hospitality industry epitomises the services sector and hotels are among the largest employers in the tourism industry (Bas Collins, 2007). While some tourism organisations have excellent human resource practices (e.g. Ritz Carlton), the widespread perception remains that of an industry that perpetuates poor pay, challenging working conditions and limited opportunities for growth and development, particularly for women and minorities (Baum, 2007). In a review of over 100 papers in five leading tourism and hospitality journals, Lucas and Deery (2004) noted that most researchers are concerned with issues of employee development, employee relations and employee resourcing in research between 2002 and 2003. However, it is clear that the resilience of employees in the tourism industry has not been a major concern so far for both researchers and practitioners (Brown *et al.*, 2017; Sydnor-Bousso *et al.*, 2011). For example, in another review of HRM practices in tourism in 2015, there is clear evidence that change within the industry at the global level 'was slow at best and, in many countries and organisations, entirely stalled with respect to key areas such as working conditions, remuneration, the status of work, diversity management and workplace relations' (Baum, 2015: 210). HRD in general is undervalued across an industry that relies much on low-skilled and casual workers (Ladkin, 2011). Despite the vulnerability of the tourism industry in the face of natural hazards being well recognised (Becken et al., 2014), tourism employers are reluctant to invest significantly in HRD (Ladkin, 2011).

The case study in Box 3.1 illustrates the importance of personal resilience and employee resilience in building the organisational resilience of the Antigua Boat Sheds, a tourism business that includes both a café and kayaking on the Avon River in Christchurch, New Zealand.

Box 3.1 The Antigua Boat Sheds & Café

The Antigua Boat Sheds as a tourism business has been part of Christchurch for more than 130 years. It is a family business which provides visitors with the experience of kayaking, canoeing and rowboat hiring on the Avon River in Christchurch along with a café. Despite its fair share of breakages during the February 2011 earthquakes, the business was reopened within six weeks due to the buildings suffering minor damages.

It has been said that resilient individuals are those that recognise and acknowledge the impact of adversity on others and work towards bouncing back. Talking to Mike Jones, one of the owners of Antigua Boat Sheds, it is clear that he displayed a high level of personal resilience by showing sheer determination as evidenced by the amount of time and resources he invested post-quake to restarting the business. As he said, 'it was a lot of hard work, a lot of hours to get it back again'. He also highlighted the role of personal networks in successfully restarting the business, mentioning that 'I had a good network of friends that helped us out and it was basically cleaning things up and all that sort of thing'. In times of adversity, relying on personal networks exemplifies personal resilience.

Yet, as Mike went on to say, 'we would not have been able to do this without the staff. ... A lot of the staff has been with us for a number of years. I think our longest serving member of staff is probably 11 or 12 years, with a lot of 6 plus [years].' He talked about how they, owners and employees, are a 'family', and thus helped each other much more than the average staff member would under the circumstances they were dealing with. When organisations nurture the relationships they build with employees, it is not surprising that they are willing to go the extra mile to help the organisation when faced with adversity.

But it seems that the personal resilience of Mike perhaps also contributed to the resilience displayed by his employees post-quake. As he mentioned, 'like everyone [in the city], the staff had their own issues at home [following the earthquakes], so we let them deal with those and we didn't put demands on them or anything like that'. Letting staff manage stress levels and acknowledging that they were also going through adversity seemed to have reinforced the bond between the owners and the staff. Also, reducing uncertainty about their future may have contributed to employee resilience. Like Mike said 'to our full timers [employees], I said I'm not getting rid of anyone, we've got enough money saved up that we can keep you on as long as it takes, but, it's gonna take this, we have to do this, to make it work'. It was clear that Mike had a very clear idea of what it would take for the business to bounce back and he provided the right leadership and support to his employees to facilitate this process. At the end of the day, employees are resilient, in Mike's words, 'if they enjoy the environment and know it's a nice place [to work]'.

Tourism, Individual Resilience and Employee Resilience

From an ecological resilience perspective, life is not experienced in a vacuum. Therefore, the wider sociocultural context has an impact on daily activities as well as non-routine activities such as tourism. The blurring of the role between individuals as members of society and as tourists creates complexities of clearly differentiating between the resilience of individuals and tourists. Are resilient individuals resilient tourists or vice versa? To some extent the psychology and related literature provide contradictory findings. If resilience is treated as a trait in human beings, then resilient individuals should be resilient tourists in the face of adversity, be it in response to poor service at a destination or being on site during a disaster. However, individuals are not resilient at all times and in all situations. Hence, the circumstances under which a tourist will or will not be resilient remains speculative at this stage. Arguably, familiarity with a destination would be one such factor that contributes to the resilience of tourists. This is because, in a familiar environment such as a destination, enabling factors such as familiar infrastructure, the presence of social networks and the tourist's own psychological capital should act as enablers of resilience in the face of adversity. Drawing on the coping strategies faced in normal life and positive emotions that imbue much of the tourism experience, the human being in the role of a tourist should have the ability to bounce back. Also, trait resilience has implications for the recruitment and management of employees in the tourism industry. The high level of emotional labour required in this industry would imply that employers should identify and recruit resilient individuals to work as front-line staff in sectors, for example, such as accommodation, tourist attractions, cafes and restaurants.

If resilience is a process, then both individual and tourist resilience can be developed and the interventions used to facilitate individual resilience would contribute to tourist resilience. To some extent, the tourist can also build resilience that feeds into individual resilience through tourism-related activities that build both social (e.g. volunteer tourism) and psychological capital (e.g. wellbeing retreats, health tourism). Exposure to acceptable levels of risk and the development of competencies among participants in managing risks related to adventure tourism, for example, can also be considered as building tourist resilience. Likewise, HRD practices commonly used to develop employee resilience would be applicable to the tourism industry. However, as Naswall *et al.* (2013) argued, a distinction between individual and employee resilience is necessary given that the latter refers to the capacity of employees, facilitated and supported by the organisation, to utilise resources to positively cope, adapt and thrive in response to changing work circumstances. This definition implies that a resilient individual would not necessarily be a resilient employee. The organisation's role in facilitating and supporting the development of resilience is emphasised. Human resource practices that facilitate the development of resilient employees through prioritising wellbeing, for example through work-based learning, must become common practice in the tourism industry. Evolving human resource practices geared towards only managing organisational change but ignoring the personal–employee resilience nexus seem counterintuitive to the requirements of a customer-focused and prone to disaster impacts industry such as tourism.

While there is still much to research on the resilience of tourism systems, it is clear that one of its components – the resilience of the tourist and how this contributes to the tourism system or community resilience – have been ignored. Many studies recognise the complexities associated with the role of people, organisations and communities in building and sustaining the tourism system. However, questions such as how, when and why resilient tourists should or should not contribute to the resiliency of the tourist system remain unanswered. Although some evidence exists to suggest that a high level of community resilience enhances individuals' coping during stressful situations and adversity, and is instrumental in faster post-disaster recovery (Sherrieb *et al.*, 2010), the nexus of tourist and tourism system resilience, including community resilience, remains unexplored. Touristic activities that are maintained in the face of adversity and that have positive impacts on the community may be thought of as contributing to community resilience. Volunteer tourism, for example, would be one such activity that can contribute to community resilience (see Box 3.2). Likewise, communities that have mechanisms and interventions in place to support both individuals and tourists during adverse times may be thought of as being resilient. Disaster and crisis management strategies focused on tourists would perhaps enhance community resilience. A triadic relationship between tourist, community and the tourism system seems plausible where individual tourist activities and behaviour may contribute to building community resilience. Likewise, community support and infrastructure may strengthen tourist resilience. Both tourist and community resilience contribute to tourism system resilience. The latter may also favourably impact both tourist and community resilience. For example, a resilient tourism system should be able to respond to new market opportunities that emerge in the face of disaster (e.g. dark tourism, volunteer tourism) which contribute to strengthening community resilience. Therefore, tourist, community and tourism-system resilience are probably prone to the dynamics of ecosystems and socio-ecological systems but the implications of this remain to be researched.

Box 3.2 The resilient tourist?

Empirical evidence suggests that tourists tend to have different behaviours in the event of an hazard and subsequent emergency phase. Examples include overseas volunteers going to Sri Lanka despite the outbreak of a civil war and the devastation brought by the 2004 Boxing day tsunami (GoOverseas, 2016) or travelling to Christchurch following the earthquakes of 2010 and 2011 (GoAbroad.com, 2016). Undeniably, there are visitors who seem not to enlist safety as primary issue when choosing a destination. Rather, they 'seem to be able to set their worries and anxieties aside and engage in travel even when faced by a crisis that involves risks beyond their control' (Hajibaba *et al.*, 2015: 4).

A pilot study by Hajibaba et al. (2015) seeks to elaborate the profile of the resilient tourist in order to provide destinations and place-marketing agencies with a detailed sociodemographic identikit of this narrow segment of the tourist demand. According to the authors, these visitors would still consider a stay in destinations hit by disasters and coping with recovery. It is argued that resilient tourists are key in the reduction of market share losses that are common in hazard-hit destinations, particularly during the first months following the disaster (Hajibaba et al., 2015).

Built on existing research in crisis and tourism disaster management (e.g. Beirman, 2003), the authors develop a conceptual model of the crisis-resistant tourist in which 'individuals high in resistance to change will execute trip plans despite the occurrence of a crisis' (Hajibaba et al., 2015: 6). The core of the study is based on a survey among nearly 4000 participants from the UK, Canada, the USA and Australia. The choice of up to four different markets is meant to overcome country-specific risk perceptions of current research (Hajibaba et al., 2015).

What emerges from the study is that crisis-resistant tourists proactively plan their travels and related activities during their journeys. They are aware of the risks but are still willing to take highly physical risks with outdoor activities.

Conclusion

Similarly to other concepts such as organisational resilience, individual resilience has been the subject of intense study in psychology and related fields. At least two well-established schools of thought have emerged over the years – the trait and process views of resilience. The notion that both views are complementary is gaining some momentum in the psychology and human resource fields. However, it is clear from this chapter that research on the personal resilience of the tourist, or tourist resilience – noting that there is perhaps a distinction to be made between the two – remains so far an enigma in tourism studies. Yet, an emerging research strand also acknowledges that individual and employee resilience are not necessarily one and the same thing. In a similar way, notions of tourist resilience, community resilience and tourism system resilience may be intuitively linked, but the mechanisms through which they are impacted remains to be identified. Therefore, it is perhaps an opportune time to make a call for researchers to investigate these complex relationships (Table 3.2). To some extent this chapter has offered some insights into how individual resilience is conceptualised and

Table 3.2 Fundamental questions related to individual and employee resilience

Who?	Who determines what are the desirable traits and behaviours in individuals and employees?
	Whose resilience is prioritised (individual versus employee)?
	Who is excluded and included in notions of individual and employee resilience?
What?	What perturbations should individuals and employees be resilient to?
	What levels of panarchy are included in considering individual and employee resilience?
	Is the focus on individual or employee resilience generic or specific?
	What are the circumstances (social, psychological, organisational, cultural) under which resilient individuals become resilient employees, and vice versa?
When?	When and how does individual resilience translate into employee resilience?
	What is the relative focus on rapid-onset disturbances and slow-onset changes?
	Is the focus on short- or long-term individual and employee resilience?
	Is the focus on the resilience of present or future generations?
Where?	Is greater emphasis given to individual resilience in some places than others?
	Is the resilience of some individuals and employees prioritised over others?
	Does building resilience in some individuals and employees affect the resilience of others elsewhere?
Why?	What is the goal of building individual and employee resilience?
	What are the underlying motivations for building individual and employee resilience?
	What is the relative balance between process and outcome?

measured while outlining how the concept may be related to tourist resilience and the linkages between the former and the community as well as tourism system resilience. It is now up to researchers in the field of tourism and elsewhere to further the research agenda on these relationships.

Further reading

A very useful account of the way in which ideas of individual resilience have shifted over the past two decades is:

O'Dougherty Wright, M., Masten, A.S. and Narayan, A.J. (2013) Resilience processes in development: Four waves of research on positive adaption in the context of adversity. In S. Goldstein and R.B. Brooks (eds) *Handbook of Resilience in Children* (pp. 15–38). Boston, MA: Springer.

An overview of some of the HRM challenges to make managers more resilient is:

Branicki, L., Steyer, V. and Sullivan-Taylor, B. (2016) Why resilience managers aren't resilient, and what human resource management can do about it. *International Journal of Human Resource Management*; doi:10.1080/09585192.2016.1244104.

On some of the determinants of individual resilience at various scales, see:

Bonanno, G.A., Romero, S.A. and Klein, S.I. (2015) The temporal elements of psychological resilience: An integrative framework for the study of individuals, families, and communities. *Psychological Inquiry* 26 (2), 139–169.

For a further understanding of the role and influence of leadership styles on psychological resilience, see:

Nguyen, Q., Kuntz, J.R., Näswall, K. and Malinen, S. (2016) Employee resilience and leadership styles: The moderating role of proactive personality and optimism. *New Zealand Journal of Psychology* 45 (2), 13–21.

4 Organisational Resilience in Tourism

The purpose of this chapter is to review the concept of 'organisational resilience' within and outside the field of tourism and hospitality. The first section of the chapter reviews some of the main definitions of organisational resilience and identifies commonalities and differences in the conceptualisation of the term. Using this information, the second section identifies the key factors within an organisation that contribute to its resilience, followed by different ways of measuring organisational resilience. The third section proposes a conceptual model that highlights the role of people, processes and networks in building resilience in the tourism and hospitality industry. The fourth section challenges some of the existing notions of organisational resilience, while the chapter concludes with final thoughts on the conceptual and empirical development of the term and fruitful areas of research within tourism and hospitality studies.

The conceptual vagueness of the term 'resilience' has been noted in previous tourism studies (Bec *et al.*, 2016; Becken, 2013; Strickland-Munro *et al.*, 2010; Strunz, 2012; see also Chapter 2). Given this vagueness, it is not surprising that notions of resilience were initially associated in the management literature with an organisation's resistance to shocks (Annarelli & Nonino, 2016). Terms such as resilience and robustness were used interchangeably but there is a difference between the two (Christopher & Peck, 2004; Sheffi & Rice, 2005). Robustness is about physical strength whereas resilience is about the ability to return to a normal state or a better one post-disturbance (Annarelli & Nonino, 2016). As noted in Chapter 2, resilience has become a well-used term in several disciplines but without always understanding the precise meaning of it or having an agreed definition. As such, organisational resilience also suffers from the same conceptual vagueness and has become another loosely defined term which is applied differently in the fields of HR, operations and supply chain management, and tourism. Competing views of the term have led to diverse ways of conceptualising and operationalising the term in various disciplines. Studies on organisational resilience in the tourism and hospitality industry specifically are limited (Orchiston *et al.*, 2016).

The importance of resilient tourism organisations can be seen from the impacts that a sudden change in the environment can have on the tourism and hospitality sector as whole. For example, despite the hospitality sector reporting that it had the highest number of organisations planning for the unexpected compared to several other industries, 94% of businesses were affected by the September 2010 earthquake in Canterbury, New Zealand, with an average of eight days of closure following the earthquake (Kachali *et al.*, 2012). Hystad and Keller (2008), investigating the long-term impacts of a forest fire in 2003 on tourism businesses near Kelowna, British Columbia, Canada, found that two and half years later permanent changes to tourism businesses included reduced numbers of employees, permanent closure of businesses and changes in product focus. Given both the financial and non-financial impacts that disasters, for example, can have on the livelihood of organisations, building organisational resilience seems intuitive. From the simple notion of resistance to shocks in the early days, organisational resilience now includes notions of recovery ability, recovery times and costs of recovery (Annarelli & Nonino, 2016). Understanding these can facilitate how long-term structural changes as well as short-term adverse impacts can be managed within organisations. However, there is limited evidence about whether certain organisation types are more adaptable and hence resilient in the face of disasters, for example (Whitman *et al.*, 2014).

Box 4.1 Improving tourism enterprises' responsiveness to extreme natural events

According to Specht (2008), it is increasingly likely that tourism enterprises will experience an extreme natural event (ENE) at some stage. In response, she identified a number of factors that were characteristic of the susceptibility of enterprises to such events, which she equated to their resilience:

(1) *Awareness*. Ensure that the industry and staff of the industry are aware of the ENEs most likely in their operational area, their nature and likely effects. Understand the statistics.
(2) *Exposure*. Ensure that built structures are appropriate and well maintained and activities professionally conducted and sensitive to the type of ENE for the area. Reduce risk where possible.

(3) *Warning.* Ensure that communication networks with civil defence, emergency, meteorological and natural hazard advisory services are in place and systematically attended to, especially when an ENE is most likely. Do not ignore warnings when they occur.
(4) *Organisational structure.* Ensure that there is room for flexibility in the organisation, with wide staff capabilities and awareness of operational tasks and procedures and good relationships with other organisations in the area of operation.
(5) *Staff.* Ensure that staff morale is high at all times, and that staff are well trained in basic emergency procedures and multitasking. Retain staff for as long as possible, and ensure that they are well versed in the geography of the local area and well connected.
(6) *Mitigation strategy.* Prepare a strategy in case of emergency in liaison with emergency services and others in the industry.
(7) *Media.* Have a good relationship at industry level with the media, ensuring that factual and accurate reports are disseminated. Collaborate with the media in the recovery phase.
(8) *Recovery.* Be responsible for your own recovery. Collaborate with emergency services and other organisations, and conduct a post-mortem, reviewing all actions and revising them for the future.

Definitions and Conceptualisations of Organisational Resilience

While resilience and vulnerability have implications for decision making at the community level, these terms are equally relevant for organisations. Organisational resilience has implications for mitigation strategies, disaster impact management and the recovery of organisations in the face of natural hazards (Prayag & Orchiston, 2016). Organisational resilience is also central to sustainable tourism management (Biggs *et al.*, 2012) and competitive advantage (Lee *et al.*, 2013). Therefore, building a resilient organisation should be a strategic initiative which changes the way a company operates and increases its competitiveness (Sheffi & Rice, 2005). While the term 'organisational resilience' has become established in the management literature, other terms such as 'enterprise' resilience (Biggs *et al.*, 2012) and 'business resilience' (Foster & Dye, 2005) have been used to describe firm-level resilience.

Several competing definitions of the term exist. For example, Mallak (1998a) defines resilience as the ability of the organisation to expeditiously design and implement positive adaptive behaviours matched to the immediate situation, while enduring minimal stress. McMannus *et al.* (2008: 82) defines organisational resilience as 'a function of an organisation's overall situation awareness, management of keystone vulnerabilities and adaptive capacity in a complex, dynamic and interconnected environment'. The notions of vulnerability and adaptive capacity in this definition of resilience stem from research on socio-ecological systems. Along the same line of thought, Seville *et al.* (2008) suggest that organisational resilience reflects the ability of an organisation not only to survive but to be able to thrive through times of adversity. This definition is embedded in notions of recovery and growth in the face of challenges. Other researchers portray organisational resilience as the ability of an organisation to develop competencies that allow it to keep up with changing dynamics, thus implicitly assuming that an organisation bounces back from disturbances and rebuilds itself (Lengnick-Hall *et al.*, 2011; Paton & Johnston, 2001). However, this perspective suggests a reactive approach to the environment as opposed to the proactive approach suggested by Vargo and Seville (2011), whereby the organisation initiates, restores or redesigns responses in accordance with environmental jolts (Whitman *et al.*, 2013). As such, the organisation has the flexibility and agility to restore or renew structure and relations.

From the operations management literature, organisational resilience has been defined as building on structural reliance (redundancy), organisational capability (requisite variety) and processual continuity (resources) to continue to exist despite facing difficulties (Börekçi *et al.*, 2014). Structural redundancy as per this definition involves technical, social and economic redundancies being independent from machine, personal and functional requirements (Glassop, 2007). Organisational capabilities encompass product and customer varieties, and financial risk management capabilities to deal with unexpected events. Process continuity ensures that there is a continuous flow of technical, social and economic resources (Börekçi *et al.*, 2014). Another definition from Lengnick-Hall *et al.* (2011) suggests that organisational resilience is the firm's ability to effectively absorb, develop situation-specific responses to, and ultimately engage in transformative activities to capitalise on disruptive surprises that potentially threaten organisational survival. Notions of managing and responding to the unexpected seem to be associated with resilience across several fields of studies. From an ecological resilience perspective, organisational resilience would imply engineering flexible systems and processes that continue to function in the face of the unexpected. Improving resilience in this context would also imply increasing the ability of an organisation to withstand the consequences of change before suffering irreparable damage (Dalziell & McManus, 2004). As such, in the tourism field Biggs *et al.* (2012: 647) define enterprise resilience as 'one that is able to remain in a stable state, maintaining or growing its income and employee numbers despite disturbance'.

A closer look at the tourism literature reveals that the role and contribution of organisational resilience to, for example, community resilience and destination resilience remain to be clarified. Organisation and community resilience feed off one another to build the resilience of tourism systems. Alternatively, if the tourism system is resilient, does this imply that communities benefiting from tourism and tourism business within those communities are resilient? To date, there is no clear answer to this question, given that the existing studies within the tourism field have been conducted at the micro level, although further thoughts on this are provided in the final chapter. Also, with the exceptions of Biggs *et al.* (2012), Dahles and Susilowati (2015) and Orchiston *et al.* (2016), the topic remains sparsely researched in tourism. This is not surprising given that different notions of 'resilience' coexist within the tourism field, sometimes even in the same paper. For example, crisis management literature in tourism often perceives resilience in engineering resilience terms of a return to 'normality' (Scott & Laws, 2006). Other researchers perceive resilience as the capacity to recover from crisis, implying that organisations can emerge with a different business model, source of competitive advantage and organisational structure, and will basically differ from the pre-crisis period, almost implying the adaptive capacity of organisations to change (Orchiston *et al.*, 2016). Another view is that resilience brings a fundamentally different state for an organisation whereby the business concept changes drastically through new methods of operations, new markets and new networks, among others (Dahles & Susilowati, 2015). Nonetheless, existing conceptualisations in tourism more or less mirror other fields of studies within the broader management literature.

Annarelli and Nonino (2016) also make a distinction between static and dynamic resilience whereby the former refers to strategic initiatives for resilience linked to the operational management of internal and external resources whereas the latter refers to the dynamic capabilities of the organisation to manage disruptions and unexpected events. The notion of the static versus dynamic view of organisational resilience co-exists with the passive versus active view. According to Pasteur (2011) and Somers (2009), passive resilience is demonstrated after the occurrence of a disturbance, reflecting how quickly an organisation returns to normal without incurring major loss or damage or discontinuity (Sawalha, 2015), whereas active resilience implies going beyond the 'bounce back' through a deliberate effort to improve the organisation's ability to cope with adversity (Sawalha, 2015). The maturity of the organisation favours more active than passive resilience (Sawalha, 2015). According to these views, the response of an organisation to unexpected events would constitute static resilience given that such responses are founded on preparedness and preventative measures to minimise threats and to reduce impacts that may occur. Alternatively, dynamic resilience would include notions of recovery leading to short unfavourable aftermaths while maximising the organisation's speed of recovery to the original or more desirable state (Annarelli & Nonino, 2016).

Organisational Resilience: The 'View' Inside the Organisation

Notions of organisational resilience overlap with organisational agility, which is defined as the ability to cope with unexpected challenges, to survive unprecedented threats of the business environment and to take advantage of changes as opportunities (Sharifi & Zhang, 1999). A key question to ask is how can an organisation build resilience? The simplest answer seems to be related to how organisations adjust operations, management, financial resources and marketing strategies and coordinate HR to sustain themselves under dramatically changing conditions. As suggested by Foster and Dye (2005), business resilience can be built around three fundamental elements: people, core business (e.g. systems, facilities and infrastructure) and networks. Extending this view, McManus et al. (2008) suggest that a resilient organisation exhibits certain behaviours, for example a greater awareness of how different aspects of the organisation fit together, its stakeholders and the environment in which it operates on a day-to-day basis as well as during emergency situations. Resilient organisations have an increased ability to identify and manage key vulnerabilities and develop the capability to adapt to changed situations with new and innovative solutions and/or the ability to adapt tools that they already have to cope with new and unforeseen situations (McManus et al., 2008). To some, this means that an organisation has to cultivate and maintain a culture of resilience (Pasteur, 2011).

In the tourism industry, studies have found several factors contributing to the resilience of organisations, including innovation, adaptation and survival strategies (Dahles & Susilowati, 2015; Specht, 2008; see also Box 4.1). Financial (e.g. access to additional finances), social capital (family and friends support, local community, collaboration between enterprises within the sector) and human capital (staff skills, ability to cope with change) have also been found to inform resilience (Biggs et al., 2012). Factors such as type of organisation and industry sector, size of the organisation and location can also influence resilience (Prayag & Orchiston, 2016). However, there is a lack of research linking organisational resilience to industry sector resilience in the tourism industry and whether sub-sectors such as accommodation, transport or tourist attractions have different levels of resilience and how these inform the resilience of the industry. The resilience of the tourism industry vis-à-vis other industries is another area that has been sparsely researched (Prayag & Orchiston, 2016). We also understand little of the significance of different markets, especially domestic versus international visitors, as well as products for business resilience. In a nutshell, existing studies are conducted at a micro level where linkages between institutions, communities and destinations have been so far ignored.

Box 4.2 Public agency survival

Destination management and marketing organisations are often public or public – private agencies. So what are the factors that affect the survival of such organisations and other public agencies given that they are highly susceptible to political change? Or are such government organisations, as Kaufman (1976) famously posed, 'immortal'? Organisational characteristics actually appear to have relatively little influence on public agency survival (Adam et al., 2007; Lewis, 2002), although the effects of some variables do change over time. In the United States, having a committee/board structure increases a public agency's risk initially, although after 6.5 years this design feature appears to work to the advantage of agency survival. Independence shows a similar pattern. Initially a liability, it becomes an asset for survival after a slightly shorter period (Boin et al., 2010).

There is some evidence that the extent of political turnover (change of policy party in government) increases the risk of agency termination (Lewis, 2002), while termination appears less likely when politicians are fiscally constrained (Carpenter & Lewis, 2004). The results of such research are significant as they suggest that public organisation survival may be connected more to political factors than to wider economic and technological change. Providing that destination management organisations (DMOs) are perceived as continuing to attract tourists they will be regarded as serving a useful role by industry interests as well as other stakeholders; this also includes the attraction of public funds for tourism promotion and other campaigns that would otherwise not be obtainable to support industry (Hall & Veer, 2016). To this end disasters may even work in a destination management and marketing organisation's favour, given the economic value associated with tourism.

> Hall and Veer (2016) argue that it is important to distinguish between the role of events (abrupt changes) and processes (more gradual changes) (see also Hall, 2016a). Much of the focus in research on tourism and change, including organisational and policy dimensions, is on the role of high-profile high-magnitude events; however, the role of 'normal' process is perhaps even more important to understanding changes in policy and organisational states in either composition or time. Indeed, in a general public agency setting, Boin *et al.* (2010: 404) observed that with respect to organisational survival, 'the name of the game is not design for survival but design for adaptation'.

Measuring organisational resilience

The complexity of measuring organisational resilience has been recognised (McManus *et al.*, 2008). A starting point, though, is the vulnerability to resilience framework, or V2R, which is used for analysing and developing action plans to reduce vulnerability and strengthen the resilience of individuals, households and communities. The framework sets out the key factors that contribute to people's vulnerability, such as exposure to hazards and stresses (e.g. improving hazard prevention and protection), fragile livelihoods (e.g. strengthening organisational structure and promoting access to technologies), future uncertainty (e.g. improving understanding of trends and their local impacts) and weak governance (e.g. decentralised and participatory decision making) (Pasteur, 2011). The framework has been adapted for the measurement of organisational resilience. For example, Sawalha (2015) asked 20 organisations in the insurance industry of Jordan which elements of the V2R framework were associated with resilience. The study found that more than 50% of the organisations surveyed prioritised organisational structure considerations (livelihoods) and disaster and crisis management (managing future uncertainty), with little support for governance (Sawalha, 2015).

Another tool for measuring organisational resilience is McManus' (2008) Relative Overall Resilience (ROR) model which is composed of three factors (situation awareness, management of keystone vulnerabilities, and adaptive capacity) with 15 indicators. Building on this initial study, Lee *et al.* (2013) added a fourth dimension, 'resilience ethos'. The adjusted ROR model measures 13 indicators using 53 items. Of these, eight indicators (minimisation of silos, internal resources, staff engagement and involvement, information and knowledge, leadership, innovation and creativity, decision making, situation monitoring and reporting) measure the dimension of adaptive capacity, while five indicators (planning strategies, participation in exercises, proactive exposure, external resources and recovery priorities) measure the dimension of planning. The two dimensions of adaptive and planning resilience reflect core themes of 'anticipation' versus 'resilience' in the crisis management and resilience literature (Comfort et al., 2001). Whether adaptive capacity is an intrinsic part of resilience is contested (Folke, 2006).

The only quantitative tool available for the tourism and hospitality industry to measure organisational resilience is Orchiston et al.'s (2016) 13 indicators which were adapted from studies by McManus et al. (2008) and Lee et al. (2013). These authors found 'planning and culture' and 'collaboration and innovation' as the two factors underlying the organisational resilience of tourism businesses in Christchurch, New Zealand. These dimensions are different from the original 'planning' and 'adaptive' dimensions suggested in Lee et al. (2013). Also, Orchiston et al. (2016) found that at least two of the three sub-sectors (accommodation, transport and tourist attraction) rated six of the 13 indicators of resilience significantly differently. The need to develop industry-specific indicators of organisation resilience is omnipresent. More recently, Mafabi et al. (2015) measured organisational resilience using 20 items that represent three dimensions (organisational adaptation, organisational competitiveness and organisational value). The argument proposed by these authors is that a resilient organisation is one capable of responding to the demands in the environment for survival, hence its adaptive capacity, similar to McManus et al.'s (2008) conceptualisation of resilience. However, Mafabi et al. (2015) posit that factors such as ability to respond to competitors, serve customers in a short time and succeed in the face of resource constraints, among others, contribute to resilience, as they define organisational competitiveness. In this study, organisational value pertains to the ability of the firm to satisfy its customers, engage in cost control effectively, and staff being satisfied with the organisation, among others. These factors are thought to contribute to organisational resilience. However, despite this tool having a strategic flair, its main focus is on operational requirements.

Critical Infrastructures for Developing Organisational Resilience

The next section outlines the role and influence of three critical infrastructures, namely people, processes and networks in building and managing organisational resilience. Much of what has been written on the 'inside-out' view of organisational resilience suggests that without these critical

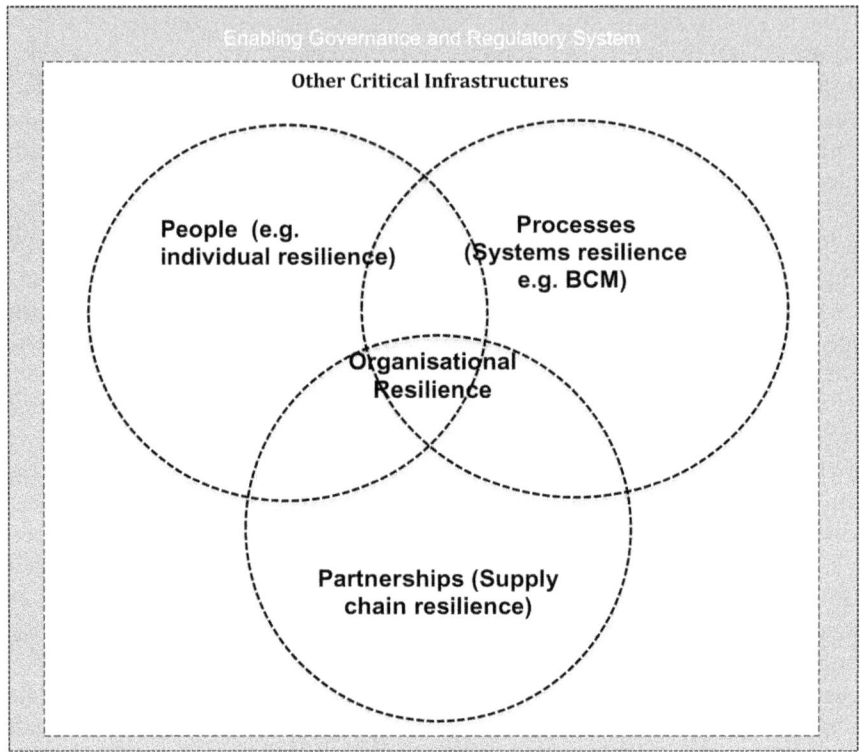

Figure 4.1 Components of organisational resilience

infrastructures there is no sustained competitive advantage, improvement in costs, operating revenue, reputation and agility (Sheffi, 2015). McLennan et al. (2013) identify eight dimensions that make institutions resilient as part of their long-term structural change. These dimensions include competition, learning, agility and adaptability, performance management, data and research capabilities, collaboration efforts, management processes and benchmarking processes. Many of these factors would fall under the role of people, processes and networks in developing organisational resilience. As shown in Figure 4.1, we argue that organisational resilience stems from interactions between these three components.

The role of people

Human capital elements have the potential to create synergistic relationships between other factors (e.g. processes and networks) that contribute to organisational resilience. In their own ways 'people' have the ability to leverage other strategic capabilities to build resilience (Lengnick-Hall et al., 2011). Specht (2008: 23) emphasised that 'best practice' with respect to resilience in the face of natural disasters 'includes ensuring a good staff morale and skill-base, good maintenance of assets, and good levels of general preparedness'. Following the earthquakes of 2010–2011 in Christchurch, New Zealand, a study by Nilakant et al. (2014) found that resilient organisations were those that understood the trajectory of employee needs, where middle managers played a key role in identifying and responding to employee needs. Organisations that provided more flexibility to assist staff in dealing with work-related and personal issues were more resilient. Other determinants of organisational resilience included offering customised human resource practices, a focus on staff wellbeing and engagement, communication and collaboration, effectively breaking down organisational silos, combining resources, and an ability to learn from within and outside the organisation. Leadership also featured prominently, with staff responding well to leaders who were visible, honest, caring and authentic in their communication, and those that empowered staff at lower levels (Nilakant et al., 2013, 2014). Basically, resilient organisations were those that were more likely to sustain a healthier workplace in the face of adversity. This is not surprising given that contextual conditions that support resilience rely on relationships within and outside an organisation to facilitate effective responses to environmental complexities (Lengnick-Hall et al., 2011).

The literature suggests four factors in the management of employees that can build resilience. When combined, these four factors promote interpersonal connections and resource supply lines that allow an organisation to act quickly under emerging conditions that are uncertain and surprising (Lengnick-Hall et al., 2011). The first factor, psychological safety, describes the degree to which people perceive that their work environment is conducive to taking interpersonal risks (Edmondson, 1999). This factor allows employees to understand the nature of risks when communicating, interacting and dealing with others. The second factor, deep social capital, evolves from face-to-face interactions and ongoing dialogues rooted in trust, honesty and respect, which enable collaborative sense making (Lengnick-Hall et al., 2011; Weick, 1993). It evolves from respectful interactions within an organisation (Ireland et al., 2002). Deep social capital facilitates growth in intellectual capital since people are more likely and able to share tacit information (Lengnick-Hall et al., 2011). The third factor, diffuse power and accountability, refers to organisations that share decision making widely, where every employee has both the discretion and the responsibility for ensuring the attainment of organisational goals. Such organisations are not managed hierarchically (Lengnick-Hall *et al.*, 2011; Mallak, 1998a). Finally, broad resource network is a key element in creating contextual conditions that support resilience development. Resilient individuals or employees are those who are capable of forging relationships with others who could share key resources (Werner & Smith, 2001), hence their ability to leverage other strategic capabilities. In the context of organisational resilience, this would imply employees being able to forge relationships with supply chain members and strategic alliances to secure the needed resources to support adaptive initiatives (Lengnick-Hall *et al.*, 2011).

The role of processes

Crises often disrupt and degrade the basic human, physical, informational and infrastructural resources of an organisation (Sheffi, 2015). Many organisations have learnt from disasters and have created more effective resources management for prevention, detection and response (Sheffi, 2015). The managerial challenge nonetheless remains to transform organisational resilience from being a set of redundant preventive actions involving resources management into a proactive strategy funded on a set of practices capable of fostering the daily effectiveness of operations and processes (Annarelli & Nonino, 2016). To this end, the notions of business continuity management (BCM) and enterprise risk management (ERM) have become fundamental for building and managing organisational resilience. BCM is a subset of ERM, with the former focusing on operational risks such as disrupted supply and production disruption, while the latter considers operational risks as well as other risks such as financial, regulatory and environmental (Sheffi, 2015). BCM arises out of an organisation's momentum to maintain continuity whereas ERM has some external drivers for its adoption and structure (Sheffi, 2015).

As a form of crisis management, BCM evolved in response to technical and operational risks that threatened an organisation's ability to recover from hazards and interruptions (Herbane, 2010). The term business continuity by itself means recovery and provides a framework for building resilience with the capability for an effective response that protects the interests of stakeholders, the environment, the organisation's reputation and brands, and other value-creating activities (Engemann & Henderson, 2011). ERM and BCM are intimately linked. ERM has led many companies to reconsider the roles of business continuity plans and emergency operations plans and to finalise processes for managing disruptions (Sheffi, 2015). Effective BCM provides an organisation with several benefits such as reduced downtime, improved business security and secure assets. From an HR perspective, the process of implementing BCM can help employees understand an organisation better and improve cross-functional training. From an operations management perspective, BCM requires a mapping of key internal and external dependencies including the critical infrastructures necessary for an organisation's survival in the face of adversity (Engemann & Henderson, 2011). Traditionally, business continuity planning (BCP) and disaster recovery planning (DRP) as the main contingency plans were carried out on different time horizons within organisations. However, the two are interdependent for building organisational resilience. These management approaches are becoming increasingly integrated to allow organisations to switch from the continuity phase to the recovery phase more smoothly and vice versa, while improving managers' understanding of the trade-offs between the continuity and recovery plans (Sahebiamnia et al., 2015). As such, an integrated approach allows organisations to create plans to respond to multiple disruptions at different scales but also to mitigate identifiable operational vulnerabilities. Consequently, organisational resilience is regarded by Lengnick-Hall et al. (2011: 244) as being 'tied to dynamic competition and the firm's ability to absorb complexity and emerge from a challenging situation stronger and with a greater repertoire of actions to draw from than were available before a disruptive event'. This has been described as the transformational view of organisational resilience (Lengnick-Hall et al., 2011).

Box 4.3 Business resilience following the 2004 southeast Asia tsunami: Evidence from reef enterprises in Phuket (Thailand)

In the aftermath of crises and disasters, the resilience of tourism businesses is essential for the wider recovery of destinations. Business resilience is defined as the 'ability to adapt to, and continue to function under changing pressures and circumstances' (Biggs et al., 2015: 65). Although socio-economic and governance contexts have a substantial influence on the resilience of tourism enterprises, specific entrepreneurial traits are similarly important for such businesses in times of uncertainty.

A study among formal and informal reef enterprises in Phuket (Thailand) measured resilience through four macro-dimensions of resilience:

- the perceived ability of their enterprises to endure change;
- levels of confidence in their enterprise;
- the perceived levels of enterprise adaptability;
- the ability to maintain options within the industry.

Findings suggest that, in case of a substantial decline in tourism numbers, formal enterprises expressed a stronger inclination to look for opportunities to move out of reef-based tourism than informal ones. Informal enterprises felt more confident about their financial condition in a shock scenario than formal enterprises. Informal enterprises also had higher lifestyle benefit scores on three different measures than formal enterprises. Informal enterprises reported higher levels of social capital than formal enterprises, expressed as a higher level of expected support from government, family and friends and local community groups (Biggs et al., 2012).

Formal and informal enterprises differed in how they responded to past shocks and in the factors that they perceived enabled them to survive. After the 2004 tsunami, the three most common responses by formal operators were cost-cutting and streamlining (54%), strengthened marketing (15%) and downsizing or temporarily closing down (13%). The top three responses by informal enterprises were downsizing or temporarily closing down (39%), relying on a second job or subsistence food production (30%) and sourcing additional funding through government support or a loan (17%). Formal and informal enterprises also differed in the factors that they perceived enabled their survival of the 2004 tsunami. The three most important survival factors reported by formal enterprises ($n = 25$) were commitment and hard work to maintain the lifestyle and enterprise (32%), the availability of past savings to draw on (12%) and the ability to cut costs (12%). The three most important survival factors reported by informal enterprises ($n = 31$) were commitment and hard work to maintain the lifestyle and enterprise (58%), government or NGO support (13%) and the ability to rely on a second source of income or subsistence (10%) (Biggs et al., 2012).

Factors mainly associated with social capital, human capital and entrepreneurial traits appear to be crucial in enhancing the resilience of reef enterprises in Phuket. Other key findings from the research are that resilience is context dependent and that human capital is decisive in the resilience of reef tourism businesses. Finally, 'lifestyle and social values are also important motivating factors for informal reef tourism enterprises and contribute to enterprise resilience' (Biggs et al., 2015: 71).

The role of networks

Organisations respond to uncertainty in different ways by, for example, centralisation of internal controls, learning and knowledge management, creativity and innovation and adapting to changing circumstances. Sources of organisational resiliency can be found when an organisation collaborates with a diverse set of independent organisations (Andrew *et al.*, 2016). The extent to which an organisation is resilient is also a function of interdependencies, that is, partnerships and cooperation with supply chain members as well as other stakeholders (e.g. NGOs, community) (Sheffi, 2015; Wu & Choi, 2005). Specht (2008) observed that in the case of extreme events:

> Good liaison with fellow operators and various agencies is a vital component of preparedness; tourism operations need to be supportive of each other and be recognised parts of the wider community. Such relationships and networks take time to develop, and continually changing staff (the norm in many tourism operations) is not conducive to an effective emergency response. Interorganisational links are often personal, dependent on trust developed between operatives. Calling Fred or Mary is usually better than calling an anonymous number. In addition, longer-term staff have a good knowledge of local geography, which is especially important when the tourist knows nothing (and maybe the emergency service operator even less). By ensuring these matters are in place, tourism operators and asset managers will retain their capability and functionality during and after an [extreme event]. (Specht, 2008: 23)

The use of social capital (Biggs *et al.*, 2012, 2015; Cheung & Chan, 2008) such as professional and informal network relationships has been found to be a valuable asset both in resolving internal organisational crises and rebuilding an organisation following an external shock (Doerfel *et al.*, 2010). Organisations that effectively use network resources are better able to adapt in times of crisis (Tierney & Trainor, 2004). A study by Stephenson *et al.* (2010) of 68 organisations in Auckland, New Zealand, showed that common weaknesses included the ability to utilise resources outside the organisation during a crisis. This highlights the importance of fostering multi-sector partnerships to enhance organisational resilience from disaster response.

Resiliency of organisations also implies resilience of supply chain partners. Accordingly, the relational dynamics with stakeholders outside the organisation are critical for developing resilience, whereby issues of competitiveness, cooperativeness and co-optiveness are considered as critical (Börekçi *et al.*, 2014). According to these authors, the resilience of one party (e.g.

supplier 1) affects and shapes not only the resilience of the buying firm but also the resilience of other suppliers. Hence, the resilience of the network system depends on an interdependent set of relationships. Specifically, building resiliency involves two broad categories of options: building redundancy and the flexibility of supply chain assets and processes. Redundant amounts of supply chain assets such as inventory, production capacity and multiple facilities offer an obvious option for crisis managers (Sheffi, 2015). The notion of supply chain resilience is relatively well researched (Ponis & Koronis, 2012) and can be defined as the ability to react to the negative effects caused by disturbances that occur at a given moment in order to maintain the supply chain's objectives (Barroso et al., 2011). It is also recognised that supply chains are complex systems comprising several interconnected agents that form a network of linkages that interact nonlinearly (Bhamra et al., 2011). This interaction gives rise to emergent behaviour in relation to resilience.

The case study in Box 4.4. illustrates the role of people, processes and networks in building organisational resilience for a restaurant, Winnie Bagoes, based in Christchurch, New Zealand.

Box 4.4 Winnie Bagoes: Gourmet pizza the Kiwi way!

Winnie Bagoes operates two branches (City branch and Ferrymead branch) in Christchurch, New Zealand, under its well-established restaurant brand name which has become synonymous with gourmet pizza offerings. The restaurant has established its competitive advantage through serving made-to-order and fresh pizza with generous toppings of high-quality ingredients. Complementing their pizza dishes, Winnie Bagoes has created a fun and social dining experience shaped by their belief that pizza is made for sharing. The September 2010 and February 2011 earthquakes severely affected hospitality firms in Christchurch, New Zealand including Winnie Bagoes' City branch. However, the Ferrymead branch was able to reopen five days after the February earthquakes while their City location remained closed. The managers relocated staff from the City branch to the Ferrymead branch immediately after reopening. Both the owner and managers at Winnie Bagoes worked hard in the post-quake environment, ensuring staff wellbeing and overseeing that operational requirements were met. As one of the managers mentioned, 'we put a lot of time and energy into training our staff to make sure the customer gets the best experience'.

> In terms of processes, Winnie Bagoes started relying more, for example, on social media for marketing purposes. As one of the manager said:
>
> ... while initially, word-of-mouth was sufficient to get customers through the door after the earthquakes, as more restaurants opened up, the business started to also use Facebook, which is our main social media avenue for connecting with customers, to just let customers know what's going on in the restaurant. Around 40% of our business is generated through social media now. In this way, Winnie Bagoes had to change the way it communicates with customers, the way it handles feedback from customers and how it incorporates such feedback in improving customer experience and developing new pizza combination/flavours.
>
> In terms of networks, Winnie Bagoes not only has a personalised approach to engaging with its suppliers but also engages with the community. For example, at the community level in the aftermath of the earthquakes, the restaurant provided pizzas to a local (Mount Pleasant) primary school and continued to sponsor four sports teams in the area. They hosted fundraising nights and sponsor pizza for schools. One of the managers mentioned that not only are customers loyal but also the suppliers, who quickly adapted after the earthquakes to facilitate the reopening of the Ferrymead branch. The personal relationship between the owner, the managers and the suppliers can be considered as factors contributing to organisational resilience.

Organisational Resilience: A Step Back to Ecological and Socio-ecological Systems

A study by Sawalha (2015), although not on the tourism industry but on the insurance industry instead, found that organisations can be grouped into three categories based on their understanding of resilience. Category 1 represented organisations that perceived resilience to be associated with the way organisations are impacted by incidents experienced in the past. Accordingly, these organisations respond in an ad hoc manner to single incidents, highlighting a lack of understanding of the drivers of resilience. This type of thinking dominates the tourism industry where resilience is perceived as the way an organisation reacts to unplanned events. Category 2 represented organisations that interpreted resilience as the management of risk and uncertainty, but this should not be the only concern for developing and implementing resilience. Category 3 organisations were more objective in their interpretation of organisational resilience and understood both the proactive and reactive sides of resilience (Sawalha, 2015). It is clear from existing studies on resilience in the tourism industry that issues of what the term means to organisations and how it is implemented are lacking.

To this end and in light of the existing conceptualisation and operationalisation of organisational resilience in related literatures, it is worthwhile revisiting some of the underpinning notions of resilience in their original form to inform organisational resilience thinking in tourism. As noted in Chapter 1, system thinking is not unfamiliar to tourism studies (Farrell & Twining-Ward, 2004). Studies on the interactions between tourism systems and their environments permeate the literature (Leiper, 1989). In ecosystem dynamics there seems to be some consensus regarding the properties of resilience. First, it is about the amount of change the system can undergo to retain the same controls on structure and function. The organisational resilience literature has embraced this idea of critical infrastructures, people and processes being managed to control the extent of change within the system. Secondly, another property of resilience is the degree to which the system is capable of self-organisation. This aspect has not been taken on board in existing studies and remains an area that requires research. The capacity of self-organisation at the firm level may well be strongly influenced by pre-existing network and business-to-business relations and the level of trust that has been developed between organisations. Thirdly, the degree to which the system can build the capacity to learn and adapt (Carpenter et al., 2001; Ponis & Koronis, 2012) is often reflected in organisational resilience literature through the concept of adaptive capacity. Although ecological resilience ideas of vulnerability and adaptive capacity are embedded in existing conceptualisations of organisational resilience, what is significant is adaptation and self-organisation in the system as it moves between states rather than adaptive capacity per se (Hall, 2016a). This challenges the adaptive capacity dimension which has been measured in organisational resilience studies so far.

As is recognised in ecosystem dynamics, a system may have 'multiple' stable states. Each separable stable state is induced by a change from the original state and would have a life cycle of its own (Farrell & Twining-Ward, 2004). Hence, self-organisation becomes critical to reach 'a' stable state. This aligns with the idea in the social sciences that there is no common path to resilience but the only commonality is that resilient choices are counter-intuitive given normal operating conditions (Meyer, 1982). Hence, similar to thinking on socio-ecological systems, organisational resilience thinking should include concepts such as climax, equilibrium and optimality in its discourse. For self-organisation to occur, values and beliefs, knowledge, skills and learning, leadership, social networks, organisational infrastructure and engaged governance are some important characteristics that must be cultivated within and between players in the system (Berkes & Ross, 2013). Also, current conceptualisations tend to suggest that 'all' organisations will survive if they are resilient. In ecosystems, weaker species must die to allow the system to reach a new stable state. Sheffi (2015) argues that, similar to the evolution of species, the more competitive and prone to failure individual players in an industry are, the more robust the industry as a whole is (Sheffi, 2015). Similarly, Hall (2016a) argues:

> There is no intrinsic relationship between organisational resilience and improving the resilience of a community *per se*. Not all organisations need to survive for a community to be resilient. At the community level the issue becomes more *which* organisations need to survive and which organisations will be born with what characteristics and values to replace those that have died in order to maintain or enhance system properties and develop a system that accepts change and unpredictability and is designed to be safe to fail. (Hall, 2016a: 285)

Hence, some organisations must fail in order to allow a new stable state to emerge.

The resilience of one system at one scale influences its resilience at other scales (Woods, 2007). So instead of organisations seeking to identify factors that will lead to 'a' single equilibrium state, multiple stable states should coexist for the continued existence of the ecosystem (Gunderson *et al.*, 2002). Yet not much is known about the resilience of tourism industries worldwide despite some studies showing that sectors/industries matter in understanding the impacts on and recovery of businesses following a disaster (Brown *et al.*, 2015; Prayag & Orchiston, 2016). Organisational resilience is closely linked to industry resilience. For example, the accommodation and transport industries are interlinked for tourism purposes; the vulnerability of one has a cascading effect on organisations in the other industry. Differences in organisational resilience between the informal and formal sectors within the same industry have also been noted in previous studies (Biggs *et al.*, 2012). On a larger scale, some studies suggest that resilient industries and businesses contribute to resilient communities (Cutter *et al.*, 2008; McManus *et al.*, 2008) although, as noted above, not all organisations need to survive for a community to be resilient (Hall, 2016a). In terms of the emergent properties of a tourism system, the issue therefore becomes more of *which* organisations need to survive and which organisations will be born with what characteristics and values to replace those that have died in order to maintain or enhance system properties (Hall, 2016a). The resilience of an organisation requires renewal, transformation and dynamic creativity from the inside out (Lengnick-Hall *et al.*, 2011).

Box 4.5 Can post-disturbance business survival be explained ecologically?

One area of ecology that may help shed light on organisational survivability is that of island biogeography (Hall, 2016a). The concept of island biogeography examines the relationships between species and a given area (MacArthur & Wilson, 1963, 1967). The conventional expression of the species–area relationship is $S = CA^z$, where S and A are species count and area, respectively, and C and z are fitted species-specific constants. However, an 'island' is any appropriate bounded space (Whittaker & Fernández-Palacios, 2007). Although the model is limited in terms of its predictive capacity for equilibrium, it is valid in suggesting that, although fluctuations will occur over time, there is a limit to the species diversity of a given area (Cox & Moore, 2010). This is very important for species survival, because every species runs the risk of extinction; the more species that arrive in a location the more species there are at risk. Furthermore, 'as more species arrive, the average population size of each will diminish as competition increases – and a smaller population is at greater risk of extinction than a larger population' (Cox & Moore, 2010: 240; Figure 4.2).

Hall (2012, 2015) used island biogeographical theory to illustrate issues of adaptation, resilience and vulnerability of 'island' economies, while the implications of the theory for resilience and disaster ecology were discussed in Hall (2016a). Using this approach, the 'equilibrial' number of businesses and organisations for a given set of resources in a specific space is reached at the intersection of the rate of immigration of new firms and capital, and the emigration or closure (extinction) of businesses, along with the capacity of businesses and organisations to innovate and adapt (which is analogous to species evolution over time and the occupation of new ecological niches). Immigration rates are postulated to vary as a function of distance (regulatory, economic, cultural, perceptual or Euclidean) and closure rates are functions of island area and resources which determine the competition for finite capital in its

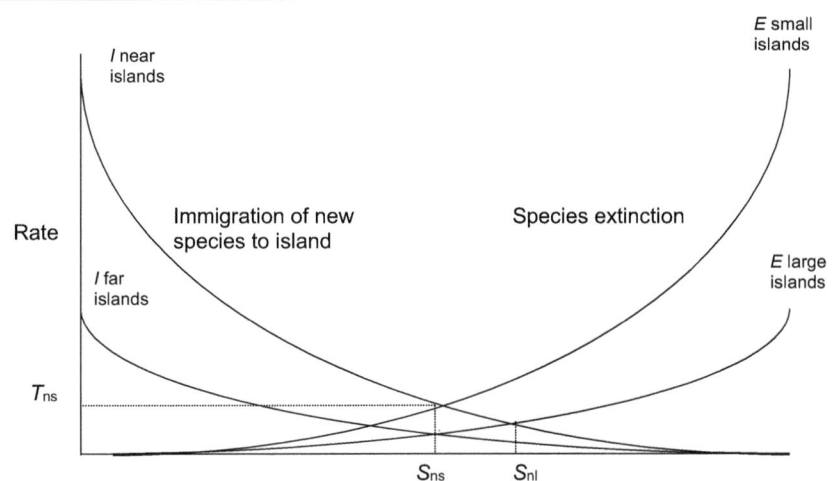

Figure 4.2 Equilibrium model of single island biota
Notes: The equilibrial species number is reached at the intersection between the curves of the rate of immigration of new species to the island and the curve of extinction of species on the island. Immigration rates are postulated to vary as a function of distance, and extinction rate as a function of island area. (One of the axiomatic laws of ecology is that the supply of resources is finite. Resource supply, interspecific and intraspecific competition, and predation, including disease, limit reproduction). The model predicts different values for S (number of species), which can be read off the ordinate, and for turnover rate (T) (the number of species that become extinct and are replaced by immigrants and speciation over unit time). Each combination of island area and isolation should produce a different and unique combination of S and T. For reasons of uncluttered illustration only limited values are shown. The equilibrium point at which I equals E is never completely constant as it will shift over time in relation to a range in external and internal factors, including disturbance. Time lags and fluctuations in carrying capacity and growth rates are all possible and make it difficult to predict exactly when population levels will be limited. However, the key point is that there is a 'capacity' as to how many species and their populations can successfully inhabit a finite area over time because of availability and stability of habitat and/or resources at the same trophic level.
Source: Dodds (2009); Hall (2015, 2016a); Whittaker and Fernández-Palacios (2007).

various forms, e.g. economic capital, human capital, natural capital. Although heuristic, the model can potentially predict different values for S (e.g. number of firms and/or capital) and for turnover rate (T) (the number of firms that close and are replaced by immigrants and innovation over unit time), given assumptions about the equilibrium nature of the bounded space. The equilibrium point at which I equals E is, of course, never completely constant as it will shift over time in relation to external and internal factors. Nevertheless, there is a 'capacity' limit as to how many businesses and organisations – as well as individuals – can inhabit a finite area over time (Hall, 2015) or, in broader ecological economic terms, without there being substantial importing of external resources, e.g. energy, food, water and/or economic capital, to maintain a given population base (Hall, 2016a) (Figure 4.3).

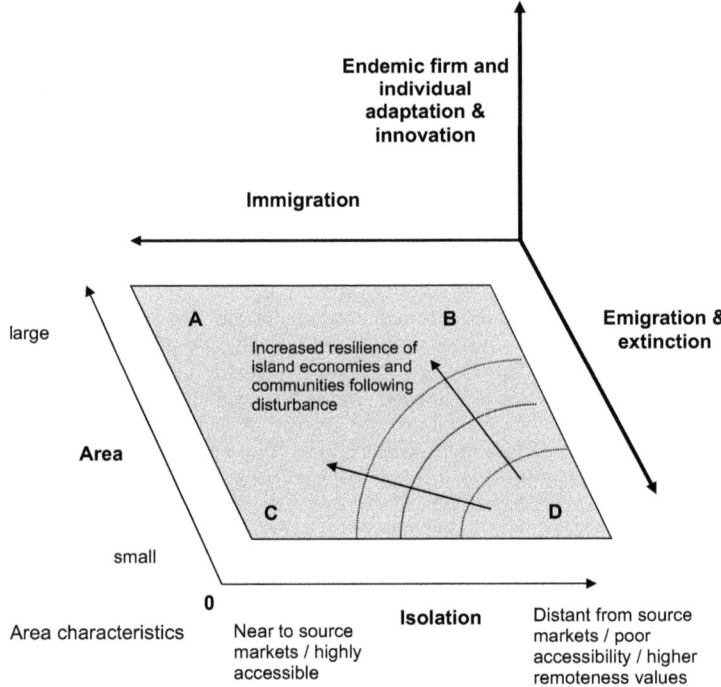

Figure 4.3 Island biogeographical perspectives on economic endemism, immigration, emigration and extinction
Notes: Community characteristics of labelled regions are as follows: (A) Moderate to high economic diversity, low endemicity and low turnover; (B) Moderate to high economic diversity, high endemicity and low turnover; (C) Moderate to low economic diversity, low endemicity and high turnover; (D) Low economic diversity, low endemicity and high turnover – a depauperate island economy. Economic diversity is the number and variety of different businesses and organisations. Endemicity is the development of businesses unique to the location as a result of adaptation and innovation. Immigration refers to the inflow of firms, people and/or funds and remittances. Emigration refers to the departure of firms, people and/or funds. Extinction refers to firms' ceasing to operate.
Source: After Hall (2012, 2015, 2016a).

Some businesses occupy a specialised niche in order to survive. In ecology the more specialised a species is the less adaptable it tends to be to disturbance or new species interactions (Concepción et al., 2015). In the case of loss of habitat or co-evolutionary interactions due to disturbance, for example, species survival may be linked to the capacity to disperse to patches with reduced levels of competition (thereby reducing specialisation). However, in other cases disturbance may reduce the number of inter- and extra-species competitors and potentially increase the survival rates of individuals, assuming resource levels stay constant. In such a situation, the increased capacity for individual survival may have very little to do with the inherent characteristics of the individual or the species (except luck), and is instead a function of wider system characteristics. The system analogy here is that firms that have survived an initial disturbance have a survival advantage, at least in the short run, before new firms emerge to enter the market and increase levels of competition and the rate of firm death (Hall, 2016a). In commenting on research on tourist firm survivability Hall and Williams (2008), observed that the duration of firm life appeared to be substantially affected by the dynamics of industry evolution within particular regions and concluded, 'It may therefore be easier for new firms to survive in those regions in which the tourist industry was growing at higher rates: since their entry into the industry is less likely to inflict market share losses on their rivals, the likelihood of retaliation by incumbents will be lower' (Hall & Williams, 2008: 198). Firm survival may therefore have less to do with entrepreneurial capacities than with the condition of the wider system.

The factors that underlie species turnover and ecosystem change are complex, dynamic, multi-scaled and often stochastic. From an ecological perspective, is it the death of individuals that is significant? Or, as Holling (1973: 1) posed in his seminal paper on resilience, is it 'the numbers of organisms and the degree of constancy of their numbers? These are two very different ways of viewing the behavior of systems, and the usefulness of the view depends very much on the properties of the system concerned'. The exact same questions apply to organisations.

Conclusion

This chapter has provided an insight into the meanings attributed to the term organisational resilience and suggested that three critical infrastructures,

Table 4.1 Fundamental questions related to organisation resilience

Who?	Who determines what is desirable in the organisation system? Whose resilience is prioritised? Who is excluded and included in the organisation system? (Who are the winners and losers, especially between different parts of an organisation, and the balances between different interests?)
What?	What perturbations should the organisation system be resilient to? What networks, interests and sectors are included in or related to the organisation system? Is the focus on resilience generic or specific within and across organisations, sectors and industries?
When?	What is the relative focus on rapid-onset disturbances and slow-onset changes within the organisation, sector and industry? Is the focus on the short- or long-term resilience of the organisation? Is the focus on the resilience of present or future generations, and/or present or future organisations, sectors and industries?
Where?	What are the spatial and jurisdictional boundaries of the organisation, sectoral and industry system? Is the resilience of some areas or parts of the organisation (e.g. infrastructure and plant, supply chain, or employees) prioritised over others? Does building resilience in some areas affect resilience elsewhere?
Why?	What is the goal of building organisation resilience? What are the underlying motivations and by whom for building organisation resilience? What is the relative balance between process and outcome?

namely people, processes and partnerships, are necessary to build resilience. The chapter proposed a conceptual model and revisited some of the notions underpinning resilience in ecological and socio-ecological systems which could enhance the conceptualisation and operationalisation of the concept of organisational resilience. What is clear from existing studies is that there is some consensus on the drivers of resilience within an organisation but how these drivers interact with each other and the linkages with other systems remains murky. In a nutshell, the micro-level understanding of organisational resilience has progressed far but system-level thinking is still in its infancy and significant questions remain (Table 4.1). Hence, fruitful areas of future research within the tourism and hospitality industry include how organisations understand the term organisational resilience, industry and sector-specific drivers of resilience, and linkages between organisational, community and destination resilience.

Further reading

One aspect of the 'inside view' of organisational resilience is the role of innovation which was briefly touched on in this chapter. The following article examines the role of innovation and creativity in building organisational resilience:

Mafabi, S., Munene, J.C. and Ahiauzu, A. (2015) Creative climate and organisational resilience: The mediating role of innovation. *International Journal of Organizational Analysis* 23 (4), 564–587.

This chapter briefly examined the role of different forms of capital including financial and social capital. The following article provides further insights on the role of capital stocks in building organisational resilience:

Baral, N. and Stern, M.J. (2011) Capital stocks and organizational resilience in the Annapurna Conservation Area, Nepal. *Society & Natural Resources* 24 (10), 1011–1026.

Networks are clearly significant for organisational resilience. For an assessment of resilience in supply chains and its implications for business continuity see:

Vargas, J. and Gonzalez, D. (2016) Model to assess supply chain resilience. *International Journal of Safety and Security Engineering* 6 (2), 282–292.

The relationship between governance and organisational resilience, an issue pertinent to understanding the social interactions between firms and their networks, is examined in:

Lampel, J., Bhalla, A. and Jha, P.P. (2014) Does governance confer organisational resilience? Evidence from UK employee owned businesses. *European Management Journal* 32 (1), 66–72.

5 Destination Resilience

Introduction

Although destinations are notoriously difficult to define (Hall, 2008), they lie at the heart of much thinking about tourism and resilience. For the purposes of this chapter, destinations are defined as a distinct spatial unit, usually at subnational level, which is defined by visitors, the services provided and its governance. A destination obviously comes to exist by virtue of the people who visit it. However, also of importance are the specific tourism services, e.g. accommodation, transport, retail, attractions, public space and physical environment, which are used by tourists and the people who live in a destination permanently, and the governance and jurisdiction of the territory and the services provided.

This chapter is structured into three main parts. The first part provides an overview of the literature on resilience and tourist destinations. The chapter next discusses the different dimensions of resilience from the ecological dimension down to the individual one. It then proposes an ultimate definition of destination resilience along with a proposed framework for the understanding of resilient destinations for complex context settings coping with risks, vulnerabilities and opportunities for resilience. A series of examples of resilience at destination level from a range of places across the globe is provided as further evidence.

Conceptualising Destination Resilience

Over the last 40 years tourism has been affected, both directly and indirectly, by major global and domestic triggering events such as political turmoil, economic crises, natural disasters and the consequences of climate change (Hall, 2010c). Nevertheless, the number of international tourism arrivals has continued to increase in both absolute and relative (to global population) terms since the 1950s (UNWTO, 2014), with only a slight decrease during the peak of the 2007–2008 global financial crisis (GFC) or during previous periods of crisis, such as the 1973 Arab-Israeli war and the subsequent increase in the price of oil. The escalation of political instability following the Arab Spring, the human crisis of refugees seeking political asylum in Europe and elsewhere and the increasing fear of international terrorism has at most shifted the flow of international tourists between destinations rather than reducing the amount of travel (e.g. Visao, 2013). This is an important observation as it highlights the importance of scale in trying to understand system resilience. The simplified tourism system shown in Chapter 1 (see Figure 1.2) shows only the relationship between the tourism-generating region tourists come from and the destination they choose. In reality, there are multiple generating areas and multiple destinations – which form a choice set for potential tourists. Figure 5.1 begins to give a brief idea of the overall complexity of the global tourism system, with the multitude of tourism generating regions and multiple potential destinations giving the global system substantial stability even if particular generating regions and/or destinations are

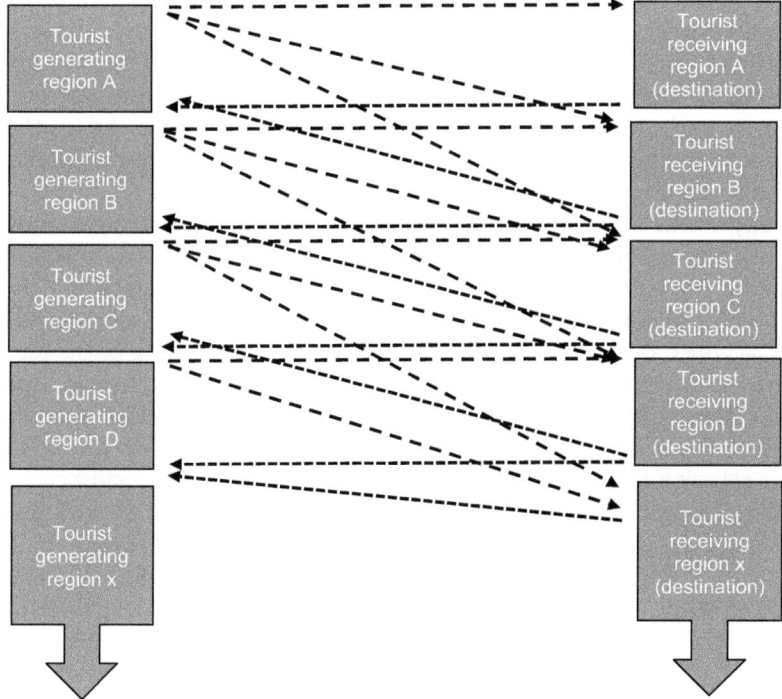

Figure 5.1 Representation of a complex tourism system

affected. It is only during a global crisis when the majority of generating regions are affected that there is a downturn in global tourism.

It has been argued that tourists are among the most vulnerable stakeholders when a given triggering event such as a natural or human-induced disaster occurs (Ma et al., 2014; Murphy & Bayley, 1989; Sönmez, 1998). Tourist destinations and tourism supply can also show high vulnerabilities (Biggs et al., 2015; Ghaderi et al., 2015; Méheux & Parker, 2006) as well as adaptability (Buultjens et al., 2014; Jopp et al., 2010) to such triggering events. Such attributes have recently been paired with the notion of resilience, particularly with respect to climate change (e.g. Becken, 2013), planning (e.g. Lew, 2014) and business adaptation (e.g. Dahles & Susilowati, 2015). At the destination level, resilience will partly be a function of individual and organisational resilience, but will also be affected by the nature of the destination system itself – the emergent effects – which stem from the density and richness of the networks between organisations and individuals in business, government, NGOs and the community within the destination region as well as the networks that exist between stakeholders in the destination and in various tourism-generating regions. As a rule of thumb, the denser and wider those networks are the more potentially resilient a destination is to perturbation. For example, a destination with, say, six main international visitor markets is potentially less susceptible to change in flows than if it only had two. Similarly, a destination which has more transport routes to access for its visitors is potentially more resilient to change than if access is limited, if one of those transport routes is affected by a disaster, such as road or rail access being lost in the event of an earthquake.

Early works (e.g. Gorica, 2008; Hobson & Essex, 2001) acknowledged the dimension of resilience in tourism but never fully addressed it nor provided a definition. Tyrrell and Johnston (2008: 16) conceived tourism resilience as 'the ability of social, economic or ecological systems to recover from tourism induced stress' – which is more resilience to tourism than the resilience of the tourism system itself, although they will be related. Cochrane (2010), instead, reprised Butler's Tourist Area Life Cycle (1980) and the 'triple-bottom line' discourse of sustainability (Elkington, 1997) in the identification of market forces, stakeholder cohesion and leadership as the cornerstones of tourism resilience.

With respect to destination resilience, a good proportion of the literature focuses on the issue of climate change (Bhandari et al., 2015; Becken, 2013; Biggs et al., 2015; Goodwin & Font, 2012; Luthe & Wyss, 2014, 2016; Méheux & Parker, 2006; Moreno & Becken, 2009; Nyaupane & Chhetri, 2009; Tervo, 2008). Other works address different kinds of disturbances, including the impact of and recovery from earthquakes and other disasters (Amore & Hall, 2016a; Becken et al., 2014; Calgaro, 2010; Causevic & Lynch, 2013; Dredge, 2015; Ghaderi et al., 2015; Mahon et al., 2013; Orchiston et al., 2016). Overall, the literature tends mainly to concentrate on the so-called macro dimensions of resilience (Norris et al., 2008), particularly the ecological and socio-ecological dimensions (Orchiston et al., 2016). Among them, Biggs et al. (2015) and Lew (2014) are strongly influenced by ecological and socio-ecological resilience theories (Adger, 2000; Folke, 2006; Gunderson & Holling, 2001; Holling, 1973). There are, nonetheless, works that acknowledge the micro dimensions of resilience, including the relevance of governance networks (Luthe & Wyss, 2016; Sheppard & Williams, 2015) and the views and perceptions of individuals (Biggs et al., 2015; Calgaro, 2010) as embedded and influenced by the particular tourist destination context.

The resilience of tourist destinations emerges from the many features of the tourist supply as well as from its demand. Moreover, it manifests itself at different scales and dimensions. Therefore, a sound assessment of destination resilience requires rigorous yet comprehensive frameworks of analysis. Only a greater understanding of the many facets of resilience can lead to an improvement in the strategies, management and sustainable development of destinations in the long term. The following sections illustrate some prominent examples as to how the dimension of resilience changes throughout the macro–micro scale continuum. Most importantly, they illustrate how even though one element of a destination may be affected by change or disaster, other parts may be able to respond and even thrive under new conditions.

Ecological Dimensions of Destination Resilience

As noted in Chapter 2, the notion of ecological resilience is derived from the field of ecology and represents one of the mainstream paradigms in the current tourism-related literature on resilience (Lew, 2014; Orchiston et al., 2016). Focusing on the dimension of ecological resilience, Berkes (2010: 25) envisions 'ecosystems as constantly changing', while Holling (1973: 14) refers to resilience as 'the persistence of systems and of their ability to absorb change and disturbance and still maintain the same relationships between populations or state variables'. Some authors describe resilience as an attribute that enables mechanisms of change from a stage of turbulence back to a given state of equilibrium (Pimm, 1984; Scheffer et al., 2001). Others tend rather to conceive it as the intrinsic capacities of ecosystems to absorb negative impacts (Cardona, 2003) by proactively or reactively adapting to given ecosystem changes (Dovers & Handmer, 1992).

The influence of ecology in the study of destination resilience can be found in most of the dedicated literature. Becken (2013), for example, elaborates a destination resilience framework centred on the notions of ecological resilience that links climatic factors to tourism activities in the Queenstown-Wanaka region of New Zealand. Similarly, Jones et al. (2010) provide a destination model utilising the approach of Gunderson and Holling (2001) in their empirical study on regional destination resilience in Ningaloo, Australia. Luthe and Wyss (2014, 2016) use ecological resilience concepts to help examine 'how the network of tourism actors, destinations, and regions can withstand and adapt to both long- and short-term changes' (Luthe & Wyss, 2016: 26) caused by climate change.

Works on destination resilience rooted on the dimension of ecological systems advocate a multi-dimensional research approach in the understanding of key processes and dimensions of tourist destinations (Hall, 2008; Becken, 2013). Moreover, this potentially enables interdisciplinary and post-disciplinary thinking in tourism (Becken, 2013; Coles et al., 2006, 2016) and may help shed light on those cultural and natural resources that are often at the core of destination attractiveness. Not surprisingly, Luthe and Wyss (2014) acknowledge how:

> ... assessing and planning resilience is of growing importance since change processes and their interrelations have become more complex in a globalized, accelerated world, placing tourism under pressure to respond and adapt to various factors. (Luthe & Wyss, 2014: 161)

Similarly, Jopp et al. (2010) argue that planned destination resilience reduces the vulnerabilities of a destination while increasing the opportunities of thriving. However, there appear to be multiple ways of interpreting not only resilience but how destinations should be planned. Nevertheless, a useful starting point is likely to be the condition of the destination's physical environment and ecosystems and their capacity to respond to change. For example, SLR is a unidirectional hazard that, once set in motion, will continue for centuries, if not millennia, even under moderate scenarios of global warming (Scott et al., 2012). Nicholls and Tol (2006) contend that cost–benefit analyses suggest that widespread coastal protection will be an economically prudent response to avoid land loss and infrastructure damage from SLR. Nonetheless, Buckley (2008: 72–73) notes that, 'Most coastal tourism destinations ... seem to have remained remarkably blasé about rising sea levels, even though these are one of the best-documented aspects of global change'. One of the major problems is that many existing coastal resort infrastructures have already been built too close to the sea, thereby limiting the beneficial effects of coastal ecosystems, such as healthy fringing reefs, vegetated sand dunes and mangroves, which may have even been replaced by resort development, in reducing the effects of storm surges, SLR and coastal erosion. Typical hard structural coastal protection, e.g. rock walls and groynes, is not well suited to the image of coastal resorts (providing unobstructed views of the sea, maintaining unhindered access to the beach and sea, and the visual perception of a pristine beach environment) (Scott *et al.*, 2012). Furthermore, while structural protection can easily be designed to protect resort buildings, coastal squeeze (whereby the area of beach between sea level and a landward boundary such as a sea wall is lost as sea levels rise) will mean that many coastal resort destinations will lose their beaches unless they are also willing to invest heavily in beach nourishment and other strategies such as 'raising' roads and infrastructure. This may be one option for some destinations but even then it is likely short term. Instead, ensuring that coastal ecosystems are conserved and maintained provides the greatest flexibility in being able to respond to SLR.

Box 5.1 Atlantic City

According to the US National Oceanic and Atmospheric Administration, flooding events have increased sevenfold in Atlantic City since the 1950s, and are spurred on by rainfall or simply a spring tide abetted by wind. The SLR in the region is of the order of 38 mm (nearly 1.5″) a decade. The casinos and famous boardwalk are protected on the ocean side by a network of beach dunes. However, the poorer western side of the city, where few tourists go, is more vulnerable. Several times a month water swells in the bay behind Absecon Island – the barrier strip dotted by the resorts of Atlantic City, Ventnor, Margate and Longport – and with nowhere to go can enter the streets, wrecking cars and stranding residents. For example, 20 cars a month are being lost to 'nuisance flooding' on Absecon Island. According to Milman (2017):

> And yet with no overarching national sea level rise plan, and patchy commitment from states, many coastal communities are left to deal with the encroaching seas themselves. Wealthier areas are raising streets and houses, erecting walls and pumps. Those without the funds or political will have several state or federal grants they can access but often make muddled choices in the face of this Sisyphean task. ... Federal leadership for communities like Atlantic City and Miami Beach is unlikely to arrive before the situation escalates further. Donald Trump's administration has already taken aim at existing coastal resiliency funding and has disparaged basic scientific understanding of climate change. (Milman, 2017)

Social-ecological dimension of destination resilience

As noted in Chapter 2, socio-ecological systems are a particular subset of ecological resilience approaches. According to Adger *et al.* (2005: 1036), the resilience of socio-ecological systems is the capacity 'to absorb recurrent disturbances such as hurricanes or floods so as to retain essential structures, processes, and feedbacks'. The socio-ecological dimensions of resilience are not static (Waller, 2001) and are about 'the ability of the linked social–ecological system to deal with the hazard and providing insights on what makes a system less vulnerable' (Berkes, 2007: 292) and thrive more under changing conditions. A resilient social ecological system (also referred to as an SES) is able to innovate itself through reflective learning and adapt to different grades of stability (Luthe & Wyss, 2016).

The socio-ecological dimension of resilience is often referred to in literature on tourist destinations. With respect to the issue of climate change, Jopp *et al.* (2010), for example, stress the importance of both the biophysical and the social impacts in affecting the vulnerability of destinations. They further argue that destination resilience is achievable through a holistic approach which is resistant to changes and which increases 'the readiness to capitalize on opportunities presented' (Jopp *et al.*, 2010: 591). The result is a Regional Tourism Adaptation Framework (RTAF) that considers assessment and adaptive planning as pivotal in increasing destination's resilience. The framework is applied in the Surf Coast destination in Australia to assess the destination's socio-ecological context and identify a range of adaptation options to capitalise on the effects of climate change (Jopp *et al.*, 2013). In contrast, Njoroge (2014) asserts that most of the destination resilience frameworks, including the RTAF, are far from being sustainable. He proposes an enhanced Regional Tourism Sustainable Adaptation Framework (RTSAF) which increases the destination's resilience 'without jeopardizing its economic viability, social justice and environmental integrity' (Njoroge, 2014: 23). In particular, it acknowledges the relevance of sustainable adaptation as well as the input from global and national stakeholders with respect to climate change 'to help regional tourism managers achieve sustainability in adaptation process' (Njoroge, 2014: 29).

The socio-ecological resilience of destinations is similarly addressed with respect to destinations affected by natural disasters. Calgaro (2010) utilises the work of Pelling (2003b) to explain how resilience has to be achieved by addressing 'the underlying ... environmental linkages that form the foundations of vulnerability' (Calgaro, 2010: 6). She then proposes a destination vulnerability assessment (DVA) established specifically to assess the social and environmental resilience of destinations to sudden shocks and stressors, with findings from the post-2004 Boxing Day tsunami in three destinations in Thailand (Box 5.2) (Calgaro, 2010; Calgaro *et al.*, 2014). Similarly, Amore (2016a) reprises the paradigm of crisis-driven urbanisation (Gotham & Greenberg, 2014) to illustrate how stressors such as natural disasters should be viewed as the outcome of governance failure. Such an approach towards vulnerability assessment, which can also be found in Gurtner (2007), is implemented in post-earthquake Christchurch, New Zealand to illustrate how the loss of a great extent of the built heritage in the city is the result of a flawed governance approach that overlooked the geotechnical conditions of the city that were already recognised by experts (Amore, 2016a).

Box 5.2 Assessing the socio-ecological vulnerability of destinations: Evidence from Khao Lak, Patong and Phi Phi Don (Thailand)

On 26 December 2004 a severe tsunami hit the southeast Asia region, killing at least 185,000 people and displacing nearly 1.75 million. Renowned destinations such as Phuket (Thailand), Bali (Indonesia), the Maldives and Sri Lanka were hit, with sharp subsequent losses in the local tourism industry (see Calgaro *et al.*, 2014). Following the disaster, the Stockholm Environment Institute (SEI) launched a research programme (Sustainable Recovery and Resilience Building in the Tsunami Affected Region) between 2005 and 2008 'to build long-term resilience to coastal hazards among vulnerable communities' (Thomalla *et al.*, 2009: 1). Among the research aims, those of destination vulnerability and resilience foresaw the development of the Destination Sustainability Framework (DSF) to three localities in Thailand: Khao Lak, Patong and Phi Phi Don.

The analysis of destination vulnerability in these three destinations shows that 'place-based differences and context matter in determining differential levels of destination vulnerability and resilience' (Calgaro, 2010: 229). Focusing on the sensitivity of the physical environment, Patong and Phi Phi Don lacked effective management solutions to cope with environmental degradation. Conversely, Khao Lak proved to be more cautious about environmental sensitivity: before the tsunami, there was not enough development to place significant pressure on the natural environment; however, the community is worried that the unmonitored rebuilding of post-tsunami development and future growth may place unsustainable pressure on fragile coastal ecosystems (Calgaro, 2010).

With regard to social resilience, Patong proved to be more resilient due to its long-established business base but turned out to be less socially

> cohesive than Khao Lak and Phi Phi Don. In Khao Lak, destination recovery was possible thanks to, mainly, strong family networks which provided the necessary financial and moral support to businesses (see also Biggs *et al.*, 2012; Box 4.2). Another important factor was the international aid from tourism-generating countries, particularly among loyal visitors. Finally, Phi Phi Don had a similar business base strength to Patong but the concentration of land ownership and power in the hands of few dominant landowner families meant that recovery was unequal at the expense of the rest of the community (Calgaro, 2010).

The examples provided here highlight the importance of linking the ecological and the social dimensions of resilience as two sides of the same coin. Vulnerability (and, hence, resilience) is also context specific and calls for an appraisal of elements of the physical environment as well as of societal ones. The latter are bound to the policy environment and the governance of places. Specifically with tourism destinations, it is important to acknowledge the many potential dimensions of resilience and the stakeholders whose values and influence can affect – positively or negatively – the resilience of a given destination.

Social-political dimensions of destination resilience

Pelling (2003a: 8) conceives resilience within the broader context of globalisation, highlighting both the strengths and the vulnerabilities of transnational populations in contemporary risk society. The concept is also proposed with regard to urban risk and vulnerabilities that place 'politics (individual to global) at the centre of analysis and praxis of sustainable urbanization' (Pelling, 2003b: 18). In contrast, Lorenz (2013: 7) defines social resilience apolitically as 'the social system property of avoiding or withstanding disasters'. In the political sciences, instead, Wildavsky (1991: 77) defines resilience as 'the capacity to cope with unanticipated dangers after they have become manifest', while Obama (2011: 18) suggests that resilience is 'the ability to adapt to changing conditions and prepare for, withstand, and rapidly recover from disruption'. Governance – here defined as the process of the governing of places through laws, rules and decision making (Bevir, 2011; Rhodes, 1997) – is central to the dimension of social-political resilience. A resilient governance framework enhances the adaptive capacity (Luthe & Wyss, 2016) of destinations as well as the quality of institutional change and innovation in times of uncertainty or as result of governance failures.

With regard to tourist destinations, the political and social dimensions of resilience are acknowledged both in Calgaro's (2010) DVA and Jopp *et al.*'s

(2010) RTAF. In particular, the political dimension is addressed in recent reports issued by the Organisation for Economic Co-operation and Development (OECD) (Dredge, 2015; Haxton, 2015; Box 5.3). The reports suggest that ideal resilient destinations are those that quickly recover from crises by adopting policies that acknowledge current and future risks (Haxton, 2015: 33). Among such policies, Dredge (2015) provides examples of land use planning and hazard mitigation to tourism-relevant amenities and infrastructures as one of the many ways to seek long-term sustainability and resilience at destination level.

Box 5.3 Long-term planning for tourism growth and destination resilience: Recommendations from the OECD

Since the GFC, the OECD has released a number of reports to assist developed countries with a series of policy considerations to support economic recovery. Looking at tourism in particular, the *Review of Effective Policies for Tourism Growth* (Haxton, 2015) seeks to enhance the resilience of destinations while supporting greener, stronger and more inclusive tourism growth. The report specifically stresses how 'tourism policy needs to be considered not in isolation but within its broader policy context, with leadership from policy makers at the highest level and whose support can help ensure that the impacts on tourism of related policy initiatives are also considered' (Haxton, 2015: 8).

The report emphasises how the governance failures following the GFC and the events in the public sphere eventually led to a sense of civic mistrust. Moreover, it reinforces the need for a long-term approach in tourism policy and planning (see also Dredge, 2015; Hall, 2008). In particular, it stresses the adoption of policies to improve the efficient use of resources while tackling issues such as depletion of natural resources, water scarcity and environmental degradation (Haxton, 2015). The report exhorts countries to pursue a green growth agenda to reframe development and put a greater emphasis on the importance 'of natural capital as a factor of production and its role in enhancing well-being' (Haxton, 2015: 16).

With respect to emergency management, a greater co-ordination among tourism stakeholders at large is likely 'to improve the preparedness of tourism operations and agencies in dealing with an emergency and would assist in response and recovery activities' (Haxton, 2015: 33). Enhanced coordination inevitably advocates for policy interlinkages between tourism and emergency management policies to reduce destination vulnerability and ease recovery in the aftermath of disasters

(Haxton, 2015). An example is that of the Pacific Asia Travel Association (PATA) Rapid Response Taskforce, which envisions tourism stakeholders having an important role in the prevention, preparedness, response and recovery of disaster-prone areas.

Box 5.4 Building destination resilience in southeast Asia: The R3ADY Asia Pacific Programme

The R3ADY Asia Pacific Programme – formerly known as APDR3 – is 'committed to reducing the risks of natural disasters and building resilient communities and economies through innovative and strategic partnerships' (R3ADY, 2016c). In R3ADY's view, risk reduction and resilience is made possible by mainstreaming disaster preparedness across all sectors, and creating strong relationships between stakeholders from different sectors before a disaster.

One of the projects R3ADY currently carries out is that of Resilience in Tourism Destinations (R3ADY, 2016a). R3ADY emphasise the importance of 'shifting focus from individual preparedness planning to a collective destination-wide resilience strategy' (R3ADY, 2016a). They stress that all the critical stakeholders of a destination need to be part of the process of risk reduction and resilience. Given the importance of exploring partnerships for resilience, R3ADY have recently developed an innovative series of guidelines – R3SOURCE – that draw from the experiences, lessons and pitfalls of existing resilience partnerships (R3ADY, 2016b).

In 2015 R3ADY presented a project to enhance the resilience of destinations in two pilot destinations in southeast Asia (R3ADY, 2015). Among the locations identified for the project were renowned international destinations like Phuket (Thailand) and the Maldives. It is argued that a collective, destination-wide approach in enhancing resilience 'will benefit local communities and livelihoods, safeguard local employment, and protect assets, while preserving the beauty of Asia's top tourist destinations' (R3ADY, 2015: 1). As of March 2016, Phuket was one of the chosen destinations for a project aimed at disaster and climate resilience through building local capacity and disaster management experience (R3ADY, 2016d).

R3ADY (2016a) *Enhancing Disaster and Climate Resilience in Asia's Key Tourism Destinations*: http://r3ady.org/tourism-destination-resilience/.

R3ADY (2016b) *A Guide to Initiate and Sustain Multi-Sectoral Partnerships*: http://r3ady.org/r3source-project/.

Luthe and Wyss (2016) also shed light on the relevance of networked governance in tourism and resilience with findings from three regional DMOs in the Surselva-Gotthard tourism system in Switzerland. Their findings suggest that innovation and learning from climate change are possible when DMOs have large and diversified networks at regional and local scale, while quick responses are better implemented in less hierarchical and smaller networks (Luthe & Wyss, 2016).

When it comes to post-disaster contexts and the assessment of the vulnerability and resilience of sociopolitical contexts, there are likely to be diverging outcomes as a result of different political interests and perspectives. For example, Ghaderi *et al.*'s (2015) study in Bangkok following the floods of 2011 suggests that shortcomings in the institutional and private sector response to crisis can affect the recovery of the destination. Conversely, Gurtner (2007) shows how destination resilience in post-tsunami Phuket was possible thanks to a proactive coalescence between government, community and tourism stakeholders. In Bosnia and Herzegovina, Causevic and Lynch (2013) show rather how the top-down, post-conflict governance found in the country has had a negative impact on the governance and planning of tourism at national and regional levels. In some circumstances, the instrumentalisation of resilience is used to justify the reorganisation and recovery of destinations following a natural hazard, as has occurred in post-earthquake Christchurch, New Zealand (Amore & Hall, 2016a, 2016b; Box 5.5) and post-Hurricane Katrina New Orleans (Gotham & Greenberg, 2014). However, where this occurs there may be a significant gap between what local community interests are seeking and what particular political and real estate interests are wanting with regard to rebuild and recovery policies.

Box 5.5 Recovery for whom? Findings from post-earthquake Christchurch, New Zealand

Christchurch is the second largest city in New Zealand and the major conurbation of the South Island. Between 2010 and 2011 a repeated series of earthquakes hit the city, causing 183 deaths and the closure of most of the CBD premises until the end of 2013. These seismic events proved to be particularly negative for the local tourism industry throughout 2012 (CCT, 2012a; CERA, 2012a) and 2013 (Hatton, 2013; Orchiston & Higham, 2016; Orchiston *et al.*, 2013). According to Amore and Hall (2017), the visitor economy figures show that the recovery of the city as a destination between 2010 and 2013 lagged behind the

> forecast worst scenario of the Visitor Recovery Plan (CCT, 2012b) issued in mid-2012.
>
> Following the earthquake of 22 February 2011, the New Zealand Government established the Canterbury Earthquake Recovery Authority (CERA) as the main body to carry out the recovery, along with other government ministries, agencies and local councils in the Greater Christchurch area. One of the primary tasks was the delivery of the Recovery Strategy for Greater Christchurch (CERA, 2012b), which also includes the Cultural Recovery to resume cultural, community and sports events and activities. In April 2012, a dedicated unit within CERA – the Christchurch Central Development Unit (CCDU) – superseded Christchurch City Council in the decision making and implementation of the rebuild strategy for the central city. The CCDU Christchurch Central Recovery Plan (CCRP) (CCDU, 2012), released at the end of July 2012, included a range of 'anchor' projects with relevance to tourism, such as the Convention Centre Precinct, the Retail Precinct, the Performing Arts Precinct and sports stadia for rugby and cricket.
>
> The CCRP and the pace of the rebuild in Christchurch has aroused critical appraisal about the actual benefits of the plan and how the rhetoric of tourism and resilience have been used to justify the development of projects worth hundreds of millions of dollars. In particular, the codes for the rebuild of commercial premises in the central city and the exemptions on height limits narrow the list of plausible investors to major local landowners and international hospitality businesses. However, Christchurch is still struggling to sort out problems with housing and social services in the most affected neighbourhoods. The financial exposure of the council, together with central government insistence on city council funding for projects, further hinders the vulnerability of the city, which is likely to be affected by a new series of earthquakes in the years to come (Orchiston, 2012).

The examples provided here show how successful destination resilience calls for cooperation among public sector and businesses interests (Ghaderi *et al.*, 2012). In turn, this enhances the trust of stakeholders at large to respond together in addressing disturbances (Jones *et al.*, 2010) such as climate change and sudden disasters (Lew, 2014). There are, nevertheless, important contextual factors to consider when assessing destination resilience at the sociopolitical scale. The next section narrows down the focus further to the dimension of resilience in urban tourism destinations.

Urban dimensions of destination resilience

The resilience of cities is conceived as 'sustainable networks of physical systems and human communities ... able to survive and function under extreme and unique conditions' (Godschalk, 2003: 137). The functionality of cities in times of uncertainty is also noted in Pelling (2003b), while the emphasis on the built environment underpins the definition by Liao (2012) with respect to the resilience of cities to extreme events such as floods. Zaidi and Pelling (2015: 1219) provide a further definition of resilience as 'the capacity of the institutions of urban management and governance to identify and respond to novel and unresolved hazards and vulnerability'. Nonetheless, the resilience of cities might not necessarily result in an overall reduction in the vulnerability of urban populations. Rather, 'resilience as a mechanism of transference of vulnerability is generally beneficial for the actor taking the resilient action but may be harmful for others' (Sapountzaki, 2014: 59), especially among middle- to low-income residents (Gotham & Greenberg, 2014; Johnson, 2011; Johnson & Olshansky, 2010).

Meerow *et al.*'s (2016) comprehensive review of the urban resilience literature identified six 'tensions':

(1) equilibrium versus non-equilibrium resilience;
(2) positive versus neutral (or negative) conceptualisations of resilience;
(3) mechanism of system change (i.e. persistence, transitional or transformative);
(4) adaptation versus general adaptability;
(5) timescale of action; and
(6) how is 'urban' defined and characterised.

According to Meerow *et al.* (2016), using the resilience concept in urban research and for policy development depends on coming to terms with these tensions. Therefore they propose a new definition of urban resilience, one that explicitly includes these conceptual tensions yet remains flexible enough to be adopted by a range of disciplines and stakeholders:

> *Urban resilience refers to the ability of an urban system – and all its constituent socio-ecological and socio-technical networks across temporal and spatial scales – to maintain or rapidly return to desired functions in the face of a disturbance, to adapt to change, and to quickly transform systems that limit current or future adaptive capacity.*

In this definition, urban resilience is dynamic and offers multiple pathways to resilience (e.g. persistence, transition, and transformation). It recognizes the importance of temporal scale, and advocates general adaptability rather than specific adaptedness. The urban system is conceptualized as complex and adaptive, and it is composed of socio-ecological and socio-technical networks that extend across multiple spatial scales. Resilience is framed as an explicitly *desirable* state and, therefore, should be negotiated among those who enact it empirically. (Meerow *et al.*, 2016: 39) (emphasis in the original)

Despite an extensive literature on urban resilience (Meerow & Newell, 2016; Meerow *et al.*, 2016), the dimension of urban destination resilience is overlooked in the tourism literature. Although some of the research is undertaken in urban contexts affected by disasters, such as Bangkok (Ghaderi *et al.*, 2015), Christchurch (Becken *et al.*, 2015; Hall *et al.*, 2016b; Orchiston & Higham, 2016) and New Orleans (Gotham, 2007; Li *et al.*, 2008), the dimension of destination resilience is far from being addressed. However, findings from Christchurch suggest that, in the aftermath of the 2010 and 2011 earthquakes, there have been efforts to revitalise the badly damaged CBD with transitional projects for culture, leisure and tourism (Amore, 2016b; Finsterwalder & Hall, 2016; Hall *et al.*, 2016b). In particular, it is shown how the trajectory of the rebuild and recovery of the city following the earthquakes of 2010 and 2011 was strongly underpinned by the neoliberal development agendas of central government and other interests (Amore & Hall, 2016b), which are elsewhere referred to as 'disaster capitalism' (Klein, 2007).

As contemporary urbanisation steadily grows and affects the vulnerability of cities worldwide (Pelling, 2003b), research on the resilience of cities as tourist destinations is increasingly important. The significance of tourism for the economy of cities and the increase of risks related to disturbances such as climate change, natural disasters, political instability and terrorism need to be addressed by acknowledging the relevance of tourism stakeholders in planning for resilience and vulnerability reduction. The 100 Resilient Cities network pioneered by the Rockefeller Foundation acknowledges the relevance of tourism for the economies of cities while addressing the development of resilience strategies for cities coping with sudden shocks and chronic stressors (100 Resilient Cities, 2016). Table 5.1 provides an analysis of the resilience plans of cities that had developed them by March 2017. Of the 100 Resilient Cities, 23 had resilience plans available on the project website. Of these, nine did not mention tourism at all; remarkably, this included notable tourist destinations such as New Orleans and San Francisco. In some cases, such as Da Nang in Vietnam, tourism is regarded as a contributor to resilience because of its capacity to promote economic development. In contrast, Rio de Janeiro in Brazil was one of the few reports to acknowledge the vulnerability of tourism

Table 5.1 Tourism in the resilience plans of the Rockefeller Foundation's 100 Resilient Cities

City	Country	Mentions of tourism in text	Use of tourism
Bangkok	Thailand	58	A goal of strategic action is to expand tourism, service industries and hospitality (p. 9). Under reducing risk and adaptation goal: Cycleways to promote local tourism (p. 61). Community water resource management program to help maintain agricultural based tourism (p. 71). Management of waste collection from canal communities will help maintain tourism attractiveness (p. 75). Development of the cultural market of the city to expand tourism, service and hospitality (p. 107). Under the expansion goal: Providing skills development for tourism operators Training program for tourism vendors and service providers (p. 108) Tourism sector analysis and roadmap for tourism promotion (p. 109) Model of management and development of cultural product for tourism promotion (pilot for Bangkok Noi district) (p. 110) Resources and infrastructure for better response and preparedness Enhancing tourist safety (p. 111)
Berkeley	USA	0	–
Boulder	USA	2	Lower dependence on sales tax as a source of city revenues helps 'to insulate the city's finances from periodic declines in tourism or cyclical economic shifts' (p. 6). 'With an estimated 2.8 million visitor nights in 2013, the tourism industry contributed to an estimated $420 million total economic impact on the City of Boulder. The industry is supported by the area's scenic beauty and recreational opportunities, *(continued)*

Destination Resilience 119

Table 5.1 (Continued)

City	Country	Mentions of tourism in text	Use of tourism
			variety of entertainment and attractions, support for arts and culture, and broad range of dining, shopping and lodging options' – Boulder Economic Council (p. 35).
Bristol	England	2	Encourage domestic tourism as part of being green and smart (p. 67).
Byblos	Lebanon	15	'Economy relies mainly on tourism, retail and health' (p. 15); 'overreliance on tourism revenue is … a significant resilience challenge' (p. 38).
			Ongoing actions to 'deliver a program of events and festivals all year long to promote local culture, traditional food and music' (p. 39) as well as 'identify and integrate the assets of the regional hinterland of Byblos to foster partnerships and diversify tourism' (p. 40). Also encourage farmers to continue cultivating land within Byblos so as to link with tourism (p. 42).
Da Nang	Vietnam	18	'Despite being recognized as one of the fastest growing cities in Vietnam and one of the most attractive tourism destinations in Southeast Asia, Da Nang is vulnerable to shocks such as typhoons, floods, heat waves, droughts and saline intrusion and to long-term stresses such as typhoon and flood damaged housing, water shortages, unemployment, poor health care, and business continuity challenges' (p. 5).
			To expand its existing reputation as a tourism destination, Da Nang has recently invested in a series of big-scale tourism infrastructure projects. A new terminal for the Da Nang International Airport has been constructed, allowing the airport to serve an expected 6 to 8 million passengers, and 400,000 to one million metric tons of cargo per year. In the next decade, Da Nang International Airport is expected to see an estimated 10 to 12 million visitors per year' (p. 11).

			In the context of being an 'environmental city', 'In terms of tourism, the World Cultural Heritage Sites in Hue, Hoi An and My Son can be connected to Da Nang and Tam Ky, creating huge potential for the growth of a regional coastal tourism hub' (p. 15).
			One specific action looks to mitigate emissions in tourism services by using solar energy systems (p. 51). 'Research on "Uber model for tourism services"' is also noted (p. 71).
Dakar	Senegal	3	'The success of this plan is rooted in generating investments for profitable sectors of the economy such as agriculture, tourism, housing, social economy, mines, logistics, and industry to catalyze high and stable growth. One of the ... projects is to make Dakar a West African regional hub for companies and international institutions, for health and education services and tourism' (p. 24).
			Climate change is recognised as a threat to the tourist appeal of the city's beaches (p. 14).
Glasgow	Scotland	0	–
Christchurch	New Zealand	7	Tourism is identified as surpassing agriculture as the greatest source of overseas income (p. 15); international gateway status.
			'At a strategic level, building relationships with global consumers is essential in attracting tourism ...' (p. 69); continued investment in airport and port infrastructure is important for tourism (p. 70). An expected outcome is 'The number of tourists using Christchurch as a gateway to the South Island and New Zealand will continue to increase' (p. 71).
Medellin	Colombia	0	–
Melbourne	Australia	1	Non-urban areas are identified as supporting tourism (p. 50).
Mexico City	Mexico	1	Recovery of the Xochimilco, Tlahuac and Milpa Alta Heritage Area through the creation of the Water Resilience Strategy in the Xochimilco-Tlahuac-Milpa Alta so as to revitalise agriculture and tourism (p. 107).

(continued)

Table 5.1 (Continued)

City	Country	Mentions of tourism in text	Use of tourism
New Orleans	USA	0	–
New York	USA	5	Culture recognised as a major driver for tourism, while the city is seen as a major tourism destination.
			Airport capacity to be expanded 'To maintain our competitiveness as a center of tourism and the global economy' (p. 97).
Norfolk	USA	0	–
Oakland	USA	1	The city and region are vulnerable to external economic shocks and crises 'related to international trade, travel, tourism, logistics, and manufacturing' (p. 29).
Pittsburgh	USA	0	–
Rio de Janeiro	Brazil	7	'Sea level rise poses a serious threat to Rio's iconic beaches and their key economic pull from tourism' (p. 23); 'The sea level rise and the intensification of storm surges put at risk the coastal infrastructure and the income from tourism' (p. 35).
			Criminal acts in urban spaces 'affects negatively real estate prices, tourism and the psychological health of citizens' (p. 24).
			Insufficient sanitation has 'various negative impacts [on] human health, tourism and the city's branding' (p. 24).
			Rio aspires to 'be the main tourism, business and social center of Latin America' (p. 73).
Rotterdam	Netherlands	1	Techniques for greening roofs can contribute to the sustainability and viability of the city centre including 'a favourable climate for businesses, tourism and offers an attractive and healthy environment for young families and professionals' (p. 112).

San Francisco	USA	0	–
Semarang	Indonesia	13	Identification of ecotourism as an environmentally friendly business innovation (p. 14). 'better connection to major economic nodes and tourism attractions can improve the overall connectivity and strengthen the productivity and activities of the citizens' (p. 15).
			Encouragement of citizenry to promote Semarang's products and tourism attractions (p. 94)
			Promote Ecotourism and Edutourism Activity
			Action: Promoting the tourism area and developing a network with the business sector. This is in line with the mission of the Semarang mayor to strengthen the economy and create a supporting business climate by building on local excellence. Resilience value: Ecotourism and edutourism in Semarang have the potential to become a major tourist attraction from the area and beyond and increase the local revenue (p. 103).
			Improve Public Transport Access to Tourism Attractions
			Action: Exploring opportunities of public transport alternatives; identifying opportunities of integrated public transport; providing tourism attraction signs Resilience value: This initiative can increase the number of tourists and the city income. This initiative can also minimise traffic jams and pollution from private vehicles.
Vejle	Denmark	0	–
Wellington	New Zealand	0	–

attractions, i.e. its beaches. Overall, tourism therefore has a somewhat confused or paradoxical role in urban resilience strategies.

Organisational dimensions of destination resilience

As the previous chapter noted, research focusing on the resilience of organisations is extensive and is significant because of cross-scale and emergent linkages to destinations. The resilience of organisations can be conceptualised from at least three perspectives with relevance for destinations. As an organisational characteristic, resilience is a quality that enables enterprises to cope with unexpected events (Auerswald & van Opstal, 2009), and to 'mitigate the effects of disasters and allow organisations to adjust to possibly damaging changes post disaster' (Whitman et al., 2014: 153). Organisational resilience is also defined as 'the capacity for an enterprise to survive, adapt, and grow in the face of turbulent change' (Fiksel, 2006: 16) and can develop 'new capabilities through dynamically responding to emergent situations' (Nilakant et al., 2014: 80) which proactively help workers to 'implement positive adaptive behaviours matched to the immediate situation, while enduring minimal stress' (Mallak, 1998b: 148). Stephenson et al. (2010: 27) provide a further definition of organisational resilience as the sum of 'social and cultural factors within organisations which contribute to the organisations' ability to survive, and potentially even thrive, in times of crisis'.

With respect to tourism scholarship, the dimension of organisational resilience is, as noted in the previous chapter, very recent. With regard to natural hazards and triggering events, Dahles and Susilowati (2015) provide findings from a longitudinal qualitative research study on the resilience of small tourism businesses in Yogyakarta, Indonesia following a series of disturbances, including the 2006 earthquakes. Similarly, Biggs et al. (2012) assessed the entrepreneurial stressors to disasters with a focus on reef tourism businesses in Phuket, Thailand, in the aftermath of the 2004 tsunami and the 2008 political crisis. Focusing on the issue of climate change, Biggs (2011) and Biggs et al.'s (2015) research among reef tourism businesses in Australia's Great Barrier Reef provides findings with regard to the characteristics of insolvent and resilient enterprises. The latter, in particular, are characterised by entrepreneurial and managerial capabilities 'to maintain or grow its existing level of employment and income and stay operating in reef tourism in the face of crises and change' (Biggs et al., 2015: 66). Mair et al. (2016) suggest that the reduction of vulnerabilities and internal adaptive capacity are the key factors behind the resilience of organisations in destination contexts.

Given the characteristics of the tourism industry, with predominantly small and medium-sized businesses that gravitate around key amenities and visitor attractions, the resilience of tourism organisations is strongly context dependent. In the case of developing countries, Méheux and Parker (2006) suggest that factors such as the exposure of visitors to local hazards, the seasonality of tourism flows, the increasing competitiveness among destinations and the networked yet fragmented nature of the tourism supply all affect the resilience of small island destinations like Vanuatu (Box 5.6). Similarly, Calgaro (2010) argues that the characteristics of embedded tourism business networks affect the resilience of organisations and correspondingly the destination. Findings from three distinct destinations in Thailand following the 2004 Boxing Day tsunami highlight how factors such as the entrepreneurial traits of tourism businesses, the financial instruments set for the recovery, the shortages of skilled workforce and the support of government agencies differed greatly from context to context (Calgaro, 2010; Calgaro et al., 2014). The idiosyncrasies of destinations' contexts underpin the findings of a study undertaken in a range of small island countries in the Caribbean and the Pacific (Mahon et al., 2013), which exhorts tourism businesses to implement disaster risk reduction (DRR) strategies in order to increase the resilience of organisations in such highly vulnerable contexts. The study also argues that companies lacking DRR are more likely to shut down than organisations that implement best practices in managing risk and thus are more capable of thriving in turbulent times (Mahon et al., 2013).

Box 5.6 Business vulnerabilities in small developing island states: Evidence from Vanuatu

Tourism businesses tend to be vulnerable to exogenous hazards such as natural disasters. This is particularly evident in the so-called Small Island Developing States (SIDS) like Vanuatu, where the high exposure to climate change, earthquakes and cyclones endangers the tourism business long-term sustainability. A 2001 report by the National Disaster Management Office lists Vanuatu as the most disaster-prone country in the South Pacific. This is particularly relevant for tourism, which is crucial for the socio-economic development of Vanuatu.

A pilot study by Méheux and Parker (2006) on tourism businesses on one of the Vanuatu islands (Tanna) focused on 'the accuracy of the perception of natural hazards held by individuals involved in the tourism industry' (Méheux & Parker, 2006: 73). Findings were then matched with the government risk management agenda to assess the awareness of disasters among tourism businesses located on Tanna. Results suggest

> that in most cases the majority of respondents accurately perceived the likelihood of damaging hazard events (Méheux & Parker, 2006). The disaster management measures for hazards like pyroclastic flows and cyclones include emergency kits and shutters to reduce damage to infrastructure and increase the safety of visitors. Conversely, there are other disaster scenarios (e.g. volcanic earthquakes) where the likelihood of the hazard is overestimated by tourism businesses. Most importantly, tourism businesses seem to lack the necessary risk reduction measures for hazards of this kind, although this is quite surprising given the risk perceived among tourism industry stakeholders.
>
> Finally, the occurrence of tectonic earthquakes in Tanna is underestimated among local tourism businesses. Misleading assumptions like the resistance of traditional buildings to earthquakes increases the vulnerability of infrastructure and visitors to this particular kind of hazard. Notwithstanding the casualties following the 7.2 MW earthquake in the Vanuatu capital, Port Vila in 2001, tourism businesses in Tanna's overestimation of building resilience can negatively affect the sustainability of the tourism industry on the island.

In the case of DMOs, Bhandari *et al.* (2015) argue that resilient organisations of this kind should move beyond the mere marketing of destination and increase their stock of knowledge as well as their interconnectedness with other stakeholders of the destination. These, in turn, 'can facilitate destination resilience and adaptation to climate change' (Bhandari *et al.*, 2015: 99). With regard to accommodation and food and beverage businesses, Prayag and Orchiston (2016) show how the latter experienced less disturbance than the manufacturing and education sectors in the provisions of supplies, but were more vulnerable to the impacts of infrastructural damage that hit Christchurch between 2010 and 2011.

Community dimensions of destination resilience

According to Adger (2000: 361), community resilience refers to 'the ability of communities to withstand external shocks to their social infrastructure'. This dimension of resilience generally relies on sociocultural resources, among others, to mediate adversities affecting a given community (Ahmed *et al.*, 2004). Arguably, community resilience is likely to enable 'a set of adaptive capacities to a positive trajectory of functioning and adaptation after a disturbance' (Norris *et al.*, 2008: 130). Specifically to post-disaster contexts, community resilience is the intrinsic ability of communities 'to withstand an extreme natural event without suffering devastating losses, damage, diminished productivity, or quality of life' (Mileti, 1999: 32). Bruneau *et al.* (2003) identify up to four dimensions of community resilience – technological, economic, organisational and social – as the cornerstones of community seismic resilience which minimise community and location disruption and mitigate the effects of future earthquakes. Cutter *et al.* (2008) conceive the resilience of communities as the ability to absorb the impacts, adaptively respond to threats, re-organise, learn and recover from disasters.

Box 5.7 Toolkit for community-led destination resilience: The UNEP Disaster Risk Management for Coastal Tourism Destinations Responding to Climate Change

UNEP's (2009) *Disaster Risk Management for Coastal Tourism Destinations Responding to Climate Change* provides practical guidance on how to better prepare for disasters in coastal destinations. The guide is targeted at disaster managers and local, municipal and community planners, as well as other stakeholders in the tourism sector dealing with climate change related effects like SLR, cyclones and severe weather conditions.

The guidelines stress the importance of achieving destination resilience through community-based DDR. In particular, it stresses the importance of systematic data gathering, analysis and risk scenario planning to be shared at the community level. This, in turn, is expected to improve decision making and give the community a greater predictability of the anticipated outcomes. To achieve community engagement in risk reduction and resilience, the UNEP identifies the local disaster agency as the key actor in delivering a community-based risk management approach.

Human communities and systems require preventative and preparedness actions against disasters. This is achievable 'through awareness-raising of disaster events, enlightened leadership, public and private sector cooperation and commitment to a common goal' (UNEP, 2009: 91). Finally, the UNEP report is aware of the potentialities of shared knowledge. The latter permeates communities as they engage in practices of risk reduction and resilience at the destination level. Where communities are informed and proactively engage with destination resilience, critical coastline ecosystems end up improving their bottom lines in the short and long term and creating shareholder value.

The scholarship on the resilience of communities with respect to tourism destinations is at its embryonic stage (Sheppard & Williams, 2015) and tends to frame communities within the broader socio-ecological dimension of resilience (e.g. Calgaro, 2010; Calgaro et al., 2014). There are, nevertheless, studies that address the resilience of destinations from a community-based perspective. Among these, Strickland-Munro et al. (2010) develop a community-centred resilience framework for protected area tourism destinations to explicitly recognise 'system change, complexity and uncertainty, in contrast to traditional indicator-based tourism impact methods that are based on linear assessment approaches' (Strickland-Munro et al., 2010: 514). On the other hand, Lawton and Weaver's (2015) study among residents of the Gold Coast, Australia, shows commitment among the local community to identify solutions and provide support in the definition of new strategies for the management of the destination during a contentious event such as Schoolies Week (Spring Break).

A resilient community is likely to reduce the vulnerability of tourism businesses (Biggs et al., 2015). As findings from Phuket, Thailand, suggest, 'the role of the support from family and friends in enterprise resilience is [an] indication of the extent to which economic relations and actions are embedded within the social structures of places' (Biggs et al., 2015: 72). Similarly, research conducted in Whistler, Canada, shows how the local community

---

Box 5.8 Residents' role in a resilient destination: Evidence from Whistler, Canada

The resort destination of Whistler is one of the premier mountain resorts in British Columbia, Canada. Over the past years, the locality has experienced a series of shocks and stressors, including the GFC and demographic pressure during the 2010 Winter Olympic Games held in Vancouver. Research conducted by Sheppard and Williams (2015) 'sought to provide insights into those factors that may enhance the resilience of tourism destination governance systems, as well as insights into how shocks and stressors affect the resilience of such systems and the community at large' (Sheppard & Williams, 2015: 2).

The results of the research highlight the role of the community in destination resilience. The findings suggest that the will of the community to focus on immediate fiscal and economic concerns following the GFC culminated in setting aside the longer term Whistler 2020 sustainability goals. Similarly, the hosting of the Winter Olympic Games shifted the focus away from sustainability goals among Whistler residents. The latter proved once more their vulnerability to external shocks and stressors with the election of a conservative mayoralty in 2011 which further pushed aside the sustainability agenda and disestablished the Whistler 2020 Task Force.

There are nevertheless encouraging findings suggesting how the community still acknowledged the importance of pursuing a sustainable development agenda despite shocks and stressors. For example, the Whistler community favoured the implementation of a new ecosystem monitoring system to manage environmental disturbance. Similarly, the Whistler Blackcomb Sky Resort has adopted a Climate Change and Resource Efficiency Strategy. What nevertheless emerged from the interviews is a sense of weaker community participation in decision making, a more hierarchical organisation of governance, and difficulties in accessing specific information on the strategies considered to cope with sustainability, particularly destination resilience.

perceives itself as paramount to the resilience of destinations during times of disturbance (Sheppard & Williams, 2015; Box 5.8).

The cases illustrated in this section suggest that resilient destinations rely on a resilient community which, in turn, reduces vulnerabilities to disasters and chronic stressors for the many stakeholders involved in the supply of tourism services. Moreover, residents of resilient destinations are likely to show a greater adaptive capacity in understanding the opportunities and the threats of tourism development at the community level. Community traits such as the role of weak ties and the importance of social capital can enhance business resilience. However, it should not be forgotten that gaining recognition of destination vulnerabilities does not necessarily

Box 5.9 Planning a resilient destination: England's Wise Growth Action Plan

The *Strategic Action Plan for Tourism 2010–2020* (Tourism England, 2010) conceives destination resilience as one of the anchors of the 'Wise Growth Action Plan Vision'. In particular, it states that tourism growth should create 'resilience and prosperity for all [while] balancing the growth aspirations of the Strategic Framework with the principles of sustainability' (Tourism England, 2010: 1). The plan acknowledges that the strategy itself is not enough to achieve destination resilience; rather,

> it is 'the quality of dialogue and relationships' (Tourism England, 2010: 2) among destination stakeholders that is crucial in achieving resilience.
>
> Destination resilience should consider all the parties, including the visitors. The Wise Growth Action Plan reiterates that a coordinated approach to every single aspect of tourism development, the achievement of long-terms goals and the principles of sustainability all concur in making destinations resilient (Tourism England, 2010). 'Wise Growth is not about developing specific types of tourism experiences. It is about embedding the principles throughout the entire tourism offer' (Tourism England, 2010: 4). The plan's main objectives are:
>
> - embed the principles of Wise Growth into all action plans associated with the Strategic Framework for Tourism.
> - embed the principles of Wise Growth into communication strategies with visitors and residents to enable them to cherish the places the places they visit, live and work;
> - help tourism businesses engage in Wise Growth, by articulating the business case and providing access to tools and resources;
> - measure, report and communicate the impacts of Wise Growth transparently.
>
> Most of these objectives reprise those emphasised in sustainable tourism discourse. However, the plan acknowledges that sharing knowledge and increasing collaboration are crucial to channelling the interests of tourism businesses, the desires of visitors and the concerns of the local community towards a common ground upon which risks are reduced and the resilience of destinations at large increases.

occur collectively. Rather, a process is likely to differ greatly among individuals and destinations.

Individual resilience and destination resilience

As noted in Chapter 3, the dimension of individual resilience embraces the fields of psychology and child development (Sheppard & Williams, 2015). From an 'engineering resilience' perspective, a resilient individual is able to 'moderate negative effects of stress' (Wagnild & Young, 1993: 165) and reach a seeming state of stable equilibrium (Bonanno, 2004). Conceived as a more dynamic process (Luthar et al., 2000), individual resilience is 'the ability to function psychologically at a level far greater than expected given the individual's capabilities and previous experiences' (Paton et al., 2000: 173).

Scholars acknowledge the vulnerability of tourists and businesses owners (Biggs et al., 2015; Dredge, 2015) during major disasters and their significance for destinations. However, the dimension of individual resilience within such stakeholders is often overlooked. Even the RTAF (Jopp et al., 2010, 2013) does not look at the adaptation of visitors.

Biggs et al. (2015: 67) suggest that, in some circumstances, the lifestyle of reef tourism business owners in the Great Barrier Reef, Australia and Phuket, Thailand is likely to make them 'more reluctant to abandon the enterprise and the location in difficult times, thus potentially strengthening their resilience'. With respect to the tourist demand, Hajibaba et al. (2015: 48) identify 'crisis-resistant tourists as those that tend to absorb risks instead of engaging in risk avoidance strategies'. Crisis-resistant tourists are able to set aside their anxieties and travel to places during or shortly after a crisis. These tourists resemble the traits of the stalwarts, the waverers (Beirman, 2003) and the allocentric traveller (Plog, 1991). However, the relationship between destinations and travellers is one characterised by numerous feedback loops. Critical among these is the diffusion of knowledge and information about a destination which may come via word of mouth or social media as well as through more formal media channels. Indeed, there is a close relationship between the different stages of a disaster and the issue–attention cycle of media and political issues (Hall, 2002).

Summary and Conclusions

Destinations are complex units of analysis. Given their contextual nature, phenomena that occur in specific places at particular scales do not necessarily apply to others. For example, risk reduction strategies that are put in place for second-home owners to mitigate waste disposal during the peak of the season may be marginal if there is no effective regional or national strategy for the disposal of trash in public spaces such as restaurants or beaches. Similarly, the resilience of destinations is context specific and there are no given one-size-fits-all solutions. The cases highlighted throughout this chapter suggest that destinations have adopted a range of different solutions to deal with issues such as climate change, coastal erosion and shifts in tourism demand in times of crisis.

It is argued here that 'in order to increase resilience, resistance and readiness, appropriate adaptation options must be identified, assessed, implemented and evaluated' (Jopp et al., 2010: 600). The tourism literature addresses the management guidelines of destinations in a similar fashion (e.g. Clarke & Godfrey, 2002), but there is little, if no empirical evidence of their application in the empirical realm. Nevertheless, there are signs of an increasing awareness of combining destination management with resilience and risk reduction. Some scholars, for example, call for the incorporation of adaptation planning into tourism policy making (e.g. Jopp et al., 2010), while other acknowledge the importance of moving beyond the currently old-fashioned industrial focus of tourism discourse (Dredge, 2015) and positioning it within the broader policy environment (Amore & Hall, 2016a; Dredge, 2015; Hall, 2008; Hall & Veer, 2016; Haxton, 2015). Revisiting the policy framework of tourism is expected to 'promote both economic growth and a fairer distribution of benefits' (Haxton, 2015: 7).

Understanding resilience and destination resilience requires a different approach in the management, policy making and environmental awareness thus far conducted in tourism policy and planning practices. First, the paradigms of sustainability and of sustainable tourism development should promote forms of slow tourism consumption (Hall, 2009) and resource management (Higgins-Desbiolles, 2011a, 2011b). Secondly, it should be acknowledged that the current forms of destination governance put in place in most countries are deeply rooted in neoliberal and hyper-neoliberal paradigms (Amore & Hall, 2016a). A system of capital accumulation that focuses on the will of the market at the expense of the environment is very unlikely to lead to resilient tourism destinations. Using stressors and triggering events such as natural disasters as leverage to ease the implementation of market-obeying recovery strategies will not make destinations more resilient in the longer term. Rather, it will increase the vulnerability of destinations to future and unavoidable disturbances. Finally, policy frameworks tend to fail and reframe issues in the aftermath of given crises and disasters (Amore & Hall, 2016a; Hall, 2011; Jessop, 2011; Sørensen, 2006).

In light of what has been stated thus far, it can be argued that there are, at least, five necessary conditions at the basis of resilient destinations. First, a destination is resilient when it is conscious of the vulnerability of its resources, attractions and amenities to chronic stressors and potential hazards. Secondly, it should not seek development paths that deliberately advantage given stakeholders while hindering the most vulnerable. Thirdly, a resilient destination develops a long-term strategy that gives scope to adaptive countermeasures that are rooted in the principles of communicative and community planning. Fourthly, it adaptively reframes its metagovernance in order to favour cross-institutional and multi-stakeholder engagement and to overcome the fragmentation of traditional destination governance. A final

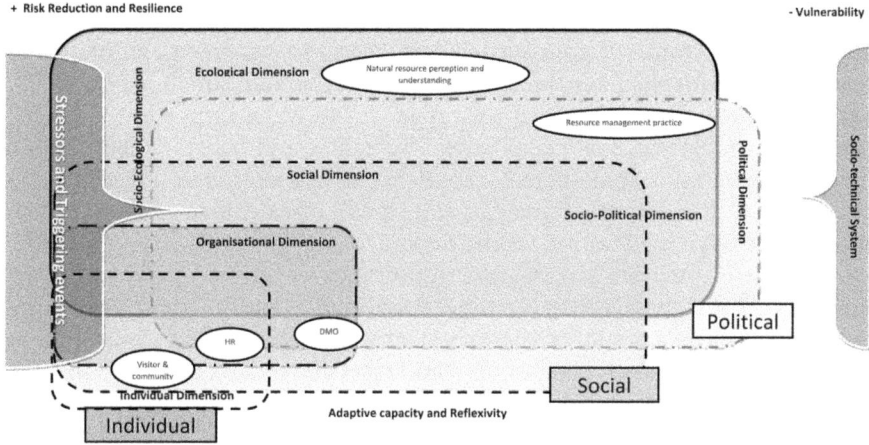

Figure 5.2 Elements in destination resilience

condition for a resilient destination is that it operates at appropriate regional and local scales.

A framework for destination resilience is provided in Figure 5.2. It is argued here that destinations best enhance their resilience when stakeholders engage in well-integrated metagovernance arenas at the regional and local

Table 5.2 Fundamental questions related to destination resilience

Who?	Who determines what is desirable in the destination system? Whose resilience is prioritised? Who is excluded and included in the destination system? (Who are the winners and losers, especially between sectors, and the balances between destination community and visitor interests?)
What?	What perturbations should the destination system be resilient to? What networks, interests and sectors are included in the destination system? Is the focus on resilience generic or specific?
When?	What is the relative focus on rapid-onset disturbances and slow-onset changes? Is the focus on short or long-term resilience? Is the focus on the resilience of present or future generations?
Where?	What are the spatial and jurisdictional boundaries of the destination system? Is the resilience of some areas prioritised over others? Does building resilience in some areas affect resilience elsewhere?
Why?	What is the goal of building destination resilience? What are the underlying motivations for building destination resilience? What is the relative balance between process and outcome?

scales (Jopp *et al.*, 2010; Luthe & Wyss, 2014, 2016). The framework acknowledges the importance of pre-disaster/perturbation assessment and preparedness to cope with the likely hazards stressed in the literature (Calgaro, 2010; Faulkner, 2001; Jopp *et al.*, 2010; Njoroge, 2014). Most importantly, it conceives metagovernance as being driven by values and beliefs (Klein, 2007). The metagovernance paradigm for tourism destinations advocates the inclusion of 'the values, norms, principles and paradigms/ideologies that underpin governance systems and governing approaches' (Amore & Hall, 2016a: 2). Finally, the framework stresses the importance of reflective learning, elsewhere known as double-loop learning: 'Double loop learning requires a paradigmatic shift as a result of the experience and so emergent knowledge is produced and ultimately new understanding is derived' (Ritchie, 2004: 679).

'Tourism is both a product and an element of a complex interdependent, interrelated system comprised of destination and society' (Gurtner, 2007: 218). Understanding destinations and destination resilience requires a framework that is empathetic to the insights from different domains of research and acknowledges the contemporary challenges that permeate from the ecological dimension down to the individual. The aim of this chapter was to help provide the 'big picture' of resilient destinations. It did so by illustrating both the macro and the micro dimensions of resilience and integrating them into a comprehensive framework. There is no magic bullet or formula for a resilient destination. However, there are certain questions that need to be considered (Table 5.2). The next chapter returns to a number of questions that have been raised through the various chapters and seeks to answer several key issues with regard to the value of the concept of resilience.

Further reading

At a destination scale there are a number of useful studies of resilience. See, for example:

Gotham, K.F. and Greenberg, M. (2014) *Crisis Cities: Disaster and Redevelopment in New York and New Orleans.* New York: Oxford University Press.

Hall, C.M., Malinen, S., Vosslamber, R. and Wordsworth, R. (eds) (2016) *Business and Post-Disaster Management: Business, Organisational and Consumer Resilience and the Christchurch Earthquakes.* Abingdon: Routledge.

Johnson, C. (2011) *The Neoliberal Deluge: Hurricane Katrina, Late Capitalism, and the Remaking of New Orleans.* Minneapolis, MN: University of Minnesota Press.

Johnson, L.A. and Olshansky, R.B. (2010) *Clear as Mud: Planning for the Rebuilding of New Orleans.* Chicago, IL: American Planning Association.

Some tourism-specific frameworks that incorporate resilience dimensions include:

Becken, S. (2013) Developing a framework for assessing resilience of tourism sub-systems to climatic factors. *Annals of Tourism Research* 43, 506–528.

Calgaro, E., Dominey-Howes, D. and Lloyd, K. (2014) Application of the Destination Sustainability Framework to explore the drivers of vulnerability and resilience in Thailand following the 2004 Indian Ocean Tsunami. *Journal of Sustainable Tourism* 22 (3), 361–383.

Jopp, R., DeLacy, T. and Mair, J. (2010) Developing a framework for regional destination adaptation to climate change. *Current Issues in Tourism* 13 (6), 591–605.

On destination management, planning and policy responses see:

Amore, A. and Hall, C.M. (2017) National and urban public policy agenda in tourism: Towards the emergence of a hyperneoliberal script? *International Journal of Tourism Policy* 7 (1), 4–22.

Bhandari, K., Cooper, C. and Ruhanen, L. (2015) The role of the destination management organization in responding to climate change: Organizational knowledge and learning. *Acta Turistica* 26 (2), 91–102.

Orchiston, C. and Higham, J.E.S. (2016) Knowledge management and tourism recovery (de)marketing: The Christchurch earthquakes 2010–2011. *Current Issues in Tourism* 19 (1), 64–84.

UNEP (2009) *Disaster Risk Management for Coastal Tourism Destinations Responding to Climate Change. A Practical Guide for Decision Makers.* Nairobi: United Nations Environment Programme.

On community-based approaches and critiques see:

Bec, A., McLennan, C.L. and Moyle, B.D. (2016) Community resilience to long-term tourism decline and rejuvenation: A literature review and conceptual model. *Current Issues in Tourism* 19 (5), 431–457.

Lew, A.A. (2014) Scale, change and resilience in community tourism planning. *Tourism Geographies* 16 (1), 14–22.

6 Conclusion: Is Resilience a Resilient Concept?

Introduction

The concept of resilience lends itself to a number of interpretations depending on the field of study, including tourism. Its multidisciplinarity and adaptability within 'systems', be they human, ecological or social, make the concept attractive to researchers. As suggested by Bhamra *et al.* (2011), is resilience a measure, a feature, a philosophy or a capability? The answer is probably all three. Norris *et al.* (2008), for example, regarded community resilience as a metaphor, a theory, a set of capacities and a strategy for disaster readiness.

Alongside the original definition of ecological resilience by Holling (1973), which is understood as the ability of systems to absorb change and still persist after an external disturbance, and its socio-ecological resilience variation (Folke, 2006), 'engineering resilience' dealing with the ability of systems to deal with disruption and speed of return to the pre-existing equilibrium has dominated research traditions (Annarelli & Nonino, 2016). With ideas of engineering resilience referring to the ability of systems to bounce back when hit by unexpected events, it is of no surprise that an exhaustive strand of research has looked at the ability of groups, individuals and organisations to anticipate risk and manage change before failures and harm occur (Hollnagel *et al.*, 2006, 2011). However, the concept is plagued by definitional issues, what it actually means in practice, and its implications for researchers, policy makers and managers. Resilience is becoming a buzzword (Pizzo, 2015). The possibility remains that the concept of resilience may share the same fate as 'sustainability' in that, although being widely adopted, the range of its application may affect its utility in that if it comes to mean everything, then it potentially means nothing (Hall, 2011).

Resilience as a Boundary Object and Bridging Concept

One of the main attractions of resilience, like sustainability, is its capacity to act as a 'boundary object' (Brand & Jax, 2007) or 'bridging concept' (Beichler *et al.*, 2014), which allows multiple disciplines and knowledge domains, including public policy areas, to interface with each other. A boundary object refers to an object or concept that resonates with different social worlds and, as a result, supports cross-disciplinary collaboration (Star & Griesemer, 1989). A boundary object's meaning is relatively flexible, which allows it to be adapted to the needs of different areas of knowledge and stakeholders, although there does need to be a degree of common ground in concept definition and understanding in order to bridge different disciplines and approaches.

Individual meanings inside this cluster of concepts are not clearly distinguishable, are partly redundant, metaphorical and evaluative (Strunz, 2012). If a concept cannot be pinned down to a single concise definition it does not mean that the concept is not useful; rather it must be thought of as a 'family' of meanings that potentially fuel creative and pragmatic problem solving. Blurred boundaries between these concepts allow for inter- and transdisciplinary research to inform conceptualisation and measurement of these concepts. Metaphors possibly open disciplinary debates and inform the evolving character of the resilience thinking perspective (Strunz, 2012).

Vale (2014: 198) argues that 'the biggest upside to resilience, however, is the opportunity to turn its flexibility to full advantage by taking seriously the actual interconnections among various domains that have embraced the same terminology'. Meerow and Newell (2016), for example, note how the concept of urban resilience has helped bring together the 'climate change adaptation' and 'disaster risk reduction' agendas, as well as security and sustainability priorities. Nevertheless, they note, 'But the term's flexibility and inherent inclusiveness has also led to conceptual confusion, especially in relation to like-minded terms such as sustainability, vulnerability, and adaptation' (Meerow & Newell, 2016: 1–2; see also Elmqvist *et al.*, 2014), while too much ambiguity can make it difficult to operationalise resilience for any specific policy context (Matyas & Pelling, 2014), meaning that it becomes an 'empty signifier' (Weichselgartner & Kelman, 2015).

The general lack of clarity with regard to meaning is only one of several critiques of the notion of resilience. There is significant concern over spatial and temporal trade-offs and inequitable benefits. For example, ecological thinking does not transfer very well to dominant modes of engineering and economic thought which focus on efficiency and return time as being the key characteristics of resilience, and which usually seek to remove any perceived system redundancies or inefficiencies, often by seeking to encourage 'market forces' (Johnson, 2011; Klein, 2007). For example, in commenting on the Christchurch earthquakes, Hayward (2013) observes:

> ... the rhetoric of resilience is used to justify authorities making decisions quickly and measuring their impact on recovery by the speed with which the city returns to a 'new normal' or experiences 'certainty' as firm centralized decision making ... the drive for efficiency is all too frequently used to justify expert command-and-control decision making with little or no meaningful local scrutiny or community leadership in decision making. (Hayward, 2013: 36)

Hayward (2013) notes the formal depoliticalisation of much of post-earthquake Christchurch by the transfer of authority to central government and by the suspension of elections on the regional council. She argues, along with others such as Brown (2012), that resilience research itself often appears 'depoliticised' (Amore & Hall, 2017), because of the dominance of policy paradigms that frame economic resilience in relation to greater engagement with the global market economy – even when that itself is the reason why local economies have received a major shock (Hall, 2016a). Brown (2014) also suggests that part of the problem has to do with the transference of an ecological concept (i.e. resilient ecosystems) to social systems, at least initially, often by researchers who are not very familiar with the debates surrounding how society functions, its inherently political and ideological implications, and the way in which such thinking may be utilised by policy makers. It may also be the case that resilience is more politically tractable than the concepts of 'vulnerability' or 'adaptation', simply because it is regarded as having a more positive connotation (McEvoy et al., 2013).

Brown (2012) suggests that much resilience thinking supports notions of 'business as usual'. Indeed, Joseph (2013) and Walker and Cooper (2011) argue that much of the resilience agenda is inherently conservative and tends to perpetuate an unjust and inequitable status quo that is interconnected with neoliberal ideas regarding the respective roles of the state and the market. Indeed, Walker and Cooper (2011) suggest that the popularity of resilience as a concept with policy makers as well as some academics is related to its ideological fit with the influential complexity theory-based financial system models of Friedrich Hayek (Meerow & Newell, 2016). Regardless of the specific ideological connections with the work of Hayek, it is clear, as per Hayward (2013) noted above, that by assuming that complex systems naturally go through adaptive cycles of collapse and reorganisation, ecological resilience theory potentially 'accepts change somewhat passively', thereby potentially precluding consideration of the social causes of crises (Evans, 2011: 224). As Vale (2014: 198) critically comments, 'It is all too easy to talk about 'bouncing back to where we were' without asking which 'we' is counted, and without asking whether 'where we were' is a place to which a return is desirable'.

Box 6.1 Policy change, public management and resilience

Although many management agencies and organisations have embraced resilience as a concept, concrete examples of actual management for resilience that have definitively reduced vulnerability and increased resilience over the long term remain rare, perhaps because of issues of time scale, difficulties in quantifying resilience and the factors that affect it, or because the concept can be variously interpreted (Hall, 2016a). As research from many environments illustrates, knowing what the stressors of a system are does not necessarily lead to appropriate intervention to reduce disturbance and therefore the likelihood of significant change in ecosystem properties. Recognising the stressors on the Great Barrier Reef, for example, does not necessarily mean that definitive action will be taken to prevent them.

Crises and disasters potentially challenge the predominance of managerial values in public administration. The policy change and agenda literature suggests that crises and disasters often have high potential for policy change. Crises can be regarded as creating windows of opportunity for policy change to occur (Schwartz & Sulitzeanu-Kenan, 2004). However, policy change is not an automatic corollary of crisis. Agenda-setting theory suggests that, while system crises will tend to focus public attention on an issue, unless there are coherent coalitions of policy actors and interests advocating for change, perceived viable solutions and/or favourable political climates, they are unlikely to lead to policy change (Birkland, 1997), e.g. the incremental policy changes made with respect to climate change and tourism (Scott *et al.*, 2016). 'Agenda-setting theory recognizes that disasters or crises do not necessarily lead to changes in dominant administrative values, such that the political climate promotes the tightening of rectitude or resilience-oriented measures at the expense of production results' (Schwartz & Sulitzeanu-Kenan, 2004: 80). When changes do occur, agenda change theorists contend that change is likely to be long lasting as it involves changes in the interrelations of interest groups and policy actors and the creation of new institutions. In contrast, the atrophy of vigilance theory posits that in hazardous or dangerous systems disaster will necessarily lead to a policy change towards the tightening of safety measures (Busenberg, 1999), such as in tourism with respect to airline security following the 9/11 terrorist attacks (Hall, 2002). As its name suggests, in the absence of further incidents or shocks to the system, vigilance will gradually be relaxed over time.

At the heart of managerialism is the idea that managers are free to manage in accordance with their professional judgement largely free of hierarchical and process stipulations (Schwartz & Sulitzeanu-Kenan, 2004). Hood (1991) suggests that environments in which production results values predominate are likely to be less capable of preventing breaches to the values of security and resilience (i.e. accident and disaster). In their study of the policy effects of disasters in Israel and the United States, Schwartz and Sulitzeanu-Kenan (2004) found that the result of challenges to existing managerial approaches that were production focused as a result of disasters appeared to depend on political culture. In the United States an increased movement in the direction of rectitude or resilience over the course of time was found following the occurrence of disasters after initial significant short-term change. In Israel they found that the managerial values and related accountability relations not only contributed to the advent of disaster but also served to impede changes designed to prevent its recurrence. In the case of tourism, each destination has its own political culture in which change is responded to, decisions are made, interests are met and courses of action decided upon.

The use of normative definitions may have its place, for example as noted above with respect to the value of resilience as a boundary object (Brand & Jax, 2007), but there are clearly significant implications with regard to differences between how systems are as compared to how they should be, as well as developing a firm understanding of the generative mechanisms of resilience in order to put concepts into practice and to achieve successful management. This is also significant because different definitions of resilience have implications for the type of management policies and strategies that are undertaken. As Grimm and Calabrese (2011: 11) observed, 'Proceeding from metaphors and thinking tools to operational concepts is challenging'. This raises some major questions, among them being the who, what, when, where and why of resilience (the five Ws of resilience) (Meerow & Newell, 2016; Vale, 2014). Nevertheless, such questions become a useful means of interrogating approaches to resilience at various scales as well as providing a basis for collaboration and mutual understanding between different stakeholders in tourism.

Figure 6.1 outlines a simple iterative process to assist planning for resilience between different stakeholders. Stage 1 deals with issues of not only defining what resilience means but also what comprises the components and boundaries of the tourism system, or whichever sub-system is being examined, as different actors may have different interpretations (see also White & O'Hare, 2014; Hall, 2016a; Meerow & Newell, 2016 with respect to similar questions). Interestingly, while tourism resilience is shown as the boundary object here, it could alternatively be, depending on the interests involved, tourism or resilience as separate definitional fields. The definitional field can also be regarded as a response to how problems and issues are defined and

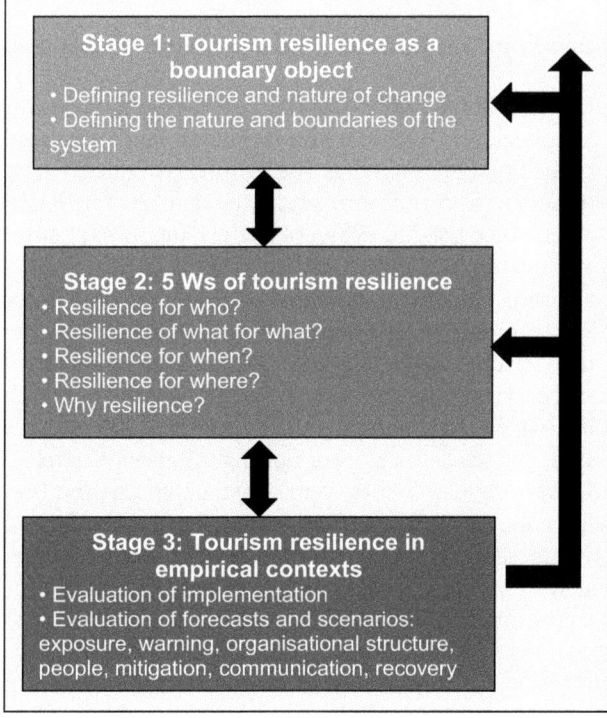

Figure 6.1 Progressing resilience in tourism

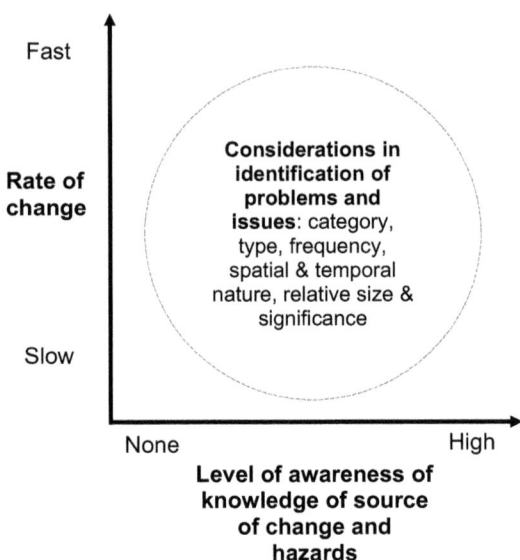

Figure 6.2 Awareness and knowledge of sources of change: Conceptual schema

bounded (Figure 6.2). Stage 2 concerns the five Ws of resilience and how they can be used to collectively consider the implications of any resilience strategy, process or initiative. Stage 3 is the empirical context of resilience in which actual practices and their impact are evaluated. The basic framework of Figure 6.2 can also be used to evaluate such issues as exposure and vulnerability, warning systems (particularly important in terms of natural hazards), organisational structure and networks, people, mitigation strategy, communication and recovery, to name just a few specific tourism resilience factors (see also Specht, 2008; Figure 6.3). Such an approach is relatively simple but can be extremely effective in improving resilience thinking and planning (Hall, 2016b). For example, following the 2004 tsunami which hit coastal Sri Lanka, the residents of poor fishing villages were relocated inland, and hotel and resort developments were constructed on land they had previously occupied (Vale, 2014). If the 'tourism system' were defined in narrow terms, this would seem to be a positive development for the hospitality sector and the system overall. However, if it were defined in broader terms to include the communities affected by tourism development, then the loss of livelihood as a result of relocation would be regarded as a negative for the system. Or, at the very least, issues of trade-off could be considered much more explicitly and transparently by working through the five Ws of resilience and the different resilience factors.

Conclusion: Is Resilience a Resilient Concept? 143

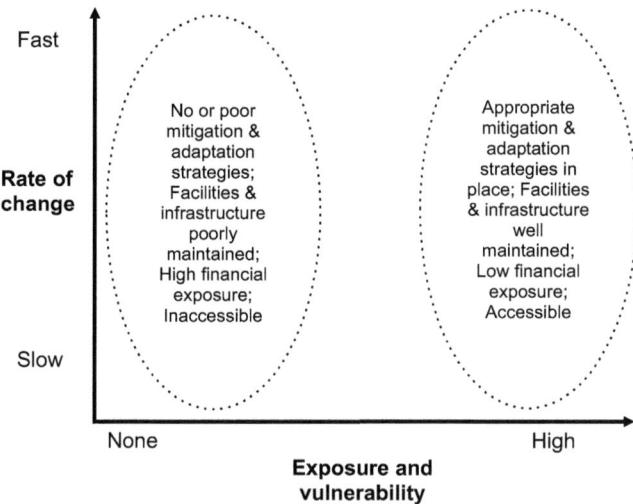

Figure 6.3a Assessing resilience factors: Exposure and vulnerability

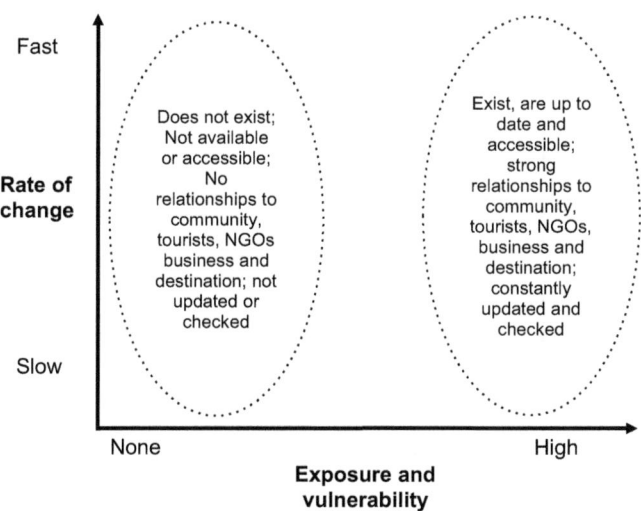

Figure 6.3b Assessing resilience factors: Hazard and risk change warning system and its relationship to tourism

144 Tourism and Resilience

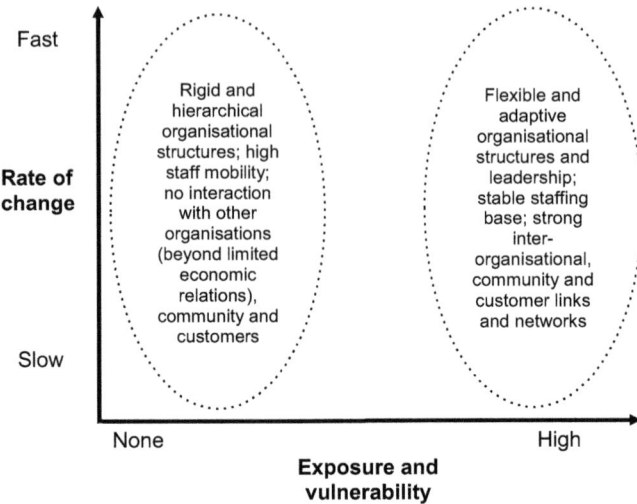

Figure 6.3c Assessing resilience factors: Organisational structures and relationships

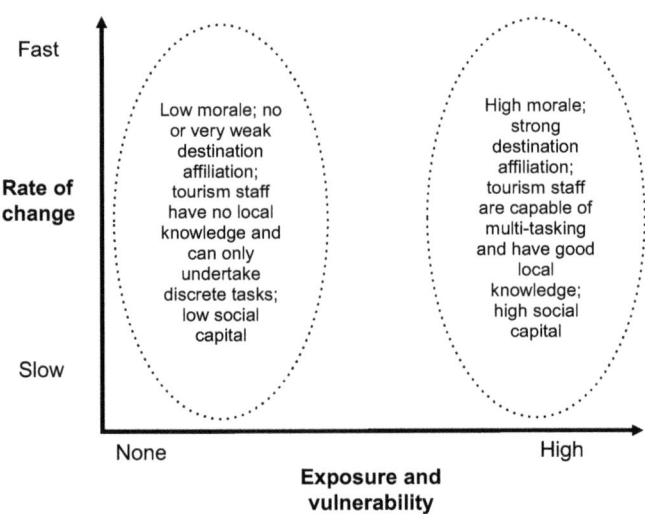

Figure 6.3d Assessing resilience factors: People

Conclusion: Is Resilience a Resilient Concept? 145

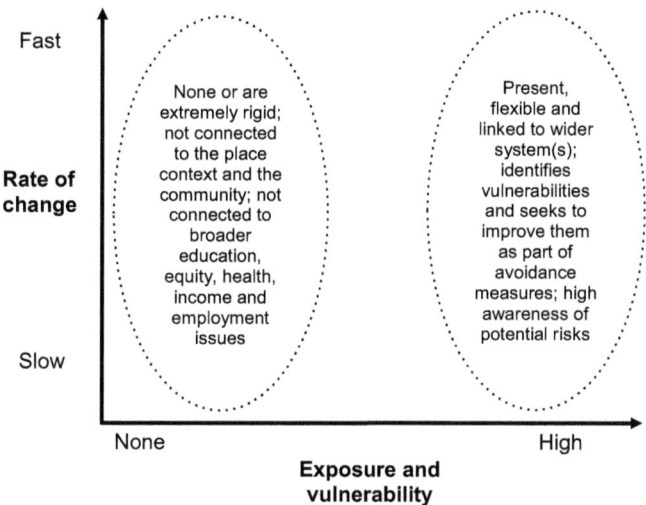

Figure 6.3e Assessing resilience factors: Mitigation and adaptation strategies

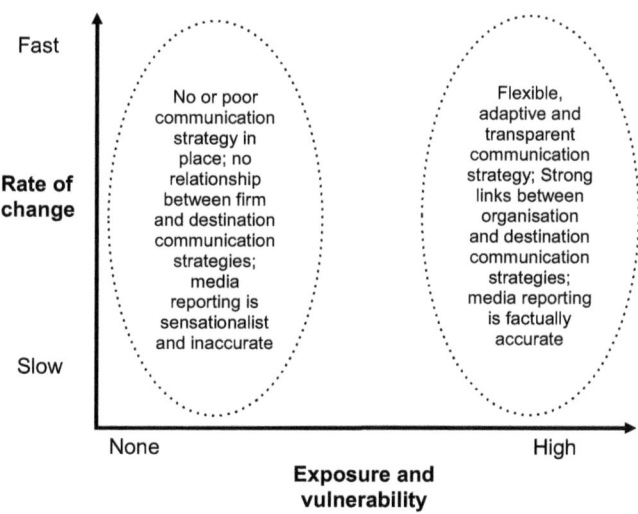

Figure 6.3f Assessing resilience factors: Communications and media

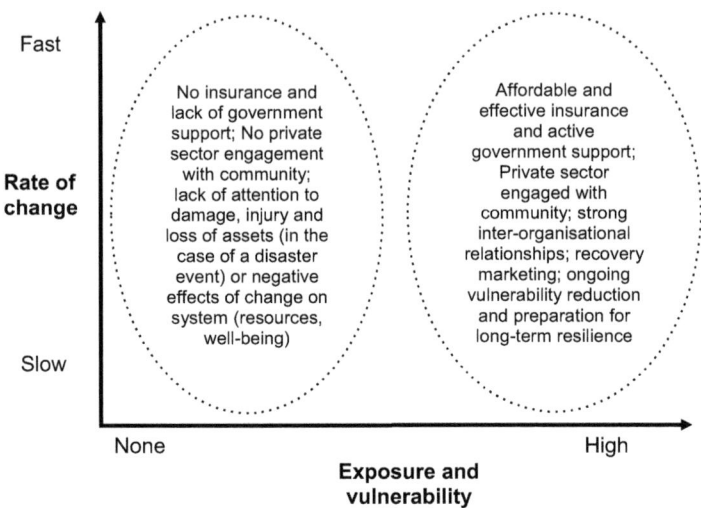

Figure 6.3g Assessing resilience factors: Recovery

Resilience and Tourism Systems

Resilience is significant for understanding how tourism organisations, destinations, communities and tourists as individuals can survive, adapt, respond and change in the face of increasing global and local change and disturbances. The wide spectrum of resilience concepts that has emerged in scientific literature attests to the contested nature of the concept. At one end, concepts such as ecological resilience are well entrenched in their respective literature and knowledge domains but other concepts such as organisational resilience and destination resilience are more 'fuzzy', although this may also be because of the fuzziness of terms such as destination as well. The latter terms add to the vague concept of 'resilience thinking' as a broad, multifaceted and loosely organised cluster of concepts (Carpenter & Brock, 2008; Carpenter et al., 2001).

Nevertheless, resilience thinking addresses the dynamics and development of complex social-ecological systems (Folke et al., 2010) in which tourism is situated. Despite the boundaries being blurred between concepts such as adaptability and vulnerability, they are integral for resilience (Folke et al., 2010; Walker et al., 2004). For example, in drawing on ecological thinking, Nelson et al. (2007) view resilience as a set of system characteristics, including the capacity to absorb change, learning and self-organisation, which give rise to the outcome of adaptedness, which they define as 'a state in which a system is effective in relating with the environment and meets the normative goals of stakeholders' (Nelson *et al.*, 2007: 400; see also Nelson *et al.*, 2010). While the disaster ecology literature highlights the importance of structure for the resilience of communities and the individuals within them, the utilisation of ecological ideas is only partial at best (Hall, 2016a).

One clear limit to resilience thinking is whether it is a desirable characteristic of people, organisations and communities at all times. For example, Pizzo (2015) highlights that some organisations and communities are undesirable (e.g. human and organ trafficking, sex tourism, drug manufacturers, etc.), but they prove to be 'resilient' over time due to their ability to transform and adapt to the 'system'. Hence, is resiliency required at all times in all situations? Literature has failed to distinguish between what is unexpected or unwanted (Pizzo, 2015).

> Ascertainment of the resilient behaviour of a community or organization after an unexpected event does not mean that all communities or organizations within the community must be resilient, nor does it imply that they must be resilient whatever the unexpected event may be, nor that they must be resilient in the same way as the one observed in previous unexpected events. (Pizzo, 2015: 134)

Clearly, such a situation brings us back to the need to be asking the five Ws of resilience. Also, individual resilience does not necessarily contribute to employee, organisational or community resilience. Similarly, a resilient community or organisation is not simply the sum of its resilient members or employees. Instead, there are clear emergent effects that need to be considered.

While resilience was introduced as a purely descriptive concept, resilience thinking has evolved into an implicit mix of normative and positive aspects (Brand & Jax, 2007; Strunz, 2012). As noted in the review of the literature on resilience by Bec *et al.* (2016), the concept has been arbitrarily adopted in the tourism literature to investigate mainly the resilience of a system following external shocks such as crises and disasters (e.g. Becken, 2013; Biggs *et al.*, 2012; Orchiston, 2013; see also Eakin *et al.*, 2012). The need for an epistemological shift in resilience thinking by integrating different ways of understanding different system structures from individuals to organisations and destinations within the larger tourism system has not yet been achieved. As the notion of panarchy highlights (see Chapter 2), change occurs cross-scale. As part of developing a better understanding of the tourism system, considerations of resilience in tourism therefore need to think of what is happening at scales above and below the main level of focus in order both to explain change and, in some cases, to intervene to create change (Hall, 2016c). In the case of tourism, at its most basic this may mean going beyond narrow considerations of human agency in considering social practices but also considering the role of structure, i.e. the socio-technical systems within which human behaviours are embedded (Hall, 2016c). Furthermore, change to a system does not just come from fast external shocks, such as a disaster or behavioural change, but also arises from slow cumulative change, as the result of, for example, evolutionary change or changes in socio-technical systems that give rise to habits and social and economic practices. The latter has been very poorly explicitly studied in the case of tourism with respect to resilience, including with respect to behavioural responses to climate change (Scott et al., 2012).

Social systems cannot be resilient if the environmental system is vulnerable (Ruiz-Ballesteros, 2011). Social systems act differently from ecosystems but the two are symbiotic and therefore ecological and social concepts of resilience need to be integrated to further understand the resilience of tourism systems. Socio-ecological perspectives of resilience recognise that change is inevitable and embrace transformation and adaptation to address and manage change (Hegney et al., 2007). Despite an emphasis by some commentators on the potentially conservative nature of resilience approaches (Brown, 2012), stability and control are not inherently central to socio-ecological interpretations of resilience. Instead, vulnerability theory is emphasised in the analysis of a community's environmental characteristics before a crisis occurs, whereas resilience theory emphasises adaptive capability when experiencing a disturbance and after a crisis (Tsao & Ni, 2016).

An important observation from the panarchical nature of tourism-related resilience is that there is the risk that separate groups, organisations or destinations may actually become less resilient the more they interact and engage with larger regional, national and global systems, leading to increased vulnerability to change (Adger, 2006; Bec et al., 2015). For example, local destination marketing organisations can become less resilient when interacting with the national destination marketing organisations and changes in international markets, creating ripple effects on organisational, destination and community resilience. According to Cochrane (2010), the three main components of a resilient tourism system are: an awareness of market forces and the ability to harness them; stakeholder cohesion and associative working, where different groups based on their roles and strengths work in a coordinated way to use resources sustainably; and strong and consistent leadership expressed through clear vision and good management, either from individuals or institutions. These components occur at a micro scale in organisations and destinations. However, there is also a need to recognise how organisational resilience and destination resilience can impact the broader macro-scale resilience of the tourism system.

Resilience: Sustainability 2.0?

Resilience and sustainability are related concepts but they are not the same (Table 6.1). Resilience thinking is valuable because of its focus on connectedness and the need to move away from the continual separation of ecological, social and economic impacts (Folke *et al.*, 2010). Strong definitions of sustainability emphasise that the stocks of natural capital need to be maintained at or above existing threshold levels. With a resilience capacity, the system is able to keep its current equilibrium state and endure external perturbations – either from nature or from human activities (Xu *et al.*, 2015). This is significant because sustainable development requires both ecosystems and socio-economic systems to be resilient, with development being based on the goods and services (capacity) that ecosystems can provide, with such development in turn affecting the condition of ecosystems (Gunderson & Holling, 2002).

Sustainable development can only be achieved in sufficiently resilient socio-ecosystems (Ruiz-Ballesteros, 2011). Socio-ecological systems display three inherent properties which influence the dynamics between organism and environment. The first is a natural potential for change, that is, the capacity for the system to create a fundamentally new system when the existing system is untenable (Walker *et al.*, 2006). The second property is the ability to adapt where the system has some level of internal control that determines the degree to which the system can control its fate before succumbing to the effect of external variables (Ruiz-Ballesteros, 2011). The adaptability of such systems is a function of the individuals and groups managing them (Walker *et al.*, 2006), and is related to learning capacity (Gooch & Warburton, 2009). Thirdly, these systems display a capacity for resilience. Sustainability management, therefore, needs to be focused on building resilience (Folke *et al.*, 2003) in order to secure societal development and avoid vulnerability (Xu *et al.*, 2015). Nevertheless, in spite of the similarities between resilience and sustainability, they are not identical concepts and cannot be substituted for each other. Xu *et al.* (2015) argue that the main difference is that resilience thinking does not emphasise the long-term time dimension and equity, whereas intergenerational equity is the core concept of sustainability.

> Resilience places more focus on the state of a system when facing disturbances. In fact, in some cases the system remains resilient as long as the critical tipping points are not passed, even though the stock of resources is reduced and less available than previously. Such a system is not sustainable based on the principle of intergenerational equity. (Xu *et al.*, 2015)

Table 6.1 Comparisons between resilience and sustainability

	Resilience	Sustainability
Similarities		
Objective	A desirable ecological resilience can sustainably supply sufficient resources and keep its functions to meet the demands of social and economic wellbeing without shifting the regimes in the face of perturbations and unforeseen shocks.	Strong definition of sustainability includes the criterion that stocks of natural capital are maintained at or above existing threshold levels for human wellbeing.
Dependency relationship	Basic ecosystem functions should not be affected by human activities or other disturbance beyond their thresholds and socio-economic systems would not collapse because of changes in the states of ecosystems (precondition of sustainability).	The sustainability of a system relies on its own resilience while such resilience depends on a wide range of properties which affect the system itself (the goods and services that ecosystems can provide).
Starting points	The first important thing for applying resilience thinking to practice is to define resilience in terms 'of what to what'.	The sustainable state of both social and environmental systems (sustainability of what) to both present and future generations (sustainability to what).
Differences		
Intergenerational equity	Resilience thinking does not conceptually emphasise intergenerational equity.	Intergenerational equity is the core concept of sustainability.
Desirable state	Does not specify a desirable state.	Interested in the desirability of any state as well as transitions.
Methodological approach	Primarily relates to cross-scale external factors as well as internal factors that potentially lead to 'tipping points'.	Primarily relates to the evolution, and co-evolution, of complex systems that embed natural, social and environmental components and dimensions.

Source: After Xu et al. (2015).

Resilience therefore contributes to rather than implies sustainability (Strunz, 2012). Resilience thus would be an indicator of sustainability as it allows a system to have a future.

Resilience is a 'relational' concept; that is, without other aspects such as vulnerability and adaptive capacity it ceases to have such strong conceptual power. Resilience is related to vulnerability approaches that have roots in complexity science. However, the relationship between resilience and vulnerability is ambiguous given that the latter has been labelled as the opposite of resilience (Gallopin, 2006). A resilient system may be less vulnerable but a vulnerable system may also be resilient (Gallopin, 2006). A resilient system is not invulnerable to change and external shocks but rather it has the capacity to manage the impacts and adapt to the circumstances. From this perspective, resilience maintains the connection between the elements in a system in the face of vulnerability.

Resilience therefore contributes to thinking about sustainability as well as providing a basis for decision making for sustainability but it does not replace the concept. Instead, the concept of resilience potentially reinforces the need for better understanding of systems and the interconnection between the different dimensions or 'pillars' of sustainability and the central role that the environment and natural capital plays.

Resilience and System Thinking

Resilience thinking provides a way of understanding human and natural systems as complex systems that are continually adapting and evolving (Walker et al., 2006). System thinking therefore potentially acts as a bridge between the social and biophysical sciences in helping to understand how individual and organisational resilience links to, for example, community resilience and destination resilience. At play are significant 'ecological' and 'social' linkages which are affected by the wider system and cross-scale relations. Nevertheless, much existing resilience research in tourism both in its theoretical and empirical treatments of the subject tends to ignore the important system-level characteristics (e.g. governance, organisational learning) that influence the development of resilience both among actors and at a wider system level. For example, the relationships between personal resilience, organisational resilience, community resilience and destination resilience are not well articulated. This is surprising given the significance of panarchy and emergence in resilience thinking (see Chapter 2). Although other factors will also be relevant, it does suggest that emergent properties at the individual level will be significant for organisational-level systems and that, similarly, emergence at the organisational level will be significant for destinations. Similarly, in reverse, the global tourism system will 'structure' or set the conditions within which the destination system operates back down through to organisations and individuals. Yet instead of taking a multi-scale approach, much research on resilience in tourism – as well as its portrayal in the literature – only tends to be conducted at a single level in relation to an external perturbation *at that level*, rather than examining the role and function of cross-scale effects. One potential implication of such an approach is that tourism needs to give greater awareness to the implications of the wider system (what in the terms of the simple model of a tourism system would be described as the environment) within which it operates, its effects on tourism, and tourism's effects on the macro-system.

In ecology, resilience is neither a positive nor a negative (Hall, 2016a). It is in the adoption of more normative socio-ecological and other approaches, such as those informed by disaster capitalism and neoliberalism (Amore & Hall, 2017; Klein, 2007), that consideration of the role of human agency in not only formulating notions of resilience but also, critically, their application and value, becomes extremely important. This is especially the case when the focus shifts from the resilience of a system to the resilience or survival of a particular firm, organisation or individual. This shift in thinking also moves from the more stochastic understanding of change in ecology to one which is often much more deterministic and in which communities, organisations and individuals supposedly possess the attributes with which to adapt to external change. However, it is also a shift in thinking that requires a much more considered critique of the implications of normative approaches for tourism, including the values, interests and power relations that may be implicit within them. As we have stressed elsewhere, the five Ws of resilience become an important means to interrogate exactly what the implications of any particular approach to resilience actually are. An important part of making resilience thinking more transparent and outlining the various assumptions within it is that the notion of resilience used will also influence the selection of tools that are regarded as part of making destinations, organisations, individuals and communities more resilient.

Table 6.2 highlights the connectivity between understandings of individual decision making, forms of governance regarded as appropriate for achieving greater social resilience, level of analysis and tool selection to generate change. The utilitarian approach can be regarded as akin to an engineering approach, while the systems of provision approach is arguably the most akin to a socio-ecological resilience approach because of its emphasis on changing the wider system so as to influence what is perceived as desirable change at lower scales. In terms of approaches, ecological resilience, for

Table 6.2 Approaches to resilience and change

Approach	Resilience thinking	Scale of analysis and intervention	Understanding of individual decision making	Dominant forms of governance	Tools to achieve increased resilience
Utilitarian	Engineering resilience	Individual, organisation	Cognitive information processing on basis of rational utility maximisation	Markets (marketisation and privatisation of state instruments)	Information provision, tax incentives, pricing, education
Social & psychological	Engineering resilience, trait based, and first and second wave approaches to individual resilience	Individuals, family, owner-operated micro businesses	Response to psychological needs, behaviour and social contexts, including cultural differentiation and behaviour as a marker of social meaning and identity Dominant paradigm of 'ABC': attitude, behaviour and choice	Markets (marketisation and privatisation of state instruments) Networks (public–private partnerships)	Social marketing in order to encourage behavioural change Nudging – making better choices through manipulating an individual's or family's environment
Systems of provision/ institutions	Socio-ecological resilience and third and fourth wave approaches to individual resilience	Community, society, network	Routine habits as constrained and shaped by socio-technical infrastructure and institutions	Hierarchies (nation state and supranational institutions) Communities (public–private partnerships, communities)	Institutional design; improving public health and education services; access to emergency services; improving neighbourhood quality; creating employment opportunities; prevention of and protection from oppression or political violence; protective child policies; low acceptance of physical violence

Source: After Hall (2014); O'Dougherty Wright et al. (2013).

example, focuses on factors such as diversity, connectivity and heterogeneity which are assumed to contribute to greater resilience. This means that redundancy in critical functional groups, which allows for a diversity of responses to different forms of disturbance and environmental variability but maintains similar effects on ecosystem function, is regarded as leading to increased resilience (Brand & Jax, 2007). However, such ecological resilience thinking, which also applies to social, infrastructural and supply-chain resilience, does not transfer very well to dominant modes of engineering and economic thought that focus on efficiency, equilibrium and return time as being the key characteristics of resilience, and that usually seek to remove any perceived system redundancies or inefficiencies (Hall, 2016a).

If correct, Table 6.2 raises some interesting questions and reinforces some of the observations made above. In particular, when seeking to encourage greater resilience in individuals, tourism-related organisations and destinations, the focus may well need to be on the wider systems of provision, i.e. society and regions at large, rather than just understanding tourism resilience and the tourism system from a narrow perspective; that is, the environment (both 'human' and 'natural') is an integral and active part of the tourism system and is more than just a passive backdrop against which tourism occurs. However, what is also important is that, if authorities, experts and public agencies are so bound up in one way of thinking about resilience and only see solutions within their particular framework, they may miss or, if highly ideological, deliberately avoid, other ways of improving resilience (Shove, 2010). Therefore, developing a capacity to learn and to do so as widely as possible becomes a desirable attribute in resilience thinking.

A Community-based Approach to Tourism Resilience?

Organisational resilience and community resilience are interrelated and interdependent. Organisational resilience is a critical component of a community's ability to plan for, respond to, and recover from emergencies and crises (Lee *et al.*, 2013). An understanding of resilient individuals provides a useful starting place for defining resilient organisations (see Chapters 3 and 4). Actions and interactions among employees and other stakeholders underpin the emergence of an organisation's collective capacity for resilience (Morgeson & Hoffman, 1999). The relationship between resilience and organisational resilience reflects the typical interaction between systems and sub-systems (Lengnick-Hall *et al.*, 2011). Learned resourcefulness, ingenuity and bricolage (the imaginative use of materials for previously unintended purposes) are all related traits and characteristics which enable individuals and organisations to engage in the disciplined creativity needed to devise unconventional, yet robust, responses to unprecedented challenges (Lengnick-Hall & Lengnick-Hall, 2003).

Community resilience has been defined as the existence, development and engagement of community resources to thrive in an ever-changing and unpredictable environment (Magis, 2010). The idea of community cohesion leading to resilient communities also applies to the destination level. Social resilience relates to the ability of communities to cope with external stress or disturbances resulting from social, political and environmental change (Adger, 2000). A destination – from a network perspective – can often be regarded as a community of sorts, with common interests as well as differences of opinion, but also, most importantly given some of the research undertaken on resilience in tourism, as a shared place (Biggs et al., 2012, 2015).

A resilient community, organisation or destination requires strong interconnectivity. This is similar to individual resilience which is much dependent on formal and informal relationships (Biggs et al., 2012). Nevertheless, social capital requires skilful investment and management for accumulation for use in times of need (Reich, 2006). Therefore, the development of trust between actors and actor engagement and learning are important for resilience (Adger, 2000), especially because when actors trust one another there is an increased likelihood of working towards common goals and outside everyday silos (Hall, 2008). From a tourism perspective, this should not be regarded as a surprising observation; rather it should be standard tourism planning and business practice. Perhaps, as in many things, the focus needs to be not so much on finding new ways to do things but on making sure that the strategies that we know work and helping to ensure that tourism businesses, employees and destinations survive and grow: collaboration; providing a decent standard of living and quality of life for employees and managers; developing trust and talking between actors; and caring about customers, staff and the community.

All Change? Or No Change?

Resilience – the magnitude of disturbance that can be tolerated before a system moves to a different state controlled by a different set of processes (Gunderson & Holling, 2002) – acquires different meanings when applied to the context of a specific, time-determined crisis generated by an unforeseeable event or unwanted change. Recourse to resilience to resolve individual, organisational, community and destination problems in the aftermath of a disaster or crisis is not as 'obvious' as is often presented in the literature

(Pizzo, 2015) and by policy makers. Moving towards resilience per se could therefore mean nothing. Resilience cannot be assumed as an extended concept applicable to all types of systems and events (i.e. disasters). Its meaning must be specifically defined, its properties articulated in each situation and the conditions under which resiliency is experienced well understood (Meerow & Newell, 2016; Pizzo, 2015).

In psychology, resilience is more developmental in nature – an ability to use internal and external resources to deal with stress and stressors. This may provide a useful framing for much tourism research although it does not

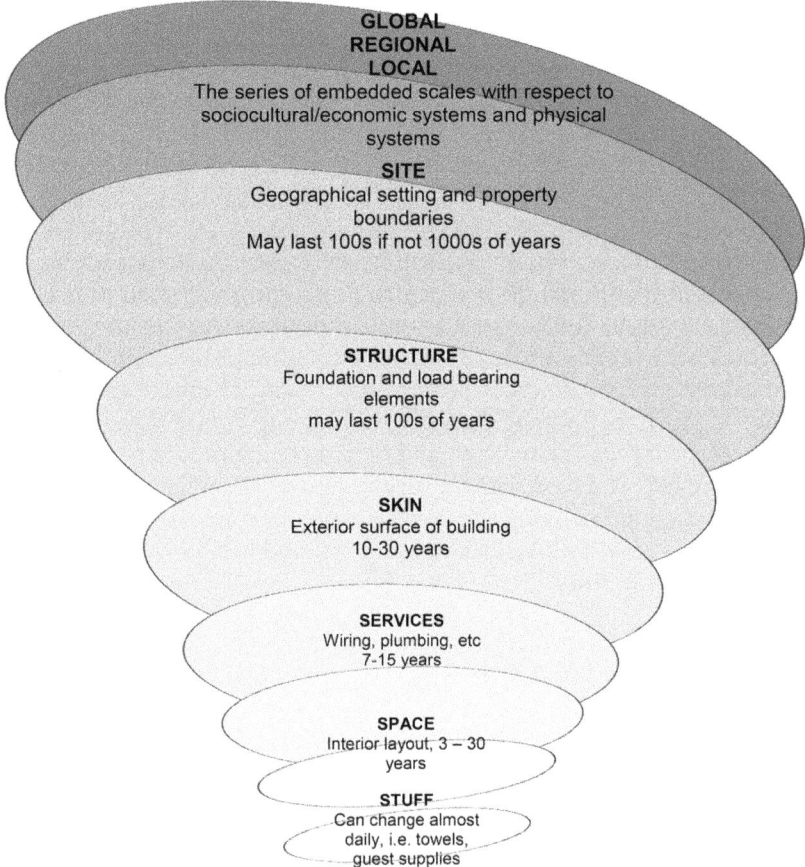

Figure 6.4 Urban hotel design panarchy
Source: After Hall (2008).

attend so much to issues of stability and change which are more the focus of ecological approaches to resilience. Surprisingly, much of the resilience literature, including in tourism, does not question what normality is. Perhaps that is because, in a *Hitchhiker's Guide to the Galaxy* kind of way, we are unable to determine exactly what normality is, or we are somewhat concerned by how absurd it really is! Nevertheless, notions such as 'bounce back' and 'adaptive capacity', for example, make the implicit assumption that there is a return to a 'new' normal (Pizzo, 2015). The notion of what is normal and what is change is really one of perspective and the time and spatial scale that is being used (Figure 6.4). Much tourism is built on the unsafe assumption that growth is normal. As we have discussed in this book, understanding changes in tourism numbers and crisis in tourism is partly an outcome of scale, as while individual locations and destinations may suffer, wider growth has continued. Nevertheless, growth cannot last for ever.

No population, including that of tourists, can increase indefinitely. This law is axiomatic and reflects the fact that the world's resources as well as local supply rates of resources are finite (Dodds, 2009). Therefore, change – moving from one state to another – is actually the norm. But what is important, from a human and ethical perspective, is what sort of change and what sort of state we want to move to and how we are going to get there. It is perhaps this normative issue that lies at the heart of much discussion about resilience, as it does about sustainability. The challenge for the tourism industry, as well as tourism researchers, is to seriously address these questions at all levels of the tourism system.

Further reading

Useful critiques of the notion of resilience at a regional scale along with their implications for planning and policy include:

Christopherson, S., Michie, J. and Tyler, P. (2010) Regional resilience: Theoretical and empirical perspectives. *Cambridge Journal of Regions, Economy and Society* 3, 3–10.
Hudson, R. (2010) Resilient regions in an uncertain world: Wishful thinking or practical reality? *Cambridge Journal of Regions, Economy and Society* 3, 11–25.
White, I. and O'Hare, P. (2014) From rhetoric to reality: Which resilience, why resilience, and whose resilience in spatial planning? *Environment and Planning C: Government and Policy* 32 (5), 934–950.

The role of place with respect to community resilience is highlighted in:

Cutter, S.L., Barnes, L., Berry, M., Burton, C., Evans, E., Tate, E. and Webb, J. (2008) A place-based model for understanding community resilience to natural disasters. *Global Environmental Change* 18 (4), 598–606.

Time is a critical variable in seeking to understand change and resilience. See:

Gibbs, L., Waters, E., Bryant, R.A., Pattison, P., Lusher, D., Harms, L. and Forbes, D. (2013) Beyond bushfires: Community, resilience and recovery – a longitudinal mixed method study of the medium to long term impacts of bushfires on mental health and social connectedness. *BMC Public Health* 13 (1), 1036.

On the implications of ecological approaches to understanding resilience for organisations, see:

Glassop, L. (2007) The three Rs of resilience: Redundancy, requisite variety and resources. In R. Kay and K.A. Richardson (eds) *Building and Sustaining Resilience in Complex Organisations. International Workshop on Complexity and Organizational Resilience* (pp. 19–34). Marblehead, MA: ISCE Publishing.

Valuable general resources on disaster risk reduction, recovery and resilience include:

Committee on Post-Disaster Recovery of a Community's Public Health, Medical, and Social Services (2015) *Healthy, Resilient, and Sustainable Communities After Disasters: Strategies, Opportunities, and Planning for Recovery*. Washington DC: Board on Health Sciences Policy; Institute of Medicine, National Academies Press. Available: https://www.ncbi.nlm.nih.gov/books/NBK316521/

Twigg, J. (2015) *Disaster Risk Reduction*. London: Humanitarian Policy Group, Overseas Development Institute. Available: http://goodpracticereview.org/wp-content/uploads/2015/10/GPR-9-web-string-1.pdf

References

100 Resilient Cities (2016) *100 Resilient Cities. About Us*. Retrieved from http://www.100resilientcities.org/about-us#/-_/ (accessed 1 April).
Adam, C., Bauer, M.W., Knill, C. and Studinger, P. (2007) The termination of public organizations: Theoretical perspectives to revitalize a promising research area. *Public Organization Review* 7 (3), 221–236.
Adger, W.N. (2000) Social and ecological resilience: are they related? *Progress in Human Geography* 24 (3), 347–364.
Adger, W.N. (2006) Vulnerability. *Global Environmental Change* 16 (3), 268–281.
Adger, W.N., Hughes, T.P., Folke, C., Carpenter, S.R. and Rockstrom, J. (2005) Social-ecological resilience to coastal disasters. *Science* 309 (5737), 1036–1039.
Ahern, J. (2011) From fail-safe to safe-to-fail: Sustainability and resilience in the new urban world. *Landscape and Urban Planning* 100 (4), 341–343.
Ahern, N.R., Kiehl, E.M., Lou Sole, M. and Byers, J. (2006) A review of instruments measuring resilience. *Issues in Comprehensive Pediatric Nursing* 29 (2), 103–125.
Ahmed, R., Seedat, M., van Niekerk, A. and Bulbulia, S. (2004) Discerning community resilience in disadvantaged communities in the context of violence and injury prevention. *South African Journal of Psychology* 34 (3), 386–408.
Amore, A. (2016a) The governance of built heritage in the post-earthquake Christchurch CBD. In C.M. Hall, S. Malinen, R. Vosslamber and R. Wordsworth (eds) *Business and Post-Disaster Management: Business, Organisational and Consumer Resilience and the Christchurch Earthquakes*. Abingdon: Routledge.
Amore, A. (2016b) Regeneration from the rubble: Culture and creative urban renewal in post-earthquake Christchurch, New Zealand. In C. Marques (ed.) *Planeamento Cultural Urbano em Áreas Metropolitanas: Revitalização dos Espaços Pós-Suburbanos*. Lisbon: Editora Caleidoscopo.
Amore, A. and Hall, C.M. (2016a) From governance to meta-governance in tourism? Re-incorporating politics, interests and values in the analysis of tourism governance. *Tourism Recreation Research* 41 (2), 1–14.
Amore, A. and Hall, C.M. (2016b) 'Regeneration is the focus now': Anchor projects and delivering a new CBD for Christchurch. In C.M. Hall, S. Malinen, R. Vosslamber and R. Wordsworth (eds) *Business and Post-Disaster Management: Business, Organisational and Consumer Resilience and the Christchurch Earthquakes*. Abingdon: Routledge.
Amore, A. and Hall, C.M. (2017) National and urban public policy agenda in tourism: Towards the emergence of a hyperneoliberal script? *International Journal of Tourism Policy* 7 (1), 4–22.

Anderson, L.G., Rocliffe, S., Haddaway, N.R. and Dunn, A.M. (2015) The role of tourism and recreation in the spread of non-native species: A systematic review and meta-analysis. *PLoS ONE* 10, e0140833. doi:10.1371/journal.pone.0140833.

Andrew, S., Arlikatti, S., Siebeneck, L., Pongponrat, K. and Jaikampan, K. (2016) Sources of organisational resiliency during the Thailand floods of 2011: A test of the bonding and bridging hypotheses. *Disasters* 40 (1), 65–84.

Annarelli, A. and Nonino, F. (2016) Strategic and operational management of organizational resilience: Current state of research and future directions. *Omega* 62, 1–18.

Armitage, D. and Johnson, D. (2006) Can resilience be reconciled with globalization and the increasingly complex conditions of resource degradation in Asian coastal regions? *Ecology and Society* 11 (1), 2.

Arntz, M., Gregory, T. and Zierahn, U. (2016) The risk of automation for jobs in OECD countries: A comparative analysis. OECD Social, Employment and Migration Working Paper No. 189. Paris: OECD Publishing.

Associated Press (2017) Huge fleet of icebergs hits North Atlantic shipping lanes. *The Guardian*. See https://www.theguardian.com/environment/2017/apr/06/huge-fleet-icebergs-north-atlantic-shipping-lanes (accessed 6 April).

Auerswald, P.E. and van Opstal, D. (2009) Coping with turbulence: The resilience imperative. Paper presented at the World Economic Forum Annual Meeting. *Innovations: Technology, Governance, Globalization*, Special Issue for the World Economic Forum Annual Meeting.

Avey, J.B., Luthans, F. and Jensen, S.M. (2009) Psychological capital: A positive resource for combating employee stress and turnover. *Human Resource Management* 48 (5), 677–693.

Baggio, R. (2007) Symptoms of complexity in a tourism system. See arXiv:physics/07010 63v2[physics.soc-ph].

Baggio, R. (2008) Symptoms of complexity in a tourism system. *Tourism Analysis* 13 (1), 1–20.

Baldwin, R. (2016) *The Great Convergence: Information Technology and the New Globalization*. Cambridge, MA: Harvard University Press.

Bardoel, E.A., Pettit, T.M., de Cieri, H. and McMillan, L. (2014) Employee resilience: An emerging challenge for HRM. *Asia Pacific Journal of Human Resources* 52 (3), 279–297.

Barnosky, A.D., Matzke, N., Tomiya, S., et al. (2011) Has the Earth's sixth mass extinction already arrived? *Nature* 471 (7336), 51–57.

Barroso, H.P., Machado, V.H. and Machado, V.C. (2011) Supply chain resilience using the mapping approach. In P. Li (ed.) *Supply Chain Management* (pp. 161–184). Rijeka: InTech (open access). See http://www.intechopen.com/articles/show/title/supply-chain-resilience-using-the-mapping-approach (accessed 1 April).

Bas Collins, A. (2007) Human resources: A hidden advantage? *International Journal of Contemporary Hospitality Management* 19 (1), 78–84.

Baum, T. (2007) Human resources in tourism: Still waiting for change. *Tourism Management* 28 (6), 1383–1399.

Baum, T. (2015) Human resources in tourism: Still waiting for change? A 2015 reprise. *Tourism Management* 50, 204–212.

BBC (2014) Small Data: Have we lost half the world's animals? *BBC News Magazine Monitor*, 6 October.

Beasley, M., Thompson, T. and Davidson, J. (2003) Resilience in response to life stress: The effects of coping style and cognitive hardiness. *Personality and Individual Differences* 34 (1), 77–95.

Bec, A., McLennan, C.L. and Moyle, B.D. (2016) Community resilience to long-term tourism decline and rejuvenation: A literature review and conceptual model. *Current Issues in Tourism* 19 (5), 431–457.

Becken, S. (2001) *Energy Consumption of Tourist Attractions and Activities in New Zealand: Summary Report of a Survey.* Lincoln: Landcare Research and Lincoln University.

Becken, S. (2013) Developing a framework for assessing resilience of tourism sub-systems to climatic factors. *Annals of Tourism Research* 43, 506–528.

Becken, S., Mahon, R., Rennie, H.G. and Shakeela, A. (2014) The tourism disaster vulnerability framework: An application to tourism in small island destinations. *Natural Hazards* 71 (1), 955–972.

Becken, S., Scott, N., Ritchie, B. and Campiranon, K. (2015) The development of new tourism networks to respond to and recover from the 2011 Christchurch earthquake. In B.W. Ritchie and K. Compiranon (eds) *Tourism Crisis and Disaster Management in the Asia-Pacific* (pp. 190–205). Wallingford: CABI.

Beichler, S., Hasibovic, S., Davidse, B.J. and Deppisch, S. (2014) The role played by social-ecological resilience as a method of integration in interdisciplinary research. *Ecology and Society* 19 (3), 1–8.

Beirman, D. (2003) *Restoring Tourism Destinations in Crisis: A Strategic Marketing Approach.* Sydney: Allen & Unwin.

Benson, C., Twigg, J., with Rossetto, T. (2007) *Tools for Mainstreaming Disaster Risk Reduction: Guidance Notes for Development Organisations.* International Federation of Red Cross and Red Crescent Societies. Geneva: ProVention Consortium.

Bergeman, C.S. and Wallace, K.A (1999) Resiliency in later life. In T.L Whitman, T.V. Merluzzi and R.D. White (eds) *Life-Span Perspectives on Health and Illness* (pp. 207–225). Mahwah, NJ: Lawrence Erlbaum.

Berinsky, A.J., Huber, G.A. and Lenz, G.S. (2012) Evaluating online labor markets for experimental research: Amazon.com's Mechanical Turk. *Political Analysis* 20 (3), 351–368.

Berkes, F. (2007) Understanding uncertainty and reducing vulnerability: Lessons from resilience thinking. *Natural Hazards* 41 (2), 283–295.

Berkes, F. (2010) Shifting perspectives on resource management: Resilience and the reconceptualization of 'natural resources' and 'management'. *Mast* 9 (1), 13–40.

Berkes, F. and Ross, H. (2013) Community resilience: Toward an integrated approach. *Society & Natural Resources* 26 (1), 5–20.

Bevir, M. (2011) Governance as theory, practice, and dilemma. In M. Bevir (ed.) *The SAGE Handbook of Governance* (pp. 1–15). London: SAGE.

Bhamra, R., Dani, S. and Burnard, K. (2011) Resilience: The concept, a literature review and future directions. *International Journal of Production Research* 49 (18), 5375–5393.

Bhandari, K., Cooper, C. and Ruhanen, L. (2015) The role of the destination management organization in responding to climate change: Organizational knowledge and learning. *Acta Turistica* 26 (2), 91–102.

Biggs, D. (2011) Understanding resilience in a vulnerable industry: The case of reef tourism in Australia. *Ecology and Society* 16 (1), 30.

Biggs, D., Hall, C.M. and Stoeckl, N. (2012) The resilience of formal and informal tourism enterprises to disasters: Reef tourism in Phuket, Thailand. *Journal of Sustainable Tourism* 20 (5), 645–665.

Biggs, D., Hicks, C.C., Cinner, J.E. and Hall, C.M. (2015) Marine tourism in the face of global change: The resilience of enterprises to crises in Thailand and Australia. *Ocean & Coastal Management* 105, 65–74.

Birkland, T.A. (1997) *After Disaster: Agenda Setting, Public Policy, and Focusing Events.* Washington, DC: Georgetown University Press.
Birkmann, J. (ed.) (2006) *Measuring Vulnerability to Natural Hazards: Towards Disaster Resilient Societies.* New Delhi: TERI Press.
Blaikie, P., Cannon, T., Davis, I. and Wisner, B. (1994) *At Risk: Natural Hazards, People's Vulnerability and Disasters.* London: Routledge.
Block, J. and Kremen, A.M. (1996) IQ and ego-resiliency: Conceptual and empirical connections and separateness. *Journal of Personality and Social Psychology* 70 (2), 349–361.
Boin, A., Kuipers, S. and Steenbergen, M. (2010) The life and death of public organizations: A question of institutional design? *Governance* 23 (3), 385–410.
Bonanno, G.A. (2004) Loss, trauma, and human resilience: Have we underestimated the human capacity to thrive after extremely aversive events? *American Psychologist* 59 (1), 20–28.
Bonanno, G.A., Galea, S., Bucciarelli, A. and Vlahov, D. (2007) What predicts psychological resilience after disaster? The role of demographics, resources, and life stress. *Journal of Consulting and Clinical Psychology* 75 (5), 671–682.
Börekçi, D.Y., Say, A.I., Kabasakal, H. and Rofcanin, Y. (2014) Quality of relationships with alternative suppliers: The role of supplier resilience and perceived benefits in supply networks. *Journal of Management & Organization* 20 (6), 808–831.
Bowler, T. (2017) Will globalisation take away your job? *BBC News*, 1 February.
Brand, F. (2005) *Ecological Resilience and its Relevance within a Theory of Sustainable Development.* UFZ Report No. 03/2005. Leipzig: Helmholtz-Zentrum für Umweltforschung.
Brand, F.S. and Jax, K. (2007) Focusing the meaning(s) of resilience: Resilience as a descriptive concept and a boundary object. *Ecology and Society* 12 (1), 1–23.
Brawn, J.D., Robinson, S.K. and Thompson III, F.R. (2001) The role of disturbance in the ecology and conservation of birds. *Annual Review of Ecology and Systematics* 32, 251–276.
Brown, C., Stevenson, J., Giovinazzi, S., Seville, E. and Vargo, J. (2015) Factors influencing impacts on and recovery trends of organisations: Evidence from the 2010/2011 Canterbury earthquakes. *International Journal of Disaster Risk Reduction* 14, 56–72.
Brown, K. (2012) Policy discourses of resilience. In M. Pelling, D. Manuel-Navarrete and M. Redclift (eds) *Climate Change and the Crisis of Capitalism: A Chance to Reclaim Self, Society and Nature.* New York: Routledge.
Brown, K. (2014) Global environmental change. I: A social turn for resilience? *Progress in Human Geography* 38 (1), 107–117.
Brown, K. (2016) *Resilience, Development and Global Change.* Abingdon: Routledge.
Brown, L. (2008) *Plan B 3.0: Mobilizing to Save Civilization.* New York: W.W. Norton.
Brown, N.A., Rovins, J.E., Feldmann, S., Orchiston, C. and Johnston, D. (2017) Exploring disaster resilience within the hotel sector: A systematic review of literature. *International Journal of Disaster Risk Reduction* 22, 362–370.
Bruneau, M., Chang, S.E., Eguchi, R.T., *et al.* (2003) A framework to quantitatively assess and enhance the seismic resilience of communities. *Earthquake Spectra* 19 (4), 733–752.
Buckley, R. (2008) Misperceptions of climate change damage on coastal tourism: Case study of Byron Bay, Australia. *Tourism Review International* 12, 71–88.
Busenberg, G.J. (1999) The evolution of vigilance: Disasters, sentinels and policy change. *Environmental Politics* 8 (4), 90–109.
Butler, R.W. (1980) The concept of a tourist area cycle of evolution: Implications for management of resources. *The Canadian Geographer/Le Géographe canadien* 24 (1), 5–12.

Buultjens, J., Ratnayake, I. and Gnanapala, A.C. (2014) From tsunami to recovery: The resilience of the Sri Lankan tourism industry. In B.W. Ritchie and K. Campiranon (eds) *Tourism Crisis and Disaster Management in the Asia-Pacific*. Wallingford: CABI.

Calgaro, E. (2010) Building resilient tourism destination futures in a world of uncertainty: Assessing destination vulnerability in Khao Lak, Patong and Phi Phi Don, Thailand to the 2004 Tsunami. PhD thesis, Macquarie University, Sydney.

Calgaro, E., Dominey-Howes, D. and Lloyd, K. (2014) Application of the Destination Sustainability Framework to explore the drivers of vulnerability and resilience in Thailand following the 2004 Indian Ocean Tsunami. *Journal of Sustainable Tourism* 22 (3), 361–383.

Cardona, O.D. (2003) *The Notions of Disaster Risk: Conceptual Framework for Integrated Management. Information and Indicators Program for Disaster Risk Management*. Manizales: Inter-American Development Bank.

Carpenter, D. and Lewis, D.E. (2004) Political learning from rare events: Poisson inference, fiscal constraints, and the lifetime of bureaus. *Political Analysis* 12, 201–232.

Carpenter, S.R. and Brock, W.A. (2008) Adaptive capacity and traps. *Ecology and Society* 13 (2), 40.

Carpenter, S., Walker, B., Anderies, J.M. and Abel, N. (2001) From metaphor to measurement: Resilience of what to what? *Ecosystems* 4 (8), 765–781.

Causevic, S. and Lynch, P. (2013) Political (in)stability and its influence on tourism development. *Tourism Management* 34, 145–157.

CCDU (2012) *Christchurch Central Recovery Plan. Te Mahere 'Maraka Ōtautahi'*. Christchurch: Christchurch Central Development Unit.

CCT (2012a) *Christchurch & Canterbury Tourism. Annual Report for the Year Ending 30 June 2012*. Christchurch: Christchurch & Canterbury Tourism.

CCT (2012b) *Greater Christchurch Visitor Recovery Plan*. Christchurch: Christchurch & Canterbury Tourism.

Ceballos, G., García, A. and Ehrlich, P.R. (2010) The sixth extinction crisis loss of animal populations and species. *Journal of Cosmology* 8, 1821–1831.

CERA (2012a) *Canterbury Economic Indicators – October 2012*. Christchurch: Canterbury Earthquake Recovery Authority.

CERA (Canterbury Earthquake Recovery Authority) (2012b) *Recovery Strategy for Greater Christchurch: Mahere Haumanutanga o Waitaha*. See http://cera.govt.nz/sites/default/files/common/recovery-strategy-for-greater-christchurch.pdf (accessed 10 April 2013).

CGIAR Research Program on Water, Land and Ecosystems (WLE) (2014) *Ecosystem Services and Resilience Framework*. Colombo: International Water Management Institute (IWMI), CGIAR Research Program on Water, Land and Ecosystems (WLE). See http://dx.doi.org/10.5337/2014.229 (accessed 1 April).

Chapin, F.S. III, Zaveleta, E., Eviner, V., et al. (2000) Consequences of changing biotic diversity. *Nature* 405, 234–242.

Cheung, C.K. and Chan, R.K.H. (2008) Facilitating achievement by social capital in Japan. *Journal of Socio-Economics* 37 (6), 2261–2277.

Christ, C., Hilel, O., Matus, S. and Sweeting, J. (2003) *Tourism and Biodiversity: Mapping Tourism's Global Footprint*. Washington, DC: Conservation International.

Christopher, M. and Peck, H. (2004) The five principles of supply chain resilience. *Logistics Europe* 12 (1), 16–21.

Christopherson, S., Michie, J. and Tyler, P. (2010) Regional resilience: Theoretical and empirical perspectives. *Cambridge Journal of Regions, Economy and Society* 3, 3–10.

Clarke, J. and Godfrey, K. (2002) *Manuale di Marketing territoriale per il turismo.* Florence: Le Monnier.
Cochrane, J. (2010) The sphere of tourism resilience. *Tourism Recreation Research* 35 (2), 173–185.
Coles, T., Hall, C.M. and Duval, D. (2006) Tourism and post-disciplinary inquiry. *Current Issues in Tourism* 9 (4–5), 293–319.
Coles, T.E., Hall, C.M. and Duval, D. (2016) Tourism and post-disciplinarity: Back to the future? *Tourism Analysis* 21 (4), 373–387
Comfort, L.K., Sungu, Y., Johnson, D. and Dunn, M. (2001) Complex systems in crisis: Anticipation and resilience in dynamic environments. *Journal of Contingencies and Crisis Management* 9 (3), 144–158.
Compact (2015) *Southeast Florida Regional Compact: Climate Change.* See http://www.southeastfloridaclimatecompact.org/wp-content/uploads/2015/10/2015 (accessed 1 April).
Concepción, E.D., Moretti, M., Altermatt, F., Nobis, M. and Obrist, M. (2015) Impacts of urbanisation on biodiversity: The role of species mobility, degree of specialisation and spatial scale. *Oikos* 124 (12), 1571–1582.
Connor, K.M. and Davidson, J.R. (2003) Development of a new resilience scale: The Connor–Davidson resilience scale (CD-RISC). *Depression and Anxiety* 18 (2), 76–82.
Cooke, F.L., Cooper, B., Bartram, T., Wang, J. and Mei, H. (2016) Mapping the relationships between high-performance work systems, employee resilience and engagement: A study of the banking industry in China. *International Journal of Human Resource Management*; doi:10.1080/09585192.2015.1137618.
Cox, C. and Moore, P. (2010) *Biogeography: An Ecological and Evolutionary Approach* (8th edn). Hoboken, NJ: John Wiley.
Cox, G.W. (2004) *Alien Species and Evolution: The Evolutionary Ecology of Exotic Plants, Animals, Microbes and Interacting Native Species.* Washington, DC: Island Press.
Cutter, S.L. and Finch, C. (2008) Temporal and spatial changes in social vulnerability to natural hazards. *Proceedings of the National Academy of Sciences* 105 (7), 2301–2306.
Cutter, S.L., Barnes, L., Berry, M., Burton, C., Evans, E., Tate, E. and Webb, J. (2008) A place-based model for understanding community resilience to natural disasters. *Global Environmental Change* 18 (4), 598–606.
Cutter, S.L., Burton, C. and Emrich, C. (2010) Disaster resilience indicators for benchmarking baseline conditions. *Journal of Homeland Security and Emergency Management* 7 (1); doi:10.2202/1547-7355.1732.
Cutter, S.L., Ash, K. and Emrich, C. (2014) The geographies of community disaster resilience. *Global Environmental Change* 29, 65–77.
Dahles, H. and Susilowati, T.-P. (2015) Business resilience in times of growth and crisis. *Annals of Tourism Research* 51, 34–50.
Daily, G. and Matson, P. (2008) Ecosystem services: From theory to implementation. *Proceedings of the National Academy of Sciences* 105, 9455–9456.
Dalziell, E.P. and McManus, S.T. (2004) Resilience, vulnerability, and adaptive capacity: Implications for system performance. Paper presented at the International Forum for Engineering Decision Making (IFED), Stoos, Switzerland, 6–8 December.
Davoudi, S., Shaw, K., Haider, L., *et al.* (2012) Resilience: A bridging concept or a dead end? 'Reframing' resilience: Challenges for planning theory and practice. Interacting traps: Resilience assessment of a pasture management system in Northern Afghanistan. Urban resilience: What does it mean in planning practice? Resilience as a useful concept for climate change adaptation? The politics of resilience for planning: A cautionary note. Edited by Simin Davoudi and Libby Porter. *Planning Theory & Practice* 13 (2), 299–333.

Davydov, D.M., Stewart, R., Ritchie, K. and Chaudieu, I. (2010) Resilience and mental health. *Clinical Psychology Review* 30 (5), 479–495.

Deutsch, L., Folke, C. and Skanberg, K. (2003) The critical natural capital of ecosystem performance as insurance for human well-being. *Ecological Economics* 44, 205–217.

de Vries, H. and Hamilton, R. (2016) Why stay? The resilience of small firms in Christchurch and their owners. In C.M. Hall, S. Malinen, R. Vosslamber and R. Wordsworth (eds) *Business and Post-Disaster Management: Business, Organisational and Consumer Resilience and the Christchurch Earthquakes* (pp. 23–34). Abingdon: Routledge.

Dodds, W.K. (2009) *Laws, Patterns and Theories in Ecology*. Berkeley, CA: University of California Press.

Doerfel, M.L., Lai, C.H. and Chewning, L.V. (2010) The evolutionary role of interorganizational communication: Modeling social capital in disaster contexts. *Human Communication Research* 36 (2), 125–162.

Doern, R. (2016) Entrepreneurship and crisis management: The experiences of small businesses during the London 2011 riots. *International Small Business Journal* 34 (3), 276–302.

Dovers, S.R. and Handmer, J.W. (1992) Uncertainty, sustainability and change. *Global Environmental Change* 2 (4), 262–276.

Dredge, D. (2015) *Short-term versus Long-term Approaches to the Development of Tourism-related Policies*. Paris: OECD Publishing.

Eakin, H., Benessaiah, K., Barrera, J.F., Cruz-Bello, G.M. and Morales, H. (2012) Livelihoods and landscapes at the threshold of change: Disaster and resilience in a Chiapas coffee community. *Regional Environmental Change* 12 (3), 475–488.

Edmondson, A. (1999) Psychological safety and learning behaviour in work teams. *Administrative Science Quarterly* 44 (2), 350–383.

Eijgelaar, E., Thaper, C. and Peeters, P. (2010) Antarctic cruise tourism: The paradoxes of ambassadorship, 'last chance tourism' and greenhouse gas emissions. *Journal of Sustainable Tourism* 18, 337–354.

Elkington, J. (1997) *Cannibals with Forks. The Triple Bottom Line of 21st Century Business*. Oxford: Capstone.

Elliott, L. (2017) The new robot revolution will take the boss's job – not the gardener's. *The Guardian*, 22 January.

Ellis, E.C., Goldewijk, K., Siebert, S., Lightman, D. and Ramankutty, N. (2010) Anthropogenic transformation of the biomes, 1700 to 2000. *Global Ecology and Biogeography* 19 (5), 589–606.

Elmqvist, T., Barnett, G. and Wilkinson, C. (2014) Exploring urban sustainability and resilience. In L.J. Pearson, P.W. Newman and P. Roberts (eds) *Resilient Sustainable Cities: A Future* (pp. 19–28). New York: Routledge.

Engemann, K.J. and Henderson, D.M. (2011) *Business Continuity and Risk Management: Essentials of Organizational Resilience*. Brookfield, CT: Rothstein.

Ernston, H. (2008) In Rhizomia – actors, networks and resilience in urban landscapes. Doctoral dissertation, Department of Systems Ecology, Stockholm University.

Evans, J.P. (2011) Resilience, ecology and adaptation in the experimental city. *Transactions of the Institute of British Geographers* 36, 223–237.

Farrell, B.H. and Twining-Ward, L. (2004) Reconceptualizing tourism. *Annals of Tourism Research* 31 (2), 274–295.

Farrell, B. and Twining-Ward, L. (2005) Seven steps towards sustainability: Tourism in the context of new knowledge. *Journal of Sustainable Tourism* 13 (2), 109–122.

Faulkner, B. (2001) Towards a framework for tourism disaster management. *Tourism Management* 22 (2), 135–147.

Fiksel, J. (2006) Sustainability and resilience: Toward a systems approach. *Sustainability: Science, Practice, & Policy* 2 (2), 14–21.
Finsterwalder, J. and Hall, C.M. (2016) Disasters, urban regeneration and the temporality of servicescapes. In C.M. Hall, S. Malinen, R. Vosslamber and R. Wordsworth (eds) *Business and Post-disaster Management: Business, Organisational and Consumer Resilience and the Christchurch Earthquakes* (pp. 230–249). Abingdon: Routledge.
Folke, C. (2006) Resilience: The emergence of a perspective for social–ecological systems analyses. *Global Environmental Change* 16 (3), 253–267.
Folke, C., Colding, J. and Berkes, F. (2003) Synthesis: Building resilience and adaptive capacity in socio-ecological systems. In F. Berkes, J. Colding and C. Folke (eds) *Navigating Social–Ecological Systems. Building Resilience for Complexity and Change* (pp. 352–387). Cambridge: Cambridge University Press.
Folke, C., Carpenter, S.R., Walker, B., Scheffer, M., Chapin, T. and Rockstrom, J. (2010) Resilience thinking: Integrating resilience, adaptability and transformability. *Ecology & Society* 15 (4), 20.
Folkman, S. and Moskowitz, J.T. (2004) Coping: Pitfalls and promise. *Annual Review of Psychology* 55, 745–774.
Foster, S.P. and Dye, K. (2005) Building continuity into strategy. *Journal of Corporate Real Estate* 7 (2), 105–119.
Fredrickson, B.L., Tugade, M.M., Waugh, C.E. and Larkin, G.R. (2003) What good are positive emotions in crisis? A prospective study of resilience and emotions following the terrorist attacks on the United States on September 11th, 2001. *Journal of Personality and Social Psychology* 84 (2), 365–376.
Gallopín, G.C. (2006) Linkages between vulnerability, resilience, and adaptive capacity. *Global Environmental Change* 16 (3), 293–303.
Gallucci, M. (2014) Miami's tourism industry isn't ready for dramatic effects of climate change. *Skift*. See http://skift.com/2014/04/22/miamis-tourism-industry-isnt-ready-for-dramatic-effects-of-climate-change/ (accessed 22 April).
GBRMA (2007) *Great Barrier Reef Climate Change Action Plan 2007–2011*. Townsville, QLD: Great Barrier Reef Marine Authority.
Geels, F.W. and Schot, J. (2007) Typology of sociotechnical transition pathways. *Research Policy* 36, 399–417
Ghaderi, Z., Mat Som, A.P. and Henderson, J.C. (2012) Tourism crises and island destinations: Experiences in Penang, Malaysia. *Tourism Management Perspectives* 2, 79–84.
Ghaderi, Z., Mat Som, A.P. and Henderson, J.C. (2015) When disaster strikes: The Thai floods of 2011 and tourism industry response and resilience. *Asia Pacific Journal of Tourism Research* 20 (4), 399–415.
Gibbs, L., Waters, E., Bryant, R.A., Pattison, P., Lusher, D., Harms, L. and Forbes, D. (2013) Beyond bushfires: Community, resilience and recovery – a longitudinal mixed method study of the medium to long term impacts of bushfires on mental health and social connectedness. *BMC Public Health* 13 (1), 1036.
Gilbert, D. and Abdullah, J. (2004) Holidaytaking and the sense of well-being. *Annals of Tourism Research* 31 (1), 103–121.
Gillespie, B.M., Chaboyer, W., Wallis, M. and Grimbeek, P. (2007) Resilience in the operating room: Developing and testing of a resilience model. *Journal of Advanced Nursing* 59 (4), 427–438.
Glasson, J., Therivel, R. and Chadwick, A. (2005) *Introduction to Environmental Impact Assessment: Principles and Procedures, Process, Practice and Prospects* (3rd edn). London: Routledge.

Glassop, L. (2007) The three Rs of resilience: Redundancy, requisite variety and resources. In R. Kay and K.A. Richardson (eds) *Building and Sustaining Resilience in Complex Organisations. International Workshop on Complexity and Organizational Resilience* (pp. 19–34). Marblehead, MA: ISCE Publishing.

GoAbroad.com (2016) *Volunteer Abroad in Christchurch*. See http://www.goabroad.com/volunteer-abroad/search/new-zealand/christchurch/volunteer-abroad-1 (accessed 1 April).

Godschalk, D.R. (2003) Urban hazard mitigation: Creating resilient cities. *Natural Hazards Review* 4 (3), 136–143.

Goldewijk, K.K., Beusen, A., van Drecht, G. and de Vos, M. (2011) The HYDE 3.1 spatially explicit database of human-induced global land-use change over the past 12,000 years. *Global Ecology and Biogeography* 20 (1), 73–86.

Gooch, M. and Warburton, J. (2009) Building and managing resilience in community-based NRM groups: An Australian case study. *Society and Natural Resources* 22 (2), 158–171.

Goodwin, H. and Font, X. (2012) *Progress in Responsible Tourism*. Oxford: Goodfellow.

GoOverseas (2016) *Volunteer in Sri Lanka*. See https://www.gooverseas.com/volunteer-abroad/sri-lanka (accessed 1 April).

Gorica, K. (2008) The evolution capacity of small and medium enterprises sector. In *Proceedings of the 1st International Conference on Tourism and Hospitality Management, 13–15 June 2008, Athens, Greece* (pp. 259–270). Athens: Tourism Research Institute.

Gössling, S. (2002) Global environmental consequences of tourism. *Global Environmental Change* 12, 283–302.

Gössling, S. (2010) *Carbon Management in Tourism: Mitigating the Impacts on Climate Change*. London: Routledge.

Gössling, S., Garrod, B., Aall, C., Hille, J. and Peeters, P. (2011) Food management in tourism: Reducing tourism's carbon 'foodprint'. *Tourism Management* 32, 534–543.

Gössling, S., Peeters, P., Hall, C.M., Dubois, G., Ceron, J.P., Lehmann, L. and Scott, D. (2012) Tourism and water use: Supply, demand, and security, an international review. *Tourism Management* 33, 1–15.

Gössling, S., Scott, D. and Hall, C.M. (2013) Challenges of tourism in a low-carbon economy. *WIREs Climate Change* 4 (6), 525–538.

Gössling, S., Hall, C.M. and Scott, D. (2015) *Tourism and Water*. Bristol: Channel View Publications.

Gotham, K.F. (2007) (Re)branding the Big Easy: Tourism rebuilding in post-Katrina New Orleans. *Urban Affairs Review* 42 (6), 823–850.

Gotham, K.F. and Greenberg, M. (2014) *Crisis Cities: Disaster and Redevelopment in New York and New Orleans*. New York: Oxford University Press.

Greenpeace (2014) Govt report whitewashes damage to Great Barrier Reef to avoid World Heritage 'In Danger' listing. Media release. Canberra: Greenpeace Australia.

Grimm, V. and Calabrese, J.M. (2011) What is resilience? A short introduction. In G. Deffuant and N. Gilbert (eds) *Viability and Resilience of Complex Systems: Concepts, Methods and Case Studies from Ecology and Society* (pp. 3–13). Heidelberg: Springer.

Grimm, V. and Wissel, C. (1997) Babel, or the ecological stability discussions: An inventory and analysis of terminology and a guide for avoiding confusion. *Oecologia* 109, 323–334.

Grimm, V., Revilla, E., Berger, U., Jeltsch, F., Mooij, W.M., Railsback, S.F., Thulk, H.H., Weiner, J., Wiegand, T. and DeAngelis, D.L. (2005) Pattern-oriented modeling of agent-based complex systems: Lessons from ecology. *Science* 310, 987–991.

Gunderson, L. (2000) Ecological resilience – in theory and application. *Annual Review of Ecological Systems* 31, 425–439.

Gunderson, L.H. and Holling, C.S. (eds) (2002) *Panarchy: Understanding Transformations in Human and Natural Systems*. Washington, DC: Island Press.

Gunderson, L.H., Holling, C.S., Pritchard, L. and Peterson, G.D. (2002) Resilience of large-scale resource systems. In L.H. Gunderson and L. Pritchard (eds) *Resilience and the Behavior of Large-scale Systems*. SCOPE (Scientific Committee on Problems of the Environment International Council of Scientific Unions) Vol. 60 (pp. 3–20). Washington, DC: Island Press.

Gurtner, Y.K. (2007) Phuket: Tsunami and tourism – a preliminary investigation. In E. Laws, B. Prideaux and K. Chon (eds) *Crisis Management in Tourism* (pp. 217–235). Wallingford: CABI.

Hajibaba, H., Gretzel, U., Leisch, F. and Dolnicar, S. (2015) Crisis-resistant tourists. *Annals of Tourism Research* 53, 46–60.

Hall, C.M. (2002) Travel safety, terrorism and the media: The significance of the issue–attention cycle. *Current Issues in Tourism* 5 (5), 458–466.

Hall, C.M. (2004) Scale and the problems of assessing mobility in time and space. Paper presented at the Swedish National Doctoral Student Course on Tourism, Mobility and Migration, hosted by Department of Social and Economic Geography, October, University of Umeå, Sweden.

Hall, C.M. (2006) Tourism urbanization and global environmental change. In S. Gössling and C.M. Hall (eds) *Tourism and Global Environmental Change: Ecological, Economic, Social and Political Interrelationships*. Abingdon: Routledge.

Hall, C.M. (2008) *Tourism Planning: Policies, Processes and Relationships*. New York: Pearson/Prentice Hall.

Hall, C.M. (2009) Degrowing tourism: Décroissance, sustainable consumption and steady-state tourism. *Anatolia* 20 (1), 46–61.

Hall, C.M. (2010a) Tourism and biodiversity: More significant than climate change? *Journal of Heritage Tourism* 5 (4), 253–266.

Hall, C.M. (2010b) Tourism and the implementation of the Convention on Biological Diversity. *Journal of Heritage Tourism* 5 (4), 267–284.

Hall, C.M. (2010c) Crisis events in tourism: Subjects of crisis in tourism. *Current Issues in Tourism* 13 (5), 401–417.

Hall, C.M. (2011) A typology of governance and its implications for tourism policy analysis. *Journal of Sustainable Tourism* 19 (4–5), 437–457.

Hall, C.M. (2012) Island, islandness, vulnerability and resilience. *Tourism Recreation Research* 37 (2), 177–181.

Hall, C.M. (2014) *Tourism and Social Marketing*. Abingdon: Routledge.

Hall, C.M. (2015) Global change, islands and sustainable development: Islands of sustainability or analogues of the challenge of sustainable development? In M. Redclift and D. Springett (eds) *Routledge International Handbook of Sustainable Development*. Abingdon: Routledge.

Hall, C.M. (2016a) Putting ecological thinking back into disaster ecology and responses to natural disasters. In C.M. Hall, S. Malinen, R. Vosslamber and R. Wordsworth (eds) *Business and Post-Disaster Management: Business, Organisational and Consumer Resilience and the Christchurch Earthquakes* (pp. 269–292). Abingdon: Routledge.

Hall, C.M. (2016b) Tourism and resilience. Paper presented at Linneaus University, Kalmar, Sweden, 4 November.

Hall, C.M. (2016c) Intervening in academic interventions: Framing social marketing's potential for successful sustainable tourism behavioural change. *Journal of Sustainable Tourism* 24 (3), 350–375.

Hall, C.M. (2017) The challenges of changing the paradigms, regimes and structures of low-carbon mobility. In D. Hopkins and J. Higham (eds) *Low-carbon Mobility Transitions* (pp. 91–103). Oxford: Goodfellows.

Hall, C.M. (2018) Resilience in tourism: Development, theory and application. In J.M. Cheer and A. Lew (eds) *Tourism, Resilience and Sustainability: Adapting to Social, Political and Economic Change* (pp. 18–33). Abingdon: Routledge.

Hall, C.M. and Lew, A. (2009) *Understanding and Managing Tourism Impacts: An Integrated Approach*. Abingdon: Routledge.

Hall, C.M. and Page, S.J. (2010) The contribution of Neil Leiper to Tourism Studies. *Current Issues in Tourism* 13 (4), 299–309.

Hall, C.M. and Saarinen, J. (2010) Geotourism and climate change: Paradoxes and promises of geotourism in polar regions. *Téoros* 29 (2), 77–86.

Hall, C.M. and Veer, E. (2016) The DMO is dead. Long live the DMO (Or, why DMO managers don't care about post-structuralism). *Tourism Recreation Research* 41 (3), 354–357.

Hall, C.M. & Williams, A. (2008) *Tourism and Innovation*. London: Routledge.

Hall, C.M., Malinen, S., Vosslamber, R. and Wordsworth, R. (2016a) Introduction: The business, organisational and destination impacts of natural disasters – the Christchurch earthquakes 2010-2011. In C.M. Hall, S. Malinen, R. Vosslamber and R. Wordsworth (eds) *Business and Post-Disaster Management: Business, Organisational and Consumer Resilience and the Christchurch Earthquakes* (pp. 3–20). Abingdon: Routledge.

Hall, C.M., Malinen, S., Vosslamber, R. and Wordsworth, R. (eds) (2016b) *Business and Post-Disaster Management: Business, Organisational and Consumer Resilience and the Christchurch Earthquakes*. Abingdon: Routledge.

Hall, C.M., Le-Klähn, D.-T. and Ram, Y. (2017) *Tourism, Public Transport and Sustainable Mobility*, Bristol: Channel View Publications.

Hall, P.A. and Lamont, M. (eds) (2009) *Successful Societies: How Institutions and Culture Affect Health*. Cambridge: Cambridge University Press.

Hall, P.A. and Lamont, M. (eds) (2013) *Social Resilience in the Neoliberal Era*. Cambridge: Cambridge University Press.

Harland, L., Harrison, W., Jones, J.R. and Reiter-Palmon, R. (2005) Leadership behaviors and subordinate resilience. *Journal of Leadership & Organizational Studies* 11 (2), 2–14.

Hartman, C. and Squires, G. (eds) (2006) *There is No Such Thing as a Natural Disaster: Race, Class, and Hurricane Katrina*. New York: Routledge.

Hatton, T. (2013) What happened to Christchurch CBD retailers? Paper presented at the 'Creating Resilience for a Hazardous World' Resilient Organizations Symposium, University of Canterbury, Christchurch, New Zealand.

Hayward, B. (2013) Rethinking resilience: reflections on the earthquakes in Christchurch, New Zealand, 2010 and 2011. *Ecology and Society* 18 (4), 34–42.

Haxton, P. (2015) *A Review of Effective Policies for Tourism Growth*. Paris: OECD Publishing.

Hegney, D.G., Buikstra, E., Baker, P., Rogers-Clark, C., Pearce, S., Ross, H., King, C. and Watson-Luke, A. (2007) Individual resilience in rural people: A Queensland study, Australia. *Rural and Remote Health* 7 (4), 1–13.

Herbane, B. (2010) The evolution of business continuity management: A historical review of practices and drivers. *Business History* 52 (6), 978–1002.

Higgins-Desbiolles, F. (2011a) Death by a thousand cuts: Governance and environmental trade-offs in ecotourism development at Kangaroo Island, South Australia. *Journal of Sustainable Tourism* 19 (4–5), 553–570.

Higgins-Desbiolles, F. (2011b) Development of Kangaroo Island: The controversy over Southern Ocean Lodge. In D. Dredge and J. Jenkins (eds) *Stories of Practice: Tourism Policy and Planning* (pp. 105–132). Burlington, VT: Ashgate.

Hjemdal, O., Friborg, O., Martinussen, M. and Rosenvinge, J.H. (2001) Preliminary results from the development and validation of a Norwegian scale for measuring adult resilience. *Journal of the Norwegian Psychological Association* 38 (4), 310–317.

Hobson, K. and Essex, S. (2001) Sustainable tourism: A view from accommodation businesses. *Service Industries Journal* 21 (4), 133–146.

Holder, J.S. (1980) Buying time with tourism in the Caribbean. *International Journal of Tourism Management* 1 (2), 76–83.

Holland, J. (2014) *Complexity: A Very Short Introduction*. Oxford: Oxford University Press.

Holling, C.S. (1973) Resilience and stability of ecological systems. *Annual Review of Ecology and Systematics* 4 (1), 1–23.

Holling, C.S. (1996) Engineering resilience versus ecological resilience. In P. Schulze (ed.) *Engineering within Ecological Constraints* (pp. 31–44). Washington, DC: National Academies Press.

Holling, C.S. (2001) Understanding the complexity of economic, ecological, and social systems. *Ecosystems* 4 (5), 390–405.

Holling, C.S. (2010) Engineering resilience versus ecological resilience. In L.H. Gunderson, C.R. Allen and C.S. Holling (eds) *Foundations of Ecological Resilience* (pp. 51–66). Washington, DC: Island Press.

Holling, C.S. and Gunderson, L.H. (2002) Resilience and adaptive cycles. In L.H. Gundersson and C.S. Holling (eds) *Panarchy: Understanding Transformations in Human and Natural Systems* (pp. 25–62). Washington, DC: Island Press.

Holling, C.S., Gunderson, L.H. and Peterson, G.D. (2002) Sustainability and panarchies. In L.H. Gundersson and C.S. Holling (eds) *Panarchy: Understanding Transformations in Human and Natural Systems* (pp. 63–102). Washington, DC: Island Press.

Hollnagel, E., Pariès, J., Woods, D.D. and Leveson, N. (eds) (2006) *Resilience Engineering: Concepts and Precepts*. Aldershot: Ashgate.

Hollnagel, E., Woods, D.D. and Wreathall, J. (eds) (2011) *Resilience Engineering in Practice: A Guidebook*. Aldershot: Ashgate.

Hood, C. (1991) A public management for all seasons? *Public Administration* 69, 3–19.

Hudson, R. (2010) Resilient regions in an uncertain world: Wishful thinking or practical reality? *Cambridge Journal of Regions, Economy and Society* 3, 11–25.

Hystad, P.W. and Keller, P.C. (2008) Towards a destination tourism disaster management framework: Long-term lessons from a forest fire disaster. *Tourism Management* 29 (1), 151–162.

IPCC (2014) *Climate Change 2014: Impacts, Adaptation, and Vulnerability. Part A: Global and Sectoral Aspects. Contribution of Working Group II to the Fifth Assessment Report of the Intergovernmental Panel on Climate Change*. Cambridge: Cambridge University Press.

Ireland, R.D., Hitt, M.A. and Vaidyanath, D. (2002) Alliance management as a source of competitive advantage. *Journal of Management* 28 (3), 413–446.

Jackson, D., Firtko, A. and Edenborough, M. (2007) Personal resilience as a strategy for surviving and thriving in the face of workplace adversity: A literature review. *Journal of Advanced Nursing* 60 (1), 1–9.

Janssen, M.A. (2007) An update on the scholarly networks on resilience, vulnerability, and adaptation within the human dimensions of global environmental change. *Ecology and Society* 12 (2), 9.

Janssen, M.A., Schoon, M.L., Ke, W. and Börner, K. (2006) Scholarly networks on resilience, vulnerability and adaptation within the human dimensions of global environmental change. *Global Environmental Change* 16 (3), 240–252.

Jenson, J.M. and Fraser, M.W. (eds) (2015a) *Social Policy for Children and Families: A Risk and Resilience Perspective* (3rd edn). Thousand Oaks, CA: SAGE.

Jenson, J.M. and Fraser, M.W. (2015b) A risk and resilience framework for child, youth, and family policy. In J.M. Jenson and M.W. Fraser (eds) *Social Policy for Children and Families: A Risk and Resilience Perspective* (3rd edn) (pp. 5–24). Thousand Oaks, CA: SAGE.

Jessop, B. (2011) Metagovernance. In M. Bevir (ed.) *The SAGE Handbook of Governance* (pp. 106–123). London: Sage.

Johnson, C. (2011) *The Neoliberal Deluge: Hurricane Katrina, Late Capitalism, and the Remaking of New Orleans*. Minneapolis, MN: University of Minnesota Press.

Johnson, E. and Miyanishi, K. (2010) Disturbance and succession. In E. Johnson and K. Miyanishi (eds) *Plant Disturbance Ecology: The Process and the Response*. New York: Academic Press.

Johnson, L.A. and Olshansky, R.B. (2010) *Clear as Mud: Planning for the Rebuilding of New Orleans*. Chicago, IL: American Planning Association.

Jones, T., Wood, D., Glasson, J. and Fulton, B. (2010) Regional planning, tourism and resilient destinations: Destination modelling for sustainable tourism planning. In R.W. Spahr and F.A.F. Ferreira (ed.) *Proceedings of IASK International Conference 'Advances in Tourism Research', 9 November* (pp. 735–750). Oviedo: International Association for Scientific Knowledge.

Jopp, R., DeLacy, T. and Mair, J. (2010) Developing a framework for regional destination adaptation to climate change. *Current Issues in Tourism* 13 (6), 591–605.

Jopp, R., DeLacy, T., Mair, J. and Fluker, M. (2013) Using a regional tourism adaptation framework to determine climate change adaptation options for Victoria's surf coast. *Asia Pacific Journal of Tourism Research* 18 (2), 144–164.

Jørgensen, S.E. and Svirezhev, Y.M. (2004) *Towards a Thermodynamic Theory for Ecological Systems*. Amsterdam: Elsevier.

Joseph, J. (2013) Resilience as embedded neoliberalism: A governmentality approach. *Resilience: International Policies, Practices and Discourses* 1 (1), 38–52.

Kachali, H., Stevenson, J.R., Whitman, Z., Seville, E., Vargo, J. and Wilson, T. (2012) Organisational resilience and recovery for Canterbury organisations after the 4 September 2010 earthquake. *Australasian Journal of Disaster and Trauma Studies* 1, 11–19.

Kaufman, H. (1976) *Are Government Organizations Immortal?* Washington, DC: Brookings Institution.

King, D.D., Newman, A. and Luthans, F. (2015) Not if, but when we need resilience in the workplace. *Journal of Organizational Behavior* 37 (5), 782–786.

Kirk, A.K. and Brown, D.F. (2003) Employee assistance programs: A review of the management of stress and wellbeing through workplace counselling and consulting. *Australian Psychologist* 38 (2), 138–143.

Klein, N. (2007) *The Shock Doctrine: The Rise of Disaster Capitalism*. New York: Metropolitan Books.

Klein, R.J.T., Nicholls, R.J. and Thomalla. F. (2003) Resilience to natural hazards: How useful is this concept? *Environmental Hazards* 5 (1), 35–45.

Knaus, C. and Evershed, N. (2017) Great Barrier Reef at 'terminal stage': Scientists despair at latest coral bleaching data. *The Guardian*, 9 April.

Ladkin, A. (2011) Exploring tourism labor. *Annals of Tourism Research* 38 (3), 1135–1155.
Lande, R. (1998) Anthropogenic, ecological and genetic factors in extinction. In G.M. Mace, A. Balmford and J.R. Ginsberg (eds) *Conservation in a Changing World*. Cambridge: Cambridge University Press.
Lasswell, H. (1936) *Politics: Who Gets What, When, How?* New York: McGraw-Hill.
Lawton, L.J. and Weaver, D.B. (2015) Using residents' perceptions research to inform planning and management for sustainable tourism: A study of the Gold Coast Schoolies Week, a contentious tourism event. *Journal of Sustainable Tourism* 23 (5), 660–682.
Lee, A.V., Vargo, J. and Seville, E. (2013) Developing a tool to measure and compare organizations' resilience. *Natural Hazards Review* 14 (1), 29–41.
Leichenko, R. (2011) Climate change and urban resilience. *Current Opinion in Environmental Sustainability* 3 (3), 164–168.
Leiper, N. (1989) Tourism and tourism systems. Occasional Paper No. 1, Department of Management Systems, Massey University, New Zealand.
Leiper, N. (1990) Tourist attraction systems. *Annals of Tourism Research* 17 (3), 367–384.
Lengnick-Hall, C.A. and Beck, T.E. (2005) Adaptive fit versus robust transformation: How organizations respond to environmental change. *Journal of Management Studies* 31 (5), 738–757.
Lengnick-Hall, C.A. and Beck, T.E. (2009) Resilience capacity and strategic agility: Prerequisites for thriving in a dynamic environment. In C. Nemeth, E. Hollnagel and S. Dekker (eds) *Resilience Engineering Perspectives: Preparation and Restoration*, Vol. 2. Aldershot: Ashgate.
Lengnick-Hall, M. and Lengnick-Hall, C. (2003) *Human Resource Management in the Knowledge Economy: New Challenges, New Roles, New Capabilities*. San Francisco, CA: Berrett-Koehler.
Lengnick-Hall, C.A., Beck, T.E. and Lengnick-Hall, M.L. (2011) Developing a capacity for organizational resilience through strategic human resource management. *Human Resource Management Review* 21 (3), 243–255.
Leroy, S.A. (2006) From natural hazard to environmental catastrophe: Past and present. *Quaternary International* 158, 4–12.
Levine, P. (2014) *Testimony of the Honorable Philip Levine, Mayor of the City of Miami Beach, Florida, before the U.S. Senate Committee on Commerce, Science and Transportation Subcommittee on Science and Space*. See https://www.commerce.senate.gov/public/_cache/files/850d66f7-dd8d-4390-b5ab-92369af604c4/AB8F70C2908499494D72B558632A499D.levine-testimony.pdf (accessed 1 April).
Lew, A.A. (1987) A framework of tourist attraction research. *Annals of Tourism Research* 14 (4), 553–575.
Lew, A.A. (2014) Scale, change and resilience in community tourism planning. *Tourism Geographies* 16 (1), 14–22.
Lew, A.A., Ng, P.T., Ni, C.C. and Wu, T.C. (2016) Community sustainability and resilience: Similarities, differences and indicators. *Tourism Geographies* 18 (1), 18–27.
Lewis, D.E. (2002) The politics of agency termination: Confronting the myth of agency immortality. *Journal of Politics* 64 (1), 89–107.
Li, W., Airriess, C.A., Leon, K., Chen, A.C. and Keith, V. (2008) *Vietnamese Americans in New Orleans East: From Vietnamese Village to Asian Quarter?* Phoenix, AZ: Arizona State University.
Liao, K.-H. (2012) A theory on urban resilience to floods: A basis for alternative planning practices. *Ecology and Society* 17 (4), 48.

Lindell, M.K. and Prater, C.S. (2003) Assessing community impacts of natural disasters. *Natural Hazards Review* 4 (4), 176–185.

Liu, Y., Wang, Z.H. and Li, Z.G. (2012) Affective mediators of the influence of neuroticism and resilience on life satisfaction. *Personality and Individual Differences* 52 (7), 833–838.

Lorenz, D.F. (2013) The diversity of resilience: Contributions from a social science perspective. *Natural Hazards* 67 (1), 7–24.

Lovejoy, T.E. (1994) The quantification of biodiversity: An esoteric quest or a vital component of sustainable development? *Philosophical Transactions of the Royal Society of London. Series B: Biological Sciences* 345 (1311), 81–87.

Lucas, R. and Deery, M. (2004) Significant developments and emerging issues in human resource management. *International Journal of Hospitality Management* 23 (5), 459–472.

Luthans, F., Vogelgesang, G.R. and Lester, P.B. (2006) Developing the psychological capital of resiliency. *Human Resource Development Review* 5 (1), 25–44.

Luthans, F., Avey, J.B., Avolio, B.J. and Peterson, S.J. (2010) The development and resulting performance impact of positive psychological capital. *Human Resource Development Quarterly* 21 (1), 41–67.

Luthar, S.S. (2006) Resilience in development: A synthesis of research across five decades. In D. Cicchetti and D.J. Cohen (eds) *Development Psychopathology: Risk, Disorder and Adaptation* (pp. 740–795). New York: Wiley.

Luthar, S.S. and Cicchetti, D. (2000) The construct of resilience: Implications for interventions and social policies. *Development and Psychopathology* 12, 857–885.

Luthar, S.S., Cicchetti, D. and Becker, B. (2000) The construct of resilience: A critical evaluation and guidelines for future work. *Child Development* 71 (3), 543–562.

Luthe, T. and Wyss, R. (2014) Assessing and planning resilience in tourism. *Tourism Management* 44, 161–163.

Luthe, T. and Wyss, R. (2016) Resilience to climate change in a cross-scale tourism governance context: A combined quantitative-qualitative network analysis. *Ecology and Society* 21 (1), 27.

Ma, E., Zhang, Y. and Qu, H. (2014) Influence of the global financial crisis (GFC) on the Chinese outbound travel market: A case study of the Shanghai regional market. In B.W. Ritchie and K. Campiranon (eds) *Tourism Crisis and Disaster Management in the Asia-Pacific*. Wallingford: CABI.

Macarthur, R.H. and Wilson, E.O. (1963) An equilibrium theory of insular zoogeography. *Evolution* 17, 373–387.

Macarthur, R.H. and Wilson, E.O. (1967) *The Theory of Island Biogeography*, Princeton, NJ: Princeton University Press.

Mace, G., Masundire, H., Baillie, J., *et al.* (2005) Biodiversity. In R. Hassan, R. Scholes and N. Ash (eds) *Ecosystems and Human Well-being: Current State and Trends: Findings of the Condition and Trends Working Group*. Washington, DC: Island Press.

Mafabi, S., Munene, J.C. and Ahiauzu, A. (2015) Creative climate and organisational resilience: The mediating role of innovation. *International Journal of Organizational Analysis* 23 (4), 564–587.

Magis, K. (2010) Community resilience: An indicator of social sustainability. *Society and Natural Resources* 23 (5), 401–416.

Maguire, B. and Cartwright, S. (2008) *Assessing a Community's Capacity to Manage Change: A Resilience Approach to Social Assessment*. Canberra: Bureau of Rural Sciences.

Mahon, R., Becken, S. and Rennie, H.G. (2013) *Evaluating the Business Case for Investment in the Resilience of the Tourism Sector of Small Island Developing States. A Background Paper*

Contributing to the Global Assessment Report on Disaster Risk Reduction (GAR) 2013. Christchurch: Lincoln University.

Mair, J., Ritchie, B.W. and Walters, G. (2016) Towards a research agenda for post-disaster and post-crisis recovery strategies for tourist destinations: A narrative review. *Current Issues in Tourism* 19 (1), 1–26.

Mallak, L. (1998a) Putting organizational resilience to work. *Industrial Management* 40 (6), 8–13.

Mallak, L.A. (1998b) Measuring resilience in health care provider organizations. *Health Manpower Management* 24 (4), 148–152.

Martens, P., Rotmans, J. and de Groot, D. (2003) Biodiversity: Luxury or necessity? *Global Environmental Change* 13, 75–81.

Masten, A.S. (1999) Commentary: The promise and perils of resilience research as a guide to preventive interventions. In M.D. Glanz and J.L. Johnson (eds) *Resilience and development: Positive life adaptations* (pp. 251–257). New York: Plenum Press.

Masten, A.S. (2007) Resilience in developing systems: Progress and promise as the fourth wave rises. *Development and Psychopathology* 19 (3), 921–930.

Masten, A.S. (2010) Ordinary magic: Lessons from research on resilience in human development. *Education Canada* 49, 28–32.

Masten, A.S. and Powell, J.L. (2003) A resilience framework for research, policy, and practice. In S.S. Luthar (ed.) *Resilience and Vulnerability: Adaptation in the Context of Childhood Adversities* (pp. 1–25). New York: Cambridge University Press.

Masten, A.S., Best, K.M. and Gaemezy, N. (1990) Resilience and development: Contributions from the study of children who overcome adversity. *Development and Psychopathology* 2 (4), 425–444.

Matyas, D. and Pelling, M. (2014) Positioning resilience for 2015: The role of resistance, incremental adjustment and transformation in disaster risk management policy. *Disasters* 39 (Suppl. I), S1–S18.

McCabe, S. and Johnson, S. (2013) The happiness factor in tourism: Subjective well-being and social tourism. *Annals of Tourism Research* 41, 42–65.

McEvoy, D., Fünfgeld, H. and Bosomworth, K. (2013) Resilience and climate change adaptation: The importance of framing. *Planning Practice and Research* 28 (3), 280–293.

McKercher, B. (1999) A chaos approach to tourism. *Tourism Management* 20 (4), 425–434.

McKinsey Global Institute (2017) *A Future That Works: Automation, Employment, and Productivity.* San Francisco, CA: McKinsey.

McLennan, C.L.J., Moyle, B.D., Ruhanen, L.M. and Ritchie, B.W. (2013) Developing and testing a suite of institutional indices to underpin the measurement and management of tourism destination transformation. *Tourism Analysis* 18 (2), 157–171.

McManus, S. (2008) Organisational resilience in New Zealand. PhD thesis, University of Canterbury, Christchurch, New Zealand.

McManus, S., Seville, E., Vargo, J. and Brunsdon, D. (2008) Facilitated process for improving organizational resilience. *Natural Hazards Review* 9 (2), 81–90.

Méheux, K. and Parker, E. (2006) Tourist sector perceptions of natural hazards in Vanuatu and the implications for a small island developing state. *Tourism Management* 27 (1), 69–85.

Meerow, S. and Newell, J.P. (2015) Resilience and complexity: A bibliometric review and prospects for industrial ecology. *Journal of Industrial Ecology* 19 (2), 236–251.

Meerow, S. and Newell, J.P. (2016) Urban resilience for whom, what, when, where, and why? *Urban Geography*; doi:10.1080/02723638.2016.1206395.

Meerow, S., Newell, J.P. and Stults, M. (2016) Defining urban resilience: A review. *Landscape and Urban Planning* 147, 38–49.

Méheux, K. and Parker, E. (2006) Tourist sector perceptions of natural hazards in Vanuatu and the implications for a small island developing state. *Tourism Management* 27 (1), 69–85.

Meyer, A.D. (1982) Adapting to environmental jolts. *Administrative Science Quarterly* 27 (4), 515–537.

Mileti, D.S. (1999) *Disasters by Design: A Reassessment of Natural Hazards in the United States*. Washington, DC: Joseph Henry Press.

Milman, O. (2015) Great Barrier Reef: Australia says Unesco decision shows it is a 'world leader'. *The Guardian*. See http://www.theguardian.com/environment/2015/jul/02/great-barrier-reef-australia-says-unesco-decision-shows-it-is-a-world-leader (accessed 2 July).

Milman, O. (2017) Climate change in the US: The dangers and the solutions. Atlantic City and Miami Beach: Two takes on tackling the rising waters. *The Guardian*, 20 March.

Montpetit, M.A., Bergeman, C.S., Deboeck, P.R., Tiberio, S.S. and Boker, S.M. (2010) Resilience-as-process: Negative affect, stress, and coupled dynamical systems. *Psychology and Aging* 25 (3), 631–640.

Moorhouse, A. and Caltabiano, M.L. (2007) Resilience and unemployment: Exploring risk and protective influences for the outcome variables of depression and assertive job searching. *Journal of Employment Counseling* 44 (3), 115–125.

Mora, S. (2009) Disasters are not natural: Risk management, a tool for development. In M. Culshaw, H. Reeves, I. Jefferson and T. Spink (eds) *Engineering Geology for Tomorrow's Cities*. Engineering Geology Special Publications Vol. 22. London: Geological Society.

Moreno, A. and Becken, S. (2009) A climate change vulnerability assessment methodology for coastal tourism. *Journal of Sustainable Tourism* 17 (4), 473–488.

Morgeson, F.P. and Hofmann, D.A. (1999) The structure and function of collective constructs: Implications for multilevel research and theory development. *Academy of Management Review* 24 (2), 249–265.

Mumby, P.J. and Steneck, R.S. (2008) Coral reef management and conservation in light of rapidly-evolving ecological paradigms. *Trends in Ecology & Evolution* 23, 555–563.

Mumby, P.J., Hastings, A. and Edwards, H.J. (2007) Thresholds and the resilience of Caribbean coral reefs. *Nature* 450, 98–101.

Mumby, P.J., Steneck, R.S. and Hastings, A. (2013) Evidence for and against the existence of alternate attractors on coral reefs. *Oikos* 122, 481–491.

Murphy, P.E. and Bayley, R. (1989) Tourism and disaster planning. *Geographical Review* 79 (1), 36–46.

Müller, F., Bergmann, M., Dannowski, R., *et al.* (2016) Assessing resilience in long-term ecological data sets. *Ecological Indicators* 65, 10–43.

Näswall, K., Kuntz, J., Hodliffe, M. and Malinen, S. (2013) Employee Resilience Scale (EmpRes): Technical report. Research Report 2013/06, Resilient Organisations, Christchurch.

Ndou, V. and Petti, C. (2006) Approaching tourism as a complex dynamic system: Implications and insights. In M. Hitz, M. Sigala and J. Murphy (eds) *Information and Communication Technologies in Tourism 2006* (pp. 26–26). Vienna: Springer Vienna.

Neal, J.D., Sirgy, M.J. and Uysal, M. (1999) The role of satisfaction with leisure travel/tourism services and experience in satisfaction with leisure life and overall life. *Journal of Business Research* 44 (3), 153–163.

Nelson, D.R., Adger, N. and Brown, K. (2007) Adaptation to environmental change: Contributions of a resilience framework. *Annual Review of Environment and Resources* 32, 395–419.

Nelson, R., Kokic, P., Crimp, S., Martin, P., Meinke, H., Howden, S.M., de Voili, P. and Nidumolu, U. (2010) The vulnerability of Australian rural communities to climate variability and change: Part II – integrating impacts with adaptive capacity. *Environmental Science & Policy* 13 (1), 18–27.

Nicholls, R. and Tol, R. (2006) Impacts and responses to sea-level rise: A global analysis of the SRES scenarios over the twenty-first century. *Philosophical Transactions of the Royal Society of London. Series A* 364, 1073–1095.

Nilakant, V., Walker, B., Rochford, K. and van Heugten, K. (2013) Leading in a post-disaster setting: A guide for human resource practitioners. *New Zealand Journal of Employment Relations* 38 (1), 1–14.

Nilakant, V., Walker, B., van Heugten, K., Baird, R. and de Vries, H. (2014) Research note: Conceptualising adaptive resilience using grounded theory. *New Zealand Journal of Employment Relations (Online)* 39 (1), 79.

Nilakant, V., Walker, B., Kuntz, J., de Vries, H., Malinen, S., Näswall, K. and van Heugten, K. (2016) Dynamics of organisational response to a disaster: A study of organisations impacted by earthquakes. In C.M. Hall, S. Malinen, R. Vosslamber and R. Wordsworth (eds) *Business and Post-Disaster Management: Business, Organisational and Consumer Resilience and the Christchurch Earthquakes* (pp. 35–47). Abingdon: Routledge.

Njoroge, J.M. (2014) An enhanced framework for regional tourism sustainable adaptation to climate change. *Tourism Management Perspectives* 12, 23–30.

Norris, F.H., Stevens, S.P., Pfefferbaum, B., Wyche, K.F. and Pfefferbaum, R.L. (2008) Community resilience as a metaphor, theory, set of capacities, and strategy for disaster readiness. *American Journal of Community Psychology* 41 (1–2), 127–150.

Nyaupane, G.P. and Chhetri, N. (2009) Vulnerability to climate change of nature-based tourism in the Nepalese Himalayas. *Tourism Geographies* 11 (1), 95–119.

Obama, B.H. (2011) *National Strategy for Counterterrorism*. Washington, DC: The White House.

Obradović, J. (2010) Effortful control and adaptive functioning of homeless children: Variable-focused and person-focused analyses. *Journal of Applied Developmental Psychology* 31, 109–117.

O'Dougherty Wright, M., Masten, A.S. and Narayan, A.J. (2013) Resilience processes in development: Four waves of research on positive adaption in the context of adversity. In S. Goldstein and R.B. Brooks (eds) *Handbook of Resilience in Children* (pp. 15–38). Boston, MA: Springer.

OECD (2013) Effective policies for growth. In *Progress Report, Annex 2, Competing Demands for Scarce Resources: A Discussion Paper*. Paris: Organisation for Economic Co-operation and Development.

O'Hare, G. and Barrett, H. (1994) Effects of market fluctuations on the Sri Lankan tourist industry: Resilience and change, 1981–1991. *Tijdschrift voor Economische en Sociale Geografie* 85 (1), 39–52.

Olsson, C.A., Bond, L., Burns, J.M., Vella-Brodrick, D.A. and Sawyer, S.M. (2003) Adolescent resilience: A concept analysis. *Journal of Adolescence* 26, 1–11.

Ong, A.D., Edwards, L.M. and Bergeman, C.S. (2006) Hope as a source of resilience in later adulthood. *Personality and Individual Differences* 41 (7), 1263–1273.

Orchiston, C. (2012) Seismic risk scenario planning and sustainable tourism management: Christchurch and the Alpine Fault zone, South Island, New Zealand. *Journal of Sustainable Tourism* 20 (1), 59–79.

Orchiston, C. (2013) Tourism business preparedness, resilience and disaster planning in a region of high seismic risk: The case of the Southern Alps, New Zealand. *Current Issues in Tourism* 16 (5), 477–494.

Orchiston, C. and Higham, J.E.S. (2016) Knowledge management and tourism recovery (de)marketing: The Christchurch earthquakes 2010–2011. *Current Issues in Tourism* 19 (1), 64–84.

Orchiston, C., Vargo, J. and Seville, E. (2013) Impacts of the Christchurch earthquakes on regional tourism activity. Paper presented at the CAUTHE Conference, 'Tourism and Global Change: On the Edge of Something Big', Christchurch, New Zealand.

Orchiston, C., Prayag, G. and Brown, C. (2016) Organizational resilience in the tourism sector. *Annals of Tourism Research* 56, 145–148.

Otto, S.P. and Day, T. (2007) *A Biologist's Guide to Mathematical Modeling in Ecology and Evolution*. Princeton: Princeton University Press.

Pahl-Wostl, C. (2000) Ecosystems as dynamic networks. In S.E. Jørgensen and F. Müller (eds) *Handbook of Ecosystem Theories and Management* (pp. 317–343). Boca Raton, FL: Lewis.

Pangallo, A., Zibarras, L., Lewis, R. and Flaxman, P. (2015) Resilience through the lens of interactionism: A systematic review. *Psychological Assessment* 27 (1), 1–20.

Pasteur, K. (2011) *From Vulnerability to Resilience: A Framework for Analysis and Action to Build Community Resilience*. Rugby: Practical Action.

Paton, D. and Johnston, D. (2001) Disasters and communities: Vulnerability, resilience and preparedness. *Disaster Prevention and Management* 10 (4), 270–277.

Paton, D., Smith, L. and Violanti, J. (2000) Disasters response: Risk, vulnerabilities and resilience. *Disaster Prevention and Management* 9 (3), 173–179.

Pavard, B. and Dugdale, J. (2006) The contribution of complexity theory to the study of socio-technical cooperative systems. In A.A. Minai and Y. Bar-Yam (eds) *Unifying Themes in Complex Systems* (pp. 39–48). Berlin: Springer.

Pelling, M. (2003a) Paradigms of risk. In M. Pelling (ed.) *Natural Disasters and Development in a Globalizing World* (pp. 1–16). London: Routledge.

Pelling, M. (2003b) *The Vulnerability of Cities: Natural Disasters and Social Resilience*. London: Earthscan.

Pendall, R., Foster, K. and Cowell, M. (2010) Resilience and regions: Building understanding of the metaphor. *Cambridge Journal of Regions, Economy and Society* 3, 71–84.

Petrucci, O. (2012) Assessment of the impact caused by natural disasters: Simplified procedures and open problems. In J.P. Tiefenbacher (ed.) *Managing Disasters, Assessing Hazards, Emergencies and Disaster Impacts*. Rijeka: InTech (open access). See http://www.intechopen.com/books/approaches-to-managing-disaster-assessing-hazards-emergencies-and-disaster-impacts (accessed 1 April).

Pickett, S.T. and White, P. (1985) Natural disturbance and patch dynamics: An introduction. In S.T. Pickett and P. White (eds) *The Ecology of Natural Disturbance and Patch Dynamics*. Orlando, FL: Academic Press.

Pimm, S.L. (1984) The complexity and stability of ecosystems. *Nature* 307 (5949), 321–326.

Pimm, S.L., Russell, G., Gittleman, J. and Brooks, T. (1995) The future of biodiversity. *Science* 269, 347–350.

Pimm, S.L., Jenkins, C., Abell, R., *et al.* (2014) The biodiversity of species and their rates of extinction, distribution, and protection. *Science* 344 (6187), 987–988.

Pizzo, B. (2015) Problematizing resilience: Implications for planning theory and practice. *Cities* 43, 133–140.

Plog, S.C. (1991) A carpenter's tools re-visited: Measuring allocentrism and psychocentrism properly ... the first time. *Journal of Travel Research* 29 (4), 51.
Ponis, S.T. and Koronis, E. (2012) Supply chain resilience: Definition of concept and its formative elements. *Journal of Applied Business Research* 28 (5), 921–929.
Prach, K. and Walker, L. (2011) Four opportunities for studies of ecological succession. *Trends in Ecology & Evolution* 26 (3), 119–123.
Pratt, G.A. (2015) Is a Cambrian explosion coming for robotics? *Journal of Economic Perspectives* 29 (3), 51–60.
Prayag, G. and Orchiston, C. (2016) Earthquake impacts, mitigation, and organisational resilience of business sectors in Canterbury. In C.M. Hall, S. Malinen, R. Vosslamber and R. Wordsworth (eds) *Business and Post-Disaster Management: Business, Organisational and Consumer Resilience and the Christchurch Earthquakes* (pp. 97–120). Abingdon: Routledge.
Pyne, S.J. (1982) *Fire in America. A Cultural History of Wildland and Rural Fire*. Princeton, NJ: Princeton University Press.
Pyne, S.J. (1991) *Burning Bush: A Fire History of Australia*. Sydney: Macmillan.
R3ADY (2015) *Enhancing Disaster & Climate Resilience in Asia's Key Tourism. Destinations – Concept & Pilot Proposal*. Washington, DC: R3ADY.
R3ADY (2016a) *Enhancing Disaster and Climate Resilience in Asia's Key Tourism Destinations*. See http://r3ady.org/tourism-destination-resilience/ (accessed 1 April).
R3ADY (2016b) *A Guide to Initiate and Sustain Multi-Sectoral Partnerships*. See http://r3ady.org/r3source-project/ (accessed 1 April).
R3ADY (2016c) Our Mission. See http://r3ady.org/our-mission/ (accessed 1 April).
R3ADY (2016d) R3ADY at PRiMO 2016. See http://r3ady.org/primo16/ (accessed 1 April).
Reich, J.W. (2006) Three psychological principles of resilience in natural disasters. *Disaster Prevention and Management* 15 (5), 793–798.
Ren, C.H. (2000) Understanding and managing the dynamics of linked crisis events. *Disaster Prevention and Management* 9, 12–17.
Rensel, J. (1993) The Fiji connection: Migrant involvement in the economy of Rotuma. *Pacific Viewpoint* 34 (2), 215–240.
Renslow, R.S., Lindemann, S.R. and Song, H.S. (2016) A generalized spatial measure for resilience of microbial systems. *Frontiers in Microbiology* 7, 443.
Resilience Alliance (2010) *Assessing Resilience in Social–Ecological Systems: Work-book for Practitioners*, Version 2.0. See http://www.resalliance.org/3871.php (accessed 1 April).
Rhodes, R.A.W. (1997) *Understanding Governance: Policy Networks, Governance, Reflexivity, and Accountability*. Philadelphia, PA: Open University Press.
Ritchie, B.W. (2004) Chaos, crises and disasters: A strategic approach to crisis management in the tourism industry. *Tourism Management* 25 (6), 669–683.
Roberts, K.H. (1990) Some characteristics of one type of high reliability organization. *Organization Science* 1 (2), 160–176.
Robertson, I.T., Cooper, C.L., Sarkar, M. and Curran, T. (2015) Resilience training in the workplace from 2003 to 2014: A systematic review. *Journal of Occupational and Organizational Psychology* 88 (3), 533–562.
Rockefeller Foundation (2016) *Resilience*. See https://www.rockefellerfoundation.org/our-work/topics/resilience/ (accessed 1 April).
Roehl, W. (1998) The tourism production system: The logic of industrial classification. In D. Ioannides and K.G. Debbage (eds) *The Economic Geography of the Tourist Industry: A Supply-side Analysis* (pp. 53–75). London: Routledge.
Ruiz-Ballesteros, E. (2011) Social-ecological resilience and community-based tourism: An approach from Agua Blanca, Ecuador. *Tourism Management* 32 (3), 655–666.

Rushe, D. and Smith, D. (2017) United Airlines CEO offers softer apology after stock nosedives. *The Guardian*. See https://www.theguardian.com/us-news/2017/apr/11/united-airlines-shares-plummet-passenger-removal-controversy (accessed 12 April).

Rutter, M. (2006) Implications of resilience concepts for scientific understanding. *Annals of the New York Academy of Sciences* 1094 (1), 1–12.

Rutty, M., Gössling, S., Scott, D. and Hall, C.M. (2015) The global effects and impacts of tourism: An overview. In C.M. Hall, S. Gössling and D. Scott (eds) *The Routledge Handbook of Tourism and Sustainability* (pp. 36–63). Abingdon: Routledge.

Sahebjamnia, N., Torabi, S.A. and Mansouri, S.A. (2015) Integrated business continuity and disaster recovery planning: Towards organizational resilience. *European Journal of Operational Research* 242 (1), 261–273.

Sapountzaki, K. (2014) 'Resilience for All' and 'Collective Resilience': Are these planning objectives consistent with one another? In P. Gasparini, G. Manfredi and D. Asprone (eds) *Resilience and Sustainability in Relation to Natural Disasters: A Challenge for Future Cities* (pp. 39–53). Dordrecht: Springer.

Sawalha, I.H.S. (2015) Managing adversity: Understanding some dimensions of organizational resilience. *Management Research Review* 38 (4), 346–366.

Scheffer, M., Carpenter, S., Foley, J.A., Folke, C. and Walker, B. (2001) Catastrophic shifts in ecosystems. *Nature* 413 (6856), 591–596.

Scheffer, M., Bascompte, J., Brock, W.A., et al. (2009) Early-warning signals for critical transitions. *Nature* 461, 53–59.

Schoon, I. (2006) *Risk and Resilience: Adaptations in Changing Times*. Cambridge: Cambridge University Press.

Schroeder, A., Persson, L. and de Roos, A.M. (2005) Direct experimental evidence for alternative stable states: A review. *Oikos* 110, 3–19.

Schwartz, R. and Sulitzeanu-Kenan, R. (2004) Managerial values and accountability pressures: Challenges of crisis and disaster. *Journal of Public Administration Research and Theory* 14 (1), 79–102.

Scott, D., Hall, C.M. and Gössling, S. (2012) *Tourism and Climate Change: Impacts, Adaptation and Mitigation*. Abingdon: Routledge.

Scott, D., Hall, C.M. and Gössling, S. (2016) A report on the Paris Climate Change Agreement and its implications for tourism: Why we will always have Paris. *Journal of Sustainable Tourism* 24 (7), 933–948.

Scott, N. and Laws, E. (2006) Tourism crises and disasters: Enhancing understanding of system effects. *Journal of Travel & Tourism Marketing* 19 (2–3), 149–158.

Secretariat of the CBD (2010) *Global Biodiversity Outlook 3*. Montreal: Secretariat of the Convention on Biological Diversity.

Secretariat of the CBD (2014) *Global Biodiversity Outlook 4*. Montréal: Secretariat of the Convention on Biological Diversity.

Selya R.M. (1978) Economic development and a clean environment in Taiwan: Toward resolving the clash. *Transition, Quarterly Journal of the Socially and Ecologically Responsible Geographers* 8 (4), 1–7.

Seville, E., Brunsdon, D., Dantas, A., Le Masurier, J., Wilkinson, S. and Vargo, J. (2008) Organisational resilience: Researching the reality of New Zealand organisations. *Journal of Business Continuity & Emergency Planning* 2 (3), 258–266.

Sharifi, A. and Yamagata, Y. (2016) On the suitability of assessment tools for guiding communities towards disaster resilience. *International Journal of Disaster Risk Reduction* 18, 115–124.

Sharifi, H. and Zhang, Z. (1999) A methodology for achieving agility in manufacturing organisations: An introduction. *International Journal of Production Economics* 62 (1), 7–22.

Shaw, K. and Maythorne, L. (2013) Managing for local resilience: Towards a strategic approach. *Public Policy and Administration* 28 (1), 43–65.

Sheffi, Y. (2015) *The Power of Resilience: How the Best Companies Manage the Unexpected.* Boston, MA: MIT Press.

Sheffi, Y. and Rice Jr, J.B. (2005) A supply chain view of the resilient enterprise. *MIT Sloan Management Review* 47 (1), 41–48.

Sheppard, V.A. and Williams, P.W. (2015) Systems-based and internal factors enhancing resort community resilience. Paper presented at Tourism Travel and Research Association: Advancing Tourism Research Globally, 2015 TTRA International Conference, Portland, Oregon, 15–17 June.

Sherrieb, K., Norris, F.H. and Galea, S. (2010) Measuring capacities for community resilience. *Social Indicators Research* 99 (2), 227–247.

Shin, J., Taylor, M.S. and Seo, M.G. (2012) Resources for change: The relationships of organizational inducements and psychological resilience to employees' attitudes and behaviors toward organizational change. *Academy of Management Journal* 55 (3), 727–748.

Shove, E. (2010) Beyond the ABC: Climate change policy and theories of social change. *Environment and Planning A* 42 (6), 1273–1285.

Simon, H.A. (1974) The organization of a complex system. In H.H. Patee (ed.) *Hierarchy Theory.* New York: George Braziller.

Smith, B.W., Dalen, J., Wiggins, K., Tooley, E., Christopher, P. and Bernard, J. (2008) The brief resilience scale: Assessing the ability to bounce back. *International Journal of Behavioral Medicine* 15 (3), 194–200.

Somers, S. (2009) Measuring resilience potential: An adaptive strategy for organizational crisis planning. *Journal of Contingencies and Crisis Management* 17 (1), 12–23.

Song, H.-S., Renslow, R.S., Fredrickson, J.K. and Lindemann, S.R. (2015) Integrating ecological and engineering concepts of resilience in microbial communities. *Frontiers in Microbiology*, 6, 1298. http://doi.org/10.3389/fmicb.2015.01298

Sönmez, S.F. (1998) Tourism, terrorism, and political instability. *Annals of Tourism Research* 25 (2), 416–456.

Sørensen, E. (2006) Metagovernance: The changing role of politicians in processes of democratic governance. *American Review of Public Administration* 36 (1), 98–114.

Specht, A. (2008) *Extreme Natural Events and Effects on Tourism: Central Eastern Coast of Australia.* Technical report. Gold Coast: CRC for Sustainable Tourism.

Stacey, R.D. (1996) *Complexity and Creativity in Organizations.* San Francisco, CA: Berrett-Koehler.

Star, S.L. and Griesemer, J.R. (1989) Institutional ecology, 'Translations' and boundary objects: Amateurs and professionals in Berkeley's Museum of Vertebrate Zoology, 1907–39. *Social Studies of Science* 19 (3), 387–420.

Stephens, J.P., Heaphy, E.D., Carmeli, A., Spreitzer, G.M. and Dutton, J.E. (2013) Relationship quality and virtuousness: Emotional carrying capacity as a source of individual and team resilience. *Journal of Applied Behavioral Science* 49 (1), 13–41.

Stephenson, A., Vargo, J. and Seville, E. (2010) Measuring and comparing organisational resilience in Auckland. *Australian Journal of Emergency Management* 25 (2), 27.

Stockholm Resilience Center (2015) *What is Resilience?* See http://www.stockholmresilience.org/21/research/research-news/2-19-2015-what-is-resilience.html (accessed 1 April).

Strickland-Munro, J.K., Allison, H.E. and Moore, S.A. (2010) Using resilience concepts to investigate the impacts of protected area tourism on communities. *Annals of Tourism Research* 37 (2), 499–519.

Strunz, S. (2012) Is conceptual vagueness an asset? Arguments from philosophy of science applied to the concept of resilience. *Ecological Economics* 76, 112–118.

Suarez, F.F. and Oliva, R. (2005) Environmental change and organizational transformation. *Industrial and Corporate Change* 14, 1017–1041.

Sutcliffe, K. and Vogus, T. (2003) Organizing for resilience. In K.S. Cameron, J.E. Dutton and R.E. Quinn (eds) *Positive Organizational Scholarship: Foundations of a New Discipline*, San Francisco, CA: Berrett-Koehler.

Swiss Re (2014) *Mind the Risk: A Global Ranking of Cities under Threat from Natural Disasters*. Zurich: Swiss Re.

Sydnor-Bousso, S., Stafford, K., Tews, M. and Adler, H. (2011) Toward a resilience model for the hospitality & tourism industry. *Journal of Human Resources in Hospitality & Tourism* 10 (2), 195–217.

Tervo, K. (2008) The operational and regional vulnerability of winter tourism to climate variability and change: The case of the Finnish nature-based tourism entrepreneurs. *Scandinavian Journal of Hospitality and Tourism* 8 (4), 317–332.

Thomalla, F., Larsen, R.K., Kanji, F., Naruchaikusol, S., Tepa, C., Ravesloot, B. and Ahmed, A.K. (2009) *From Knowledge to Action: Learning to go the Last Mile. A Participatory Assessment of the Conditions for Strengthening the Technology–Community Linkages of Tsunami early Warning Systems in the Indian Ocean*. Stockholm: Stockholm Environment Institute.

Tierney, K. and Trainor, J. (2004) Networks and resilience in the World Trade Center disaster. In *MCEER: Research Progress and Accomplishments 2003–2004* (pp. 157–172). Buffalo, NY: Multidisciplinary Center for Earthquake Engineering Research, State University of New York.

Tourism England (2010) *A Strategic Action Plan for Tourism 2010–2030*. London: Tourism England.

Tsao, C.-T. and Ni, C.-C. (2016) Vulnerability, resilience, and the adaptive cycle in a crisis-prone tourism community. *Tourism Geographies* 18 (1), 80–105.

Tugade, M.M. and Fredrickson, B.L. (2004) Resilient individuals use positive emotions to bounce back from negative emotional experiences. *Journal of Personality and Social Psychology* 86 (2), 320–333.

Tyler, D. and Dangerfield, J.M. (1999) Ecosystem tourism: A resource-based philosophy for ecotourism. *Journal of Sustainable Tourism* 7 (2), 146–158.

Tyrrell, T.J. and Johnston, R.J. (2008) Tourism sustainability, resiliency and dynamics: Towards a more comprehensive perspective. *Tourism and Hospitality Research* 8 (1), 14–24.

UNCTAD (2008) *Human Development Report 2007/8. Fighting Climate Change: Human Solidarity in a Divided World*. Geneva: United Nations Conference on Trade and Development.

UNEP (2009) *Disaster Risk Management for Coastal Tourism Destinations Responding to Climate Change. A Practical Guide for Decision Makers*. Nairobi: United Nations Environment Programme.

UNESCO (2016) *Great Barrier Reef*. See http://whc.unesco.org/en/list/154 (accessed 1 April).

UNISDR (2009) *2009 UNISDR Terminology on Disaster Risk Reduction*. Geneva: United Nations International Strategy for Disaster Reduction.

UNISDR (2015a) *Making Development Sustainable: The Future of Disaster Risk Management. Global Assessment Report on Disaster Risk Reduction*. Geneva: United Nations International Strategy for Disaster Reduction.

UNISDR (2015b) *HFA Decade. The Economic and Human Impact of Disasters in the Last 10 Years*. Geneva: United Nations International Strategy for Disaster Reduction.

UNISDR, USAID and CRED (2016) *2015 Disasters in Numbers*. Geneva: United Nations International Strategy for Disaster Reduction, US Agency for International Development and Centre for Research on the Epidemiology of Disasters.

UNWTO (2014) *Tourism Highlights, 2014 edition*. Madrid: United Nations World Tourism Organization.

UNWTO-UNEP-WMO (2008) *Climate Change and Tourism: Responding to Global Challenges*. Madrid: United Nations World Tourism Organization, United Nations Environment Programme and World Meteorological Organization.

US Senate (2014) *Leading the Way: Adapting to South Florida's Changing Coastline*. Hearings of the US Senate Committee on Commerce, Science, & Transportation. Washington, DC: United States Senate.

Vale, L. (2014) The politics of resilient cities: Whose resilience and whose city? *Building Research & Information* 42 (2), 37–41.

Vanhove, A.J., Herian, M.N., Perez, A.L., Harms, P.D. and Lester, P.B. (2016) Can resilience be developed at work? A meta-analytic review of resilience-building programme effectiveness. *Journal of Occupational and Organizational Psychology* 89 (2), 278–307.

Vargo, J. and Seville, E. (2011) Crisis strategic planning for SMEs: Finding the silver lining. *International Journal of Production Research* 49 (18), 5619–5635.

Visao (2013) Turismo. Portugal deve tirar proveito duradouro de instabilidade no medio oriente. *Visao*. See http://visao.sapo.pt/lusa/turismo-portugal-deve-tirar-proveito-duradouro-de-instabilidade-no-medio-oriente=f745111 (accessed 11 August).

Vogus, T.J. and Sutcliffe, K.M. (2007) Organizational resilience: Towards a theory and research agenda. Paper presented at ISIC, IEEE International Conference on Systems, Man and Cybernetics, 7–10 October, Montreal, Canada.

Vörösmarty, C.J., Green, P., Salisbury, J. and Lammers, R.B. (2000) Global water resources: Vulnerability from climate change and population growth. *Science* 289, 284–288.

Wagnild, G. and Young, H. (1993) Development and psychometric evaluation of the resilience scale. *Journal of Nursing Measurement* 1 (2), 165–178.

Waldrop, M.M. (1992) *Complexity: The Emerging Science at the Edge of Order and Chaos*. New York: Touchstone.

Walker, B. and Salt, D. (2006) *Resilience Thinking: Sustaining Ecosystems and People in a Changing World*. Washington, DC: Island Press.

Walker, B. and Salt, D. (2012) *Resilience Practice: Building Capacity to Absorb Disturbance and Maintain Function*. Washington, DC: Island Press.

Walker, B., Holling, C.S., Carpenter, S. and Kinzig, A. (2004) Resilience, adaptability and transformability in social-ecological systems. *Ecology and Society* 9 (2), 5.

Walker, B., Gunderson, L., Kinzig, A., Folke, C., Carpenter, S. and Schultz, L. (2006) A handful of heuristics and some propositions for understanding resilience in social-ecological systems. *Ecology and Society* 11 (1).

Walker, J. and Cooper, M. (2011) Genealogies of resilience: From systems ecology to the political economy of crisis adaptation. *Security Dialogue* 42 (2), 143–160.

Walker, P.A., Greiner, R., McDonald, D. and Lyne, V. (1998) The tourism futures simulator: A systems thinking approach. *Environmental Modelling and Software* 14 (1), 59–67.

Waller, M.A. (2001) Resilience in ecosystemic context: Evolution of the concept. *American Journal of Orthopsychiatry* 71 (3), 290–297.

Wanberg, C.R. and Banas, J.T. (2000) Predictors and outcomes of openness to changes in a reorganizing workplace. *Journal of Applied Psychology* 85 (1), 132–142.

WEF (2017) *The Inclusive Growth and Development Report 2017*. Cologny: World Economic Forum.

Wei, W. and Taormina, R.J. (2014) A new multidimensional measure of personal resilience and its use: Chinese nurse resilience, organizational socialization and career success. *Nursing Inquiry* 21 (4), 346–357.

Weichselgartner, J. and Kelman, I. (2015) Geographies of resilience: Challenges and opportunities of a descriptive concept. *Progress in Human Geography* 39 (3), 249–267.

Weick, K.E. (1993) The collapse of sensemaking in organizations: The Mann Gulch disaster. *Administrative Science Quarterly* 38 (4), 628–652.

Werner, E.E. and Smith, R.S. (2001) *Journeys from Childhood to Midlife: Risk, Resilience, and Recovery*. Ithica, NY: Cornell University Press.

White, I. and O'Hare, P. (2014) From rhetoric to reality: Which resilience, why resilience, and whose resilience in spatial planning? *Environment and Planning C: Government and Policy* 32 (5), 934–950.

Whitman, Z.R., Wilson, T.M., Seville, E., Vargo, J., Stevenson, J.R., Kachali, H. and Cole, J. (2013) Rural organizational impacts, mitigation strategies, and resilience to the 2010 Darfield earthquake, New Zealand. *Natural Hazards* 69 (3), 1849–1875.

Whitman, Z., Stevenson, J., Kachali, H., Seville, E., Vargo, J. and Wilson, T. (2014) Organisational resilience following the Darfield earthquake of 2010. *Disasters* 38 (1), 148–177.

Whittaker, R.J. and Fernández-Palacios, J. (2007) *Island Biogeography: Ecology, Evolution, and Conservation* (2nd edn). Oxford: Oxford University Press.

Wholey, D. and Brittain, J. (1989) Characterizing environmental variation. *Academy of Management Journal* 32, 867–882.

Wildavsky, A.B. (1991) *Searching for Safety*. New Brunswick: Transaction Publishers.

Williams, A. and Zelinsky, W. (1970) On some patterns of international tourism flows. *Economic Geography* 46 (4), 549–567.

Windle, G. (2011) What is resilience? A review and concept analysis. *Reviews in Clinical Gerontology* 21 (2), 152–169.

Wood, S.J. and de Menezes, L.M. (2010) Family-friendly management, organizational performance and social legitimacy. *International Journal of Human Resource Management* 21 (10), 1575–1597.

Woods, D.D. (2007) Essential characteristics of resilience. In E. Hollnagel, D. Woodsand N. Leveson (eds) *Resilience Engineering: Concepts and Precepts*. Cheltenham: Ashgate.

Worster, D. (1990) The ecology of order and chaos. *Environmental History Review* 14 (1–2), 1–18.

Wu, Z. and Choi, T.Y. (2005) Supplier–supplier relationships in the buyer–supplier triad: Building theories from eight case studies. *Journal of Operations Management* 24 (1), 27–52.

Xu, L., Marinova, D. and Guo, X. (2015) Resilience thinking: A renewed system approach for sustainability science. *Sustainability Science* 10, 123–138.

Youssef, C.M. and Luthans, F. (2007) Positive organizational behavior in the workplace: The impact of hope, optimism, and resilience. *Journal of Management* 33 (5), 774–800.

Zaidi, R.Z. and Pelling, M. (2015) Institutionally configured risk: Assessing urban resilience and disaster risk reduction to heat wave risk in London. *Urban Studies* 52 (7), 1218–1233.

Zalasiewicz, J., Williams, W., Smith, A., *et al.* (2008) Are we now living in the Anthropocene? *GSA Today* 18, 4–8.

Zautra, A.J. (2009) Resilience: One part recovery, two parts sustainability. *Journal of Personality* 77 (6), 935–1943.

Zautra, A.J. and Reich, J.W. (2010) Resilience: The meanings, methods, and measures of a fundamental characteristic of human adaptation. In S. Folkman (ed.) *The Oxford Handbook of Stress, Health, and Coping* (pp. 173–185). New York, NY: Oxford University Press.

ZSL and WWF (2014) *Living Planet Report*. London: Zoological Society of London and World Wildlife Fund.

Index

Page numbers in *italics* refer to Figures. Page numbers in **bold** refer to Tables.

accessibility 100
adaptation 35, **57**, 84, **117**, **119**, 131–132, 137, 138, 143–146, 148
   assessment as a resilience factor in tourism *145*
   business 106
   climate change 137
   community 8, 126
   defined 13
   destination 110, 126
   island economies 98, *100*
   natural 8
   organisational 85, 86, 87, 96
   personal 62, **64**, 66–67, 69
   strategies 18–19
   visitor 131
   waves of positive personal adaptation **64**
adaptive capacity 43–44, 82, 83, 86–87, 96, 112, 118, 124, 129, 151, 157
adaptive cycle 28, 46, **47**, *48*, 58–59, 139
   described 46–52
   and panarchy 46–53
adaptive scales *51*, *58*
Afghanistan **32**
Africa 12, 121
Anthropocene 2, 4–5, 9
apps 3
Arab Spring 105
Arctic 6, 7, 22–23
Asia 12
attractions 74, 85, **120**, **123**, 124, 125, 132
Australia 8–9, 12, 38, 78, 108, 110, 124, 128, 131
   Gold Coast 128
   Melbourne **121**

   Ningaloo 108
Australian Greenhouse Office (AGO) 7
automated transport 3

behavioural interventions 64, 65, 70, 71, 74, 75, **153**; *see also* social marketing
Belgium 31
biodiversity 9–12, 38, 53, **57**
   defined 10
   loss 6, 10, 12, **29**
Bosnia and Herzegovina 115
Brazil **12**, 118
   Rio de Janeiro 118, **122**
bus 3
bushfire *see* wildfire
business 4, 8, 14, 17, 20, 28, 36, **54**, **56**, 72–73, 80, 96, 97, 112, 124–126
   resilience 81, 83, 85, 87, 91–92, 98–101, 112, 124–125
business continuity management 90–91
business cycle **29**
business loss 14
business studies 32, **34**, 35, 53, **54**, **56**

Canada 38, 76, 80, 128
   British Columbia 80
   Kelowna 80
   Newfoundland 23
   Whistler 128
capacity 7, 13, 15, 82
   adaptive 43–44, 82, 83, 86–87, 96, 112, 118, 124, 129, 151, 157
   and resilience 2, 32, 33, 36, **40**, 43–44, 62, 63, 66, 67, 68, 71, 74, 83
   and sustainability 52
car *see* automobile

carbon emissions *see* emissions
carbon footprint 6; *also see* emissions
Caribbean 12
Centre for Research on the Epidemiology of Disasters (CRED) 14–16
change 1–18
  approaches to **153**
  global 13, 26, 108
  spatial scales 18
China 3, **12**, **16**
coastal areas 7, 11, **12**, 18, 55, **56**, 109–110, 111, **121**, **122**, 127, 142
  protection 108–109
climate change 6, 11, 12, 19, 22, **29**, 57, 104, 106, 108, 110, 116, 125, 126, 148
  and tourism 5–10, **12**, **52**, 57, 108, 115, 124, 127, 139
  and urban resilience 137
Colombia **121**
  Medellin **121**
complex adaptive system 25–28
  defined 25
connectivity **123**, 152, 154, 155
cruise ship 6, 23
cruise tourism 23

Denmark **123**
  Vejle **123**
destination 19, 20, 21, 26, 27, 30, 52, 55, **56**, 73–74, 75–76
  adaptation 18
  image 7
  planning 113, 129
  resilience 18, 55, 83, 104–131
  socio-ecological vulnerability 111
destination management 53, 85, 132
Destination Vulnerability Assessment (DVA) 110–111
disaster capitalism 118, 152
disasters 2, 12, 13–15, 17, 35, 36, 39, **57**, 75–76, 81, 89, 93
  death 15
  defined 13, 15, 17
  global human impact **15**
  individual resilience within 68–69
  risk reduction 12
drought 17, *120*
  defined 15
  global human impact **15**

earthquake 13, 14, 72, 75, 80, 89, 95, 106, 111, 115–116, 118, 127, 138
  defined 15
  global human impact **15**
economic development 118, 125
  tourism 118–119, 125
EM-DAT 14, 15, 16
emissions 4, 5, 6, 11; *see also* carbon footprint
  mitigation 18, **121**
employment 3, 65, 114, **120**, 124, *145*, **153**
enterprise risk management 90
Europe 3, 105
experience 24, 35, 39, 62, 63, 66–67, 70, 71, 114
  tourism 74, 94, 95
extreme natural event 80–81, 127
extreme temperature 15
  global human impact **15**

flood 14, 17, 38, 109–110, 115, **120**
  defined 15
  global human impact **15**
fossil fuel 4
fuel 5, 16
  efficiency 21

gender 67
Global Biodiversity Outlook 10
global financial crisis 105, 113, 128
global warming *see* climate change
Great Barrier Reef 7–9, 124, 131, 139
Great Barrier Reef Marine Authority (GBRMPA) 7

health 63, 65, **120**, **121**, **122**, *145*, **153**
  mental 67, 71
health tourism 74
heritage 111; *see also* World Heritage
hospitality 3, 71, 79, 80, 87, 94, 102, 116, **119**, 142
human resource development 70, 72, 74
human resource management 69–71
Hurricane Katrina 115
hyper-neoliberal 132
hyper-turbulence 29

iceberg 23
India **16**
Indian sub-continent **12**
Indonesia **16**, 111, 124
  Bali 111
  Semarang **123**
  Yogyakarta 124
informal sector 91–92, 93, 97
innovation 43–44, *48*, 84, 86, 87, 93, 99, *100*, 112, 115, **123**
insurance 86, 95, *146*
island biogeography 98–101
Israel 140

Japan 14, **16**
Jordan 86

Korea *see* South Korea

landslide 15
  defined 16
  global human impact **15**
Latin America **122**
Lebanon
  Byblos **120**

Maldives 114
marketing 85, 92, 148; *see also* pricing, promotion, social marketing
  place 76
  recovery *146*
  strategies 84
  social media marketing 95
mass movement
  defined 16
  global human impact **15**
McKinsey Global Institute 3
Mexico **16**
  Mexico City **121**

national park 11, **56**
natural disaster *see* disaster
neoliberalism **29**, 63, 118, 132, 138, 152
Netherlands
  Rotterdam **122**
networks 25, 79, 83, 84, 87, 93–96, 106, 115, 117, 142; *see also* social capital
  agent 25

communication 81
  family 112
  firm 20, 125
  governance 107
  personal 70
  social 70, 74, 97
New Zealand **12**, 38, 72, 80, 87, 89, 93, 94, 108, 111, 115–116
  Auckland 93
  Canterbury 80
  Christchurch 72, 87, 89, 94, 111, 115–116, 118, **121**
  Queenstown-Wanaka 108
  Wellington **123**
normality 83, 157

ocean acidification 7, 29; *see also* climate change
Organization for Economic Co-operation and Development (OECD) 113–114
Office of US Foreign Disaster Assistance (OFDA) 15

Pacific Asia Travel Association (PATA) Rapid Response Taskforce 114
Pakistan **16**
panarchy 46–53, 59, 147, 151, *156*
Philippines 3, **12**, **16**
pricing **153**
promotion 8, 44, 85, **119**
protected area *see* national park
public policy 33, 137
  resilience as a bridging concept for 137
public transport **123**
pyroclastic flow 126

R3ADY Asia Pacific Programme 114
rail 106
rebound effects 21
regime shift 42, 45–46; *see also* threshold
Regional Tourism Adaptation Framework (RTAF) 110
Regional Tourism Sustainable Adaptation Framework (RTSAF) 110
Relative Overall Resilience model (ROR) 86–87

188 Tourism and Resilience

resilience
  as boundary object 137
  community-based 74–76, 126–127, 136, 151, 154–155
  destination 104–133, 146, 151
  ecological 8, 28, 33, 37–38, 41–42, **42**, 47, 51, 53, 55, 58, 59, 63, 73, 82, 96, 107–109
  employee 69–76
  engineering 27, 37, 41–42, **42**, 47, 53, 63, 83, 130, 136, **153**
  individual 61–76, 130–131, 147, **153**
  organisational 79–101
  social 43–45, 62, 63, 111, 112, 152, 155
  socio-ecological 43–45, 55, 58, 95, 102, 107, 110–111, 117–118, 128, 136, 148, 149, 152
  in tourism literature 53–58
  tourist 74–75, 76, 77
  urban 117–118, 124, 137
Resilient Cities network 118–123
risk 35, 46, **57**, **64**, 70, 74, 80, 85, 89, 114, 131
  climate change 6–7, 19
  disaster 12
  extinction 10, 98
  extreme weather events 6
  financial 82
  perception 76, 126
  reduction 114, 125, 126
  society 112
  technological 3
risk management 90, 96, 125, 127
Rockefeller Foundation 36, 118, 119

safety 75, 119, 126, 140
  psychological 89
safari tourism 2
scale 11, 17–18, 25, 27, 28, 43, 50, 58, 63
  and panarchy 51–52, 58
sea level rise (SLR) 7, 18–19, 108–109
second homes 11, 131
Senegal
  Dakar **121**
slow tourism 132
social capital 84, 89, 92, 93, 129, *144*, 155; *see also* networks
social ecological system (SES) 40, 43–45, 110, 146–147

social marketing **153**
South Africa 38
Sri Lanka 75
stability 26, **27**
Stockholm Environment Institute (SEI) 40, 111
storm 7, 14, **29**, 39
  global human impact **15**
  surge 108, **122**
supply chain 36, 71, **73**, 93, 94, 154
  management 79
  members 90, 93
sustainability science 35
sustainable development 41, 129
  and panarchy 52
  and resilience 41, 69, 149–151
  in tourism 71
systems 1–2, 17, 19–22, 38–39, 118, 155–157
  complex 1, 24–25, 106, 94
  complex adaptive 25–28
  ecosystems 6, 7–8, 10, 38–39
  physical 6, 7
  socio-economic 6, 23
  system-level 20
  tourism 1–2, 17, 19–30, 106, 142, 146–149, 154
  transport 14
  vulnerability 13
Switzerland 115

taxation 119, 153
taxis 3
Thailand 91–92, 111–112, 114, 124, 125, 128, 131
  Bangkok 115, 118, **119**
  Khao Lak 111–112
  Patong 111–112
  Phi Don 111–112
  Phuket 91–92, 114, 124, 128, 131
threshold 26, 45–46, 149, **150**; *see also* regime shift
tipping point *see* threshold
tourism 53–58, 143–149, 154–155
  and destination resilience 104–134
  environmental impacts 5–13
  and individual and employee resilience 73–76

and organisational resilience 79–81, 83–85, 87, 91–94
system 1–2, 19–30, 106, 142, 146–149, 154
transport 3
trip elements 20
tsunami 16
  2004 Boxing Day tsunami 69, 75, 91–92, 110, 111–112, 115, 124, 125, 142
  defined 17
  global human impact **17**

Uber **121**
United Nations Conference on Trade and Development (UNCTAD) 14
United Nations Environment Programme (UNEP) 6, 127
United Nations Office for Disaster Risk Reduction (UNISDR) 12, 13, 14–16
United Kingdom
  Bristol **120**
  Glasgow **121**
United States Agency for International Development (USAID) 15
United States of America **12**, 14, **16**, 18–19, 38, 76, 85, 140
  Atlantic City 109
  Berkeley **119**
  Boulder **119**
  Florida 18–19
  Los Angeles
  Miami 18–19
  New Orleans 115, 118, **122**
  New York **122**
  Norfolk **122**
  Oakland **122**
  Pittsburgh **122**
  San Francisco 118
United Nations World Tourism Organisation (UNWTO) 22
urbanisation 6, 13, 118, 128
  crisis-driven 111

Vanuatu 126
  Port Vila 126
  Tanna 126
Vietnam **16**, 118
  Da Nang 118, **120**
volcanic activity **15**, **126**
  global human impact **15**
  volcanic eruption defined 16
volunteer tourism 74
vulnerability 13, 55, **57**, 72, 82, 86, 96, 115, 116, 128, 138, **143–146**, 148, 151
  biodiversity 12
  climate change **12**
  defined 13
  destination 110, 111–112, 117, 132
  disasters 12, 55, 131
  ecosystem 8
  infrastructure 126
  vulnerability to resilience framework (V2R) 86

water security **12**; *see also* drought
wildfire 15, 16, 35, 80
  global human impact **15**
work life balance 70
World Economic Forum (WEF) 3
World Heritage 7–8, **56**
World Meteorological Organization (WMO) 6
World Wildlife Fund (WWF) 10

For Product Safety Concerns and Information please contact our EU Authorised Representative:

Easy Access System Europe

Mustamäe tee 50

10621 Tallinn

Estonia

gpsr.requests@easproject.com